Praise for *Feathered Forest*

"Luminous. You can feel the deep, cool shadow of the great western forest and the flicker of bird color flashing across it. The kind of book that inspires people to contemplation but also to action."

—BILL MCKIBBEN, author of *Here Comes the Sun*

"In a feast of wonder and winged delight, Marina Richie takes us from the heights of towering old-growth forests to the depths of their tangled roots, and from the past of her childhood to a future of unraveling—or renewal. Reminding us that the choice is ours, her fascinating and well-researched book is particularly important in a harrowing time. Highly recommended."

—KATHLEEN DEAN MOORE, author of *Earth's Wild Music*

"Many people have written about birds, and many people have written about trees, but almost no one has written about birds *and* trees. Travel along with Marina Richie as she brings both these subjects together on her journeys through the forests of the Northwest. Without trees, we would not have the birds that live among us today, and without birds . . . well, we cannot imagine."

—JOAN MALOOF, author of *Nature's Temples*

"Not since Loren Eiseley has a writer so effortlessly integrated the intellect of a scientist with the soulful insights of a poet. If you are reading this line, then Marina Richie already has you by the hand. Let her guide you through the enchanting landscape she knows so well: cathedral-like canopies and birds whose songs are the 'om' of the forest."

—PETE DUNNE, author of *Under Their Wing*; former director, Cape May Bird Observatory

"The title of Marina's book reflects her complete love for the birds and the trees that support them. Her evocative writing brings to life the Pacific wilderness and amplifies the fact that her words are from the heart."

—DAVID LINDO, The Urban Birder; vice president, Wildfowl and Wetlands Trust

"Marina Richie's life-long love of trees, abundant curiosity, and decades of forays into the Pacific Northwest forests imbue her stories with wisdom, authenticity, and delight. If you're looking for the perfect guide to the ancient forests of Cascadia, look no further. *Feathered Forest* engages all our senses so that we both lose *and* find ourselves in each chapter, in each forest, and in each of the precious lives of the birds within it."

—MARIA MUDD RUTH, author of *The Bird with the Flaming Red Feet* and *Rare Bird*

"With evocative imagery and a poet's flair, Richie blends natural history and personal experiences to illuminate the threads that weave together Cascadia's ancient forests and the captivating birds that dwell in them. A story of community and connections—and the power of ancient forests to sustain biodiversity while nurturing our own well-being in a fast-changing world."

—SOPHIE OSBORN, author of *Feather Trails*

"'As alarmingly fewer birds trace our skies,' Marina Richie writes, 'isn't it time we looked up . . . and took notice?' In an adventure both personal and expansive, Richie lifts us from our earthbound anchors to explore the intricate, often unseen, and always astonishing world of birds. We witness the whirling dance of swifts, feel the drumbeats of woodpeckers, and hear the haunting music of thrushes. Within each vivid encounter with wild birds, there is a trace of deep concern for the wildness of the world. With lyrical descriptions and fine-tuned science, Richie shows a deep love for and expansive understanding of these 'troubadours of rebirth.' She tunes our ears and our hearts to hear the stories sung within the feathered forest."

—M. L. HERRING, author of *Born of Fire and Rain*

"What a glorious tangle! In these pages, Marina Richie brazenly dissolves false boundaries—between bird and forest, human and wild, observer and observed. In her beautiful telling, communion is not a metaphor but a practice: witness, listen, be changed. As the ancient forest sings a chorus of relations—owl! pine! fungus! finch!—Richie guides us along a path that leads inexorably from wonder to belonging to action."

—LYANDA LYNN HAUPT, author of *Rooted* and *Among the Birds*

"Bird by bird and tree by tree, Marina Richie weaves a magical world of our forests and the birds that require them—just as we do—for survival and well-being. A must-read for tree and bird lovers alike."

—LYNDA MAPES, author of *The Trees are Speaking*; 2025 Pulitzer Prize finalist

"[Marina Richie's] lyrical language leads us on a journey through the vertical layers of the old-growth forests and giant trees of the Pacific Northwest, introducing us to the elusive birds who depend on these threatened ecosystems for their survival. As we meet the denizens of her forests and learn about the threats that plague them today, we become as invested as she is in protecting their fragile existence. By book's end, Marina has become our teacher, our guide, our interpreter, and, most importantly, our forest companion. She has beckoned us with a call to action that we are ready to follow as we delight in this captivating and informative scientific memoir."

—TINA MORRIS, author of *Return to the Sky*

"By rhyming bird and tree, environmental and personal history, and close observation and activism, Richie has created a literary refugium. Here, readers can find a moment of respite from capitalism's disastrous monoculture and consider how we might return to interconnectedness with other species."

—THEO DOWNES-LE GUIN, head of the Ursula K. Le Guin Foundation

"Through richly detailed stories of birds and trees, Marina Richie's deeply personal account brings readers into close connection with the worlds that are ancient forests. This wonderful book is an homage to refuge and refugia, to close observation, and to the beauty of interlocking systems: feathers, ecosystems, and kinships."

—MARGUERITE HOLLOWAY, author of *Take to the Trees*

"Starting with a riveting climb up an ancient Douglas-fir and ending with the tree's destruction and a devastating fire, *Feathered Forest* is nature writing at its best: alive, absorbing, and full of consequence. The vivid, verb-driven language, where 'wings flare with fire' and the songs of finches are 'like chips of sunshine freed from clouds,' invites us into a world of birds and branches, full of bustling life. Science mixes with wonder in this beautiful book, which offers hope in our hard world."

—DAVID GESSNER, author of *Return of the Osprey* and *All the Wild That Remains*

Feathered Forest

Also by Marina Richie

Halcyon Journey: In Search of the Belted Kingfisher
(Oregon State University Press, 2022)

Feathered Forest

Aloft with Birds in Ancient Trees

Marina Richie

Foreword by David George Haskell

Chelsea Green Publishing
White River Junction, Vermont
London, UK

First published in 2026 by Chelsea Green Publishing | PO Box 4529 | White River Junction, VT 05001 | West Wing, Somerset House, Strand | London, WC2R 1LA, UK | www.chelseagreen.com
A Division of Rizzoli International Publications, Inc. | 49 West 27th Street | New York, NY 10001 | www.rizzoliusa.com

Publisher: Charles Miers
Deputy Publisher: Matthew Derr
Project Manager: Natalie Wallace
Developmental Editor: Amalia Herren-Lage
Copy Editor: Susan Campbell
Proofreader: Nancy A. Crompton
Indexer: Linda Hallinger
Designer: Jenna Richardson

ISBN 978-1-64502-295-4 (hardcover) | ISBN 978-1-64502-296-1 (ebook) | ISBN 978-1-64502-297-8 (audiobook)
Library of Congress Control Number: 2026015024 (print)

Our Commitment to Green Publishing
Chelsea Green sees publishing as a tool for cultural change and ecological stewardship. We strive to align our book manufacturing practices with our editorial mission and to reduce the impact of our business enterprise in the environment. We print our books using vegetable-based inks whenever possible. This book may cost slightly more because it was printed on paper that contains recycled fiber, and we hope you'll agree that it's worth it. *Feathered Forest* was printed on paper supplied by Marquis that is made of recycled materials and other controlled sources.

Authorized EU representative for product safety and compliance
Mondadori Libri S.p.A. | www.mondadori.it
via Gian Battista Vico 42 | Milan, Italy 20123

MIX
Paper | Supporting responsible forestry
FSC www.fsc.org FSC® C103567

Printed in Canada.
10 9 8 7 6 5 4 3 2 1   26 27 28 29 30

For Sandra Murphy
In gratitude for a friendship like feathers—
entwining, uplifting, and enfolding.

CONTENTS

FOREWORD

Old wisdom tells us: Pay attention to feathered and leafy creatures. In scriptures and creation stories from around the world, birds and trees created the world and continue to sustain us. In Mayan and Norse stories, birds perch in primordial "world trees." In tales from other cultures, birds brought the land into being, allowing trees to take root. In dozens of tales from Northern Eurasia and North America, for example, diving birds carried mud to the water's surface, creating the terrestrial world. For the Cherokee, it was the wingbeats of vultures that shaped the forested mountains of the Appalachians. In these creation stories, trees offer life, knowledge, and connection among realms. Birds complement the trees' rootedness with transforming motion and spirit. Even in scriptures that are not typically thought of as animistic, such as the texts of the Abrahamic religions, trees converse with one another, birds bring messages and divine energy, and people find hope and guidance through their sylvan and winged neighbors.

Modern science echoes these insights, though the fossil record shows that forests got here first. Rocks from 385 million years ago in what is now upstate New York are run through by meters-long roots radiating out from tree trunk bases as wide as a meter or more. Slightly older forests of palm-like trees are preserved in 390-million-year-old rocks in southern England. By 350 million years ago, Earth was largely a forested planet. Since then, forest cover has waxed and waned with changes in climate and the activities of other species. Most notably, in the last ten million years, grasses have worked with fire and grazing mammals to deforest parts of the planet, a process more recently helped by industrious humans clear-cutting, torching, and paving. But even the grassy and concrete challenges of recent years have not displaced trees as the Earth's great producers, community makers, and guardians. Almost one-third of the planet remains forested, a conservative statistic because it omits trees in cities, agricultural landscapes, and savannas. For hundreds of millions of years, trees have lofted woody scaffolds in their vaulting ambition to reach light, and, along the way, they have built soil, shaped the gaseous mix of the atmosphere, called down rain, and created opportunities for other creatures—from fungi to microbes to insects to vertebrates to other plants—to evolve and thrive. Mythologies of trees as the *axis mundi*, the central axis of the world, are no metaphors.

Trees gave birds their wings. It was partly by scrabbling up tree trunks and leaping into branches that feathered dinosaurs realized the dream of flight. Birds' perching feet, bark-clinging claws, and feathers optimized for sweeping down through the air are all gifts from trees. Once aloft, birds took on an outsized role in the planet's ecology. Their numbers are relatively few—roughly ten thousand bird species compared to four hundred thousand species of beetle, for example—but for a small crew, birds do some heavy lifting. Their hot blood gives them keen appetites. Winged hunger, assisted by nerves and muscles made swift and powerful by bodies running fever-hot, makes birds supreme dispersers of fruits and seeds, diligent and energetic pollinators, and incessant groomers of plant life, plucking insects that plague leaves and stems. Take birds away, scientific experiments tell us, and fruits languish, flowers are forlorn, and insect populations surge to pestilential levels. Although flying birds appeared only about 150 million years ago, much more recently than trees and forests, they now count alongside trees as Earthly co-creators. Birds and trees are different creatures in almost every way: how they gather food and breed, their modes of communication, their mobility, and their relationships with time. Yet the world is sustained by the synergies among these differences.

The grand stories recounted in august myths and constructed through science unfold at scales incommensurate with human existence. Hundreds of millions of years? Planet-wide forests and bird diversity? Our senses and imaginations cannot grasp such immensities, existing as they do beyond ordinary human experiences of time and space. Instead, we intersect these giant narratives through the particularities of our human-scaled lives. At these intersections, wonder blooms. In a delightful paradox, the closer we attend to the minutiae of the everyday, the more vivid and real the big picture becomes. Through these experiences, we come to understand birds and trees not simply as ideas, but as bodily and emotional truths. Creation stories, for all their grandeur, honor this granular particularity. Rare is the myth that speaks only through abstraction. Instead, *this* bird flew to *this* tree. *This* tree fruit was eaten by *this* person. We are swept into universal truths by the characters in the stories, where every protagonist has a name, a place, a role. Such is the genius of Marina Richie's writing in this volume. Her sustained attention reveals the identities and personalities of living creatures and illuminates subtle weaves of intersecting histories and energies. These portraits are fascinating and compelling in their own right. Through them, we are also brushed by truths about meaning in the wider living world. Some of these insights can be spoken, but many live in the spaces just beyond or underneath words.

One of these truths is the centrality of interconnection. As John Muir told us, "When we try to pick out anything by itself, we find it hitched to everything else in the Universe." This is a fine abstraction, but without grounding, the words dissipate. We cannot hitch our minds to formless grandiosities. It is through repeated close attention, a form of befriending of the world, that we apprehend both the veracity and limits of the abstraction. "Everything?" Well, sure, but not all strands in the living meshworks of life have the same thickness and vitality. The most important in each place are often surprising cross-connections in the living tapestry that reveal the impish and adventitious nature of evolution's creative hand. These are the "interlocking and miraculous" connections, in Richie's words, from which the feathered forest is made.

Through Marina Richie's keen observations and astute reflections, we discover one unexpected strand of ecological connection after another. Bird and fungal life are stitched together. Woodpeckers are mediators of the afterlife. Water unites. Birdsong is both language and signature of place. Human attention and care—through the work of forest-lovers, activists, scientists, managers—ravel through the woods. We are not bystanders or at-a-remove observers, we're kin and neighbors, part of the living community. Our senses offer us the surest portal to these truths, and the stories in this volume abound in sounds, textures, and aromas. Every sensory experience is an invitation to curiosity and belonging.

Repeated close attention to the community of life produces both inward and outward transformations, and these stories are invitations to both. The inward changes are shifts in our will and attention, joyful commitments to attend to the lives of others, human and more-than-human. This inner turn then leads to outward work. In what ways are we called to respond to the beauty and brokenness of the world? That calling might be heard from the raven, the chickadee, the voice of a community activist or biologist, or the sound of rain on mossy logs. Calling also arrives not as sound, but the scent of the woods, the light glancing from the filigreed marvel of a feather, or in the sight of vortices of swifts circling home.

Trees link soil and sky. Each root burrows into and enlivens the underworld where the dead go to be resurrected in new forms. From these lively tombs, trees carry energy and knowledge upward and outward, into their trunks and crowns. Through the trees' veined networks, the soil speaks to the sun, and in this conversation is born new life, not as a metaphor but as a reality made one atom, photon, and chemical bond at a time. This heavenward movement of matter and energy connects the trees with the winged ones, creatures that feel the air as a living liquid. Tomb and renewal. Sunlight and new flesh. Spirit and moving air. These meetings are the feathered forest, and each is generative and expansive, building opportunities for all life.

David George Haskell

Introduction

Did the postcard tumble into my hands, or was it hidden under a letter from my mother stuffed full of *Washington Post* news clippings? I stared at a black-and-white photo of a hippo surfacing from a silvery pool. The wrinkled brow, bulging sideways eyes, and flaring nostrils of the branchlike nose reminded me of a tree trunk. Sentient. Hippo and tree.

Flipping the card over, I read the words and then skipped outside the post office, waving the card like a permission slip. There, in that tiny town by the John Day River below the Strawberry Mountain Wilderness of northeast Oregon, the week before I would turn twenty-five, I had opened a portal. I'd heard back from Ursula K. Le Guin.

I imagine the famous author dashing off the note in her lively script, affixing a 13-cent Crazy Horse stamp, and addressing the card to me (then going by my given name, Deborah) at Box 9 in Prairie City on November 18, 1983.

> Dear Deborah, Thanks for writing! I appreciate the fellowship. Becoming a writer is sort of like becoming a tree. It takes a long time and is risky! But worth it. Keep on making new rings—, All the best, UKG

I had written to Le Guin after reading her October 6th letter to the editor in the *Oregonian* that began, "This is a lament for an old tree, a horse-chestnut tree on Northwest Thurman Street." The city of Portland had ordered the tree to be cut down after one complaint from an old man. "It was a big tree, a great one, sound-limbed, with strong roots," Le Guin wrote. As a tree-lover since childhood, I felt bereft when I read, "Waking in the night I feel the absence of those great branches outside our windows, as they say people feel pain in a limb that has been amputated, that isn't there."

In my bird-track penmanship, I remember expressing solidarity, sorrow, and my wish that I could have chained myself to the tree and prevented the killing. I also confessed I wanted to be a writer—not a dabbler, but a professional. I'd fallen for her novels at age eleven reading the Earthsea trilogy, often nestled in the fork of a maple tree. She published more than twenty novels and hundreds of short stories before her death in 2018 at the age of eighty-eight. Breaking the glass ceiling of science fiction as a woman, Le Guin changed the genre from craft to literature. She had a fierce love for wild trees that threaded through Earthsea and the heartrending adult novel, *The Word for World Is Forest*.

In that auspicious autumn of 1983, I had begun a daily practice of ascending attic stairs to sit at an antique wooden desk by a dormer window facing Strawberry Mountain looming above a range of peaks across an open valley where cattle grazed. I put sheet after sheet in a manual typewriter, composing directionless prose of elk bugling, Pileated Woodpeckers drumming, and fallen golden larch needles feathering the trails. My pages were like the leaves on the cottonwood outside the house, destined to fall and compost.

After winding up a seasonal job on the Malheur National Forest, my first unemployment paychecks arrived and with them the gift of time to write. All summer, I'd hiked on compass lines through centuries-old, red-gold ponderosas, western larch, and grand firs, clambering over downed trees, jumping over rocky streams, and stopping at set intervals to take tree measurements within the parameters of a circle. Yet, I struggled with the objective of inventorying timber for the next sale of "complete overstory removal," which meant logging all the stately elder pines. Sometimes, I would veer from my compass line to miss the biggest trees.

Few people then were considering the fate of birds and their animal kin as twinned with those of wild forests. Every day in the field, I witnessed wonders. Once, a cougar slipped across a meadow like a long whisk of sunlight. Warblers, vireos, thrushes, flycatchers, and woodpeckers were daily companions. Cultural history was literally carved into trees, such as in the wide living ponderosa I found etched with a seven-foot curvaceous woman, the work of a lonely Basque sheepherder a century earlier. I walked in the footsteps of the Northern Paiute, among the groups who identify as the Numic peoples.

The postcard from Le Guin rooted me in purpose. I applied for a reporter job at the *Blue Mountain Eagle* weekly newspaper in John Day. The editor took a leap of faith. I had a biology degree and zero journalism experience. He did know I could write letters to the editor. More likely, he was desperate to find anyone willing to work long hours for $200 a week covering news throughout the 4,500-square-miles of Grant County.

I botched my first assignment covering Senator Mark Hatfield's town hall in John Day. I'd never heard of the inverted pyramid of putting the top news first. I didn't know the basics of grounding a reader in who, what, when, where, and why, or what to quote and what to paraphrase. Typing my stories to load within a big box of a primitive computer, I'd push a button and cross my fingers. At least a quarter of the time, the article would be swallowed up. Rewriting as fast as I could often resulted in a better story.

Those two years I wrote for the *Blue Mountain Eagle* before heading to the University of Montana for journalism graduate school taught me other lessons. On an assignment, I met Bonnie Nance, a rancher caring for a rescued calf in her living room. Until then I hadn't known the tender side of ranchers. She had dark circles under her eyes from rising in the night to warm bottled milk for the motherless animal snuggled on a worn couch. Bonnie loved the land, as I did, and her life was far tougher than mine. As she cradled the calf, I felt a stirring of possibility. By tapping into our common humanity, might we come closer to sharing kinship for the natural world?

When we live in community, like the wild forest, we become interwoven, embracing what we share and our differences, too. Of all our animal kin, birds have the promise of linking us across borders to find our interdependence. I once lived next door to a crusty older man whose politics were the opposite of mine. But all gruffness slipped away one summer when he and I became co-conspirators, seeking the nest of a White-headed Woodpecker family. Whenever he spotted the uncommon bird or heard the purred *pee-kik-kik* call, he would text me, and I'd come running. When I did the same, he'd head to my tangled bird-friendly yard. Soon, I was digging up native purple asters for him. In the fall, he sent me photos of overflowing daisylike flowers. Birds led us away from prickly subjects we could not agree on and toward a common ground of caring for the more-than-human world.

When conceiving this book, I asked myself three questions: "Where do I want to immerse in nature? How can my passion for birds be part of a new journey? And how might my writing make a difference? I've long had a love for wild forests, for the birds that dwell within them, and for saving big trees and wilderness.

Enter the "feathered forest"—my term for an ecosystem as interlocking and miraculous as the feathers that are the secret to bird flight. Buffering from heat and cold like layers of downy plumage, the forest shelters her inhabitants in a changing climate with chaotic temperature extremes. To find the wild groves, I seek native trees growing in companionship and with plentiful standing dead trees, called snags. These are often the places defined as old growth, old, or ancient. My favorite scientific description comes from a 2020 British Columbia Provincial government task force:

> Old forests meld light and dark; their structural complexity can include large old living trees, large standing dead snags, long downed logs, a multi-layered canopy, horizontal patchiness with canopy gaps that allow understory growth, and hummocky micro-topography.[1]

To experience a feathered forest, I often walk alone, jot notes, and let beauty wash over me. For an example, come with me to the wild trees by Clear Lake in Oregon's western Cascades on a July day:

> The pool is the giant's oval eye tinted turquoise and azure. Douglas-fir branches sway like a hundred bird wings in the sigh of a breeze. A weave of dogwood, huckleberry, vine maple, alder, and elderberry in bloom become the basketry rimming the Great Spring, bubbling up from beneath lava right here, the McKenzie River's beginnings. I cup my hands in the water and drink icy mental clarity. Can I hear the roots drinking? No rain has fallen for more than a month, yet all feels drenched and luxuriant.
>
> Leaving the Great Spring, I slow-step back to Clear Lake. A breeze riffles strands of my shoulder-length hair. Summer heats the Oregon grape, thimbleberry, and fireweed blossoming in full columnar flourishes of magenta pink. Now a bee. A Steller's Jay flashing indigo wings as if stealing splashes of this spring. A Spotted Sandpiper—narrow of wing and spotted of breast—arrows from lake toward the spring. Aren't we all drawn to the beginnings of things? A carpenter ant, shiny and black, crawls over my leg where I'm now sitting on the raised root of a big-bellied Douglas-fir, wider in girth than I am tall at five feet, five inches. Touching the tree's channeled mossy bark, a protective shield from past fires over hundreds of years, I reflect on the meaning of origin for jay, sandpiper, ant, tree, and river. Perhaps we all feel a homeward tug, each in our own manner.
>
> On the way to the lake and the spring, I walked in a state of grace along a soft needled trail. There's something about the tall, taller, and tallest

> trees—the way I can't go far without pausing to tilt my head back and gaze up, up, and up. The way sunlight tarries on her journey downward. The way of cool shadowed nooks. The tenacity of a standing dead western hemlock white as bone leaning on another hemlock scarred and frayed yet still alive. The faint chiming of Golden-crowned Kinglets high in the canopies.

My concept of a feathered forest coalesced when I climbed a centuries-old, 200-foot Douglas-fir with an intrepid graduate student, Nina Ferrari, as she studied forest birds in their vertical world. Ascending on a rope into the canopy, my perspective shifted at every level until I was gently rocking in the tree's crown and feeling birdlike.

It was there I understood Le Guin's description of the Immanent Grove that is fundamental to her Earthsea novels. She wrote, "The forest seems to shift and move, but . . . the Grove does not move. Its roots are the roots of being. It is all the rest that moves."[2] Le Guin also penned a warning—one she witnessed as log truck after log truck rolled out of national forests filled with immense trees. "If the Grove were cut, all wizardry would fail. The roots of those trees are the roots of knowledge."[3]

Shaped by dynamic forces over the millennia, ancient forests thrum with interrelated lives, many hidden from view. Birds of the feathered forest build astonishing communities among the living, burned, and renewed trees. Nothing can be neatly divided. All parts are cycling life, death, and rebirth.

I reside with my husband a few miles south of Bend, on the eastern flanks of the Cascades in central Oregon. Some of my observations on birds, feathers, and wildness come from attending to my home yard or strolling a half mile to what I call the Turquoise Forest, a sliver of the Deschutes National Forest edged by a 7,000-year-old lava flow and home to the Grandmother Tree, an amber-barked, wide-plated and bodacious ponderosa pine..

To explore ancient groves, I took short trips in all directions of the compass, seeking those that might best exemplify the bioregion of Cascadia, comprising southeast Alaska and British Columbia, Washington, Oregon, parts of Idaho, the edges of Montana and Wyoming, and northern California, home to the planet's tallest trees—the redwoods. The region is defined by the watersheds of the Columbia and Fraser Rivers that flow into the Pacific Ocean.

Indigenous peoples lived here for thousands of years in respectful relationship with the natural world before the near genocide caused by colonialism. They are still here today, resilient and passing down traditions. I live in the traditional lands of the Confederated Tribes of Warm Springs: the Wana Łama (Warm Springs), Wasq'ú (Wasco), and Northern Paiute (Numic) people.

Many of Cascadia's forests bear the imprints of anadromous fish, which spend part of their life cycles in fresh water and part in salt. For thousands of years, Chinook, coho, pink, chum, and sockeye salmon and steelhead migrated en masse up rivers to spawn and die where they were born. Before the era of dams, Bald Eagles and trees alike grew mighty on their flesh. In return, the forests gifted the waters in nutrients, taken up by aquatic insects then eaten by young salmon returning to the sea.

The world's largest temperate rainforest falls within Cascadia, including the tallest and heaviest trees on Earth. The more than nine-hundred-year-old redwood Hyperion holds today's record as loftiest on the planet at 381 feet tall, with a diameter of 15.2 feet and more than 550 million leaves. Olympic National Park is known for record-setting trees, including western redcedar, Sitka spruce, western hemlock, Douglas-fir, and grand fir. Stretching 2,500 miles from coastal northern California to the western side of the Gulf of Alaska, the rain-soaked forests sustain the most biodiversity outside of the tropics and are the densest in carbon. No other place on our spinning planet yields this abundance.

Coastal forests with high rainfall and summer fog are interconnected with the upwelling of the Pacific Ocean bringing nutrients to the surface near land. More than a million seabirds nest on rocky islands near shore. The fate of trees and sea are entwined—one ecosystem feeds the other. The temperate rainforest also extends inland to the western Cascades, where some of the tallest and oldest Douglas-firs in the world grow.

Crossing over the Cascades, a north–south barrier to coastal rainfall, eastside forest ecosystems vary dramatically by elevation, aspect, rainfall, and geology. A half-hour drive east of Bend in the high desert are the world's oldest western juniper forests, wise in the ways of longevity where water is scarce. The Blue Mountains arc east and north from Bend for 300 miles. Connecting the Cascades to the Rockies, the Blues form Oregon's largest ecoregion, containing almost half the forests in the state.

I'm drawn to Cascadia as river-centric. A watershed is featherlike, with the river as the quill or shaft and the entering tributaries as the vane. A river desires to run free and wild down to her confluence. A forest desires to grow free and tall from roots to crowns. Birds weave desire into mossy nests. Within every ancient forest, I feel the desire to spiral upward on feathered wings.

In our industrial era of human-caused perils, feathered forests can serve as climate refugia, a geologic term for places that escape catastrophic changes. Refugia act like lifeboats for biodiversity, coming to shore when the storm is over. In the last interglacial period in Greenland (about 130,000 to 116,000 years ago), birds flew with seeds of the Greenland mountain ash to eastern North America. Those trees then vanished from Greenland during the next glacial cycle. However, the birds had inadvertently planted the ash seeds 3,000 miles away. The trees grew in refugia, buffered from changes and persisting through tough times. When the ice sheets began to melt and retreat, the descendent birds flew back with the seeds to replant them in Greenland.

I can think of no better guides to climate refugia than birds. When the colossal asteroid struck the Yucatan Peninsula 66 million years ago, the only surviving dinosaurs were birds. Feathered flights took them to the hidden places safe from fiery heat. As the planet slowly cooled and became more inviting, birds continued to diversify into today's 11,000 species. More than 400 species live part or full time in Cascadia. The most imperiled are Northern Spotted Owls and Marbled Murrelets—dependent on ancient forests.

At every level of feathered forests, birds lead to facets of climate refugia. Towering trees of many species, sizes, ages, and widths create cool microclimates not found in logged and simplified forests. Like a deep swimming pool, temperatures are colder at the bottom. Within these groves are refreshing microclimates created by springs, creeks, mossy fallen trees, and rockfall.

As no bird lives in isolation, no forest survives as a fragment. To flourish, there must be the equivalent of flocks. Turn to birds. Turn to the way of feathers. A plucked bird cannot fly any more than a clear-cut can sustain a richness of life. Turn to the way of patterns, naming, and the wisdom of trees living for centuries and, in their dying, nurturing the future.

"No way was clear, no light unbroken, in the forest," wrote Le Guin in *The Word for World Is Forest*. "Into wind, water, sunlight, starlight, there always entered leaf and branch, bole and root, the shadowy, the complex."[4]

How do we protect what we love in a time of loss? How do we mend what's broken? Three billion fewer individual birds live in North America now compared with 1970. Cascadia's great forests have dwindled by 90 percent from logging. Those are hard statistics to swallow. Perhaps we all could use a radical shift to lift us from our gravity-confined way into the realms of birds.

When my heart is breaking, I visualize ancient trees flying away to a place of safety. Set free from their roots, the great trunks with their whorled needled canopies are heading skyward. Escaping into a hidden climate refugia, they will take root once more. Hermit Warblers will teeter on tiptop branches. Spotted Owls will perch just below. Varied Thrushes will croon one-chord lullabies among unfurling ferns.

I want to be there, too, far from the artificial, plastic, concrete, and confining din of technological life. Sometimes we must . . . stop. And, in the stopping, turn our attention to the closest bird in the closest tree. Notice what happens then to our spirits. Uplift. Hold a fallen feather. Glide fingers and thumb up and down the vane to know the meaning of interlocking.

In a time of shifting baselines, it's hard to fathom what a big ancient forest looks like. Our future is uncertain as we reach one tipping point after another that signals planetary distress. And still, I choose action. From hummingbirds to hawks, birds lead us to refugia that we must protect in a time of skyrocketing temperatures, record drought, and increasingly severe wildfires driven by high winds of extreme weather. Winged messengers awaken us to the urgent need to stop burning fossil fuels and to protect wild forests with ancient trees that are capturing and storing far more carbon than younger trees.

Writing this ode to the feathered forests, I have returned to Le Guin's writing about naming and the wisdom of trees. I had lamented the loss of her postcard for decades, until a winter day in 2024 when, sorting through old folders, the card fell out. In the same file were the yellowed pages I'd typed in that attic in Prairie City. Le Guin was fifty-four when she took time to encourage an unknown young woman in a small town. It's my turn to mentor, even as I keep putting on new rings and taking risks. One of the risks is heartbreak. I choose to keep falling in love with every sunrise, every singing bird among a shiver of branches.

ONE

Tall Tree Climb

I am 175 feet up a lofty Douglas-fir and about to find myself in trouble. Red Crossbills whisk by seeking cones. Their flight calls skip through curtains of branches. Green needles interlock like feathers. Secure in my climbing harness, I drink in the full cup of jay-blue sky. Everything has a signature. Lookout Creek's soothing flow breezes upward. A Western Swallowtail butterfly sails past my hand. From far below, a Varied Thrush chords the morning in one-note praise song.

Halfway up the tree, I'd watched a Western Flycatcher at eye level as he whistled a quick uptick, *hap-PY?* Poised before a flight downward, this bird of Oregon in summer and Mexico in winter peered from a lichen-draped limb. I noted the teardrop white eye ring, peaked head, and silky plumage. Studying the wash of lemony breast feathers, olive head and back, creamy wing bars, and notched ash gray tail, I grew curious. Do the colors mimic the lichens encrusting the branches or the lichens mimic the bird? The two seemed so entwined. A female flycatcher weaves spiderweb to bind lichen with moss, leaves, and soft bark, forming a dainty cup nest. Every bird of this ancient forest is leading me through a maze of relationships.

Held in the arms of the sheltering tree, I know why I prefer the term ancient. A Douglas-fir hits a growth stride at a hundred years and keeps going for one human lifetime after another. The oldest on record was 1,400 years old when cut down in 1913 near Mount Vernon, Washington, sixty miles north of Seattle.

There's collective wisdom in centuries-old tree and forests. Here in the H.J. Andrews Experimental Forest, internationally famous for studies of ancient forests, I'm in a temperate rainforest nuzzled within the Lookout Creek watershed of Oregon's western Cascades. Beauty is defined in living trees that are straight, forked, and twisted in a carefree dance with the dying, dead, hollow, and broken-topped. The bark of long-lived trees reminds me of my deepening wrinkles—yet ten times so.

Within the heart of this 6,400 acres of rare and intact ancient forest are some of Cascadia's tallest remaining trees. Many of the Douglas-firs are more than 250 feet high. The elders are at least 400 years old, with those that have survived past big fires living for more than 750 years. This is the traditional homeland of the Kalapuya people. The Pacific Northwest Research Station, Willamette National Forest, and Oregon State University oversee the 22 square miles (15,800 acres) of the Andrews Forest. Elevations range from 1,350 feet to 5,430 feet. Douglas-firs, western redcedar, and western hemlock intermingle in the lower elevation, while higher up are noble and silver firs. Winter storms typically soak the spongy forests in rain lower down and snow, higher up. Summers tend to be dry and warm. Annual precipitation averages 84 inches. In this era of accelerating climate change, the word "typical" has become suspect.

On this not-too-hot early August day, I'm at peace within the center of a rippling sea of trees harboring thousands of life forms. A year later, in 2023, lightning would strike a tree on a ridge across Lookout Creek and spark a wildfire. So much would change, except for the vivid memory of a climb that, when I close my eyes, remains in the present tense.

Driftwood-gray spires of dead trees quill the sky. Exuberant as my twelve-year-old self after laddering up a pine, I don't feel over sixty. I've never come close to being this high up in a tree. Looking down is dizzying. Yet, I feel safe within centuries-old trees that are kin and not kin, old and not old, straight or leaning, clustered or not. Time slows down among the ancient ones. They do not rush or make to-do lists, yet everything gets done, like a gourmet chef who never hurries yet presents a bountiful feast at the exact right moment.

Two hours earlier, I had placed my hands on the trunk and silently asked the tree nicknamed "Traverse" for permission to climb, promising to be gentle on the lichen-tufted and furrowed bark. I would be the two-legged spider laddering my way up via the single-rope system that arborists call rope walking. I began far away from the trunk, walking in air, coming close to the trunk only about 80 feet up. The first limbs were at about 60 feet—part of a Douglas-fir's self-pruning strategy when branches are shaded and no longer receiving light.

Near the top, I feel an unearned confidence swaying alone, donned in a bright yellow hard hat. Far below, Nina Ferrari is climbing up a second rope.

She's the youthful, intrepid graduate student who ascends even higher giants for a sky-breaking climate study of birds at every vertical level, one never attempted before in this environment. I'm counting on her help to switch the ascender to the descender device for the rappel down.

Gazing up, I decide I can edge 10 feet higher, closer to the 200-foot treetop for a better view. But as I push the ascender up the rope and step down, the rope slides out of the ascender around my ankle. My foot dangles free. Precarious. Slight skip of a heartbeat. Nina told me this might happen. Deep breath. I can do this. Just reach down and press the rope back in. But nothing is easy here. I can't quite finagle the move. Go slow, Marina, I tell myself. The breath of the tree is my breath.

When I was in fifth and sixth grades, my family lived in a Pennsylvania farmhouse with a wide-trunked maple out front. I'd spring up to grasp the lowest branch, swing one leg up and then the other to balance before scrambling to a favorite fork in the tree. Rigging a rope to pull up books by favorite authors, from Ursula K. Le Guin to J. R. R. Tolkien, I read for hours as birds came close, from Northern Cardinals to Tufted Titmice.

Remembering the ease of childhood agility, I raise my right foot to find purchase on a sturdy branch below me. My hand is shaking. Leaning over, I flick open the ascender latch and thread the rope back in. Snap! My little triumph. Still, I am relieved to make out Nina's orange helmet visible through the needled lacery 40 feet below. While my rope-walking way up was relatively easy, her alternate system on the second rope reminded me of a frog taking small upward leaps and requiring a strong core and arms. She'd given me her preferred equipment for my novice attempt.

A jingle of carabiners announces Nina's arrival. A wisp of dark curly hair escapes from beneath her helmet. A few specks of bark spangle her shiny cheeks. Her eyes remind me of the golden-brown plumage of a Pacific Wren, dweller of moss-cloaked fallen trees, upturned roots, and a singer of melodies like a splashing icy brook.

For her climate study of birds in their three-dimensional world, Nina selected Douglas-firs as the most common conifer in the Andrews. Their sturdy straight columnar trunks are also ideal for climbing. In this 2022 season, she'd regularly summited seven ancient Douglas-firs and seven 60-to-80-year-old trees in plantations for comparison. Among the centuries-old study trees is McRae—the tallest documented tree in the Andrews Forest at 302 feet—

equaling the Statue of Liberty. Living up to her race car of a last name, Ferrari, Nina once scaled six towering study trees in a single day, an impressive feat. At 10-meter intervals up each trunk she had secured an audio recording unit for capturing bird vocalizations and sensors logging temperature and humidity. To retrieve the data took acrobatic maneuvers on the rope to swing in closer to the trunks. The trees are also far apart and require lugging heavy ropes in a pack over rough terrain and setting up for each climb.

Today, there's no rush. Suspended in deep time, we are free from the pell-mell motion of daily life often quickening toward the next task. I ask her what word describes her feeling up in the canopy. "Serene," she says without hesitation. "You are small and insignificant yet connected to this huge tree you trust to keep you alive."

Complexity reigns. Nothing stands still for long. Wind gusts knock down trees—creating gaps for wildflowers, saplings, and room for flycatchers to fly from limbs to nip insects in the openings. At night, an owl pounces on a vole. Flying squirrels glide to the forest floor seeking aromatic truffles in the life-filled soil. Native fungus, natural diseases, tunneling beetles, and dwarf mistletoe are sculptors of diversity. Below ground, a mycorrhizal network of roots laced in fungi are sharing and gaining nutrients and tapping messages. Wildfire, too, is part of the co-evolution of animals and forests. The fires burn differently depending on where, when, and how. Some can be blazing hot, while others creep along to be snuffed by rains.

On a normal day, Nina would descend and speed off to the next tree. This is a postseason climb to help my research for a birding magazine feature story. Reaching in my pocket for my iPhone to take photos, I'm sure I'll drop it. Why when leaning over a cliff do I think I'll lose my balance? Why do I teeter when crossing a rushing stream on a log that would be a cinch on land? Perhaps it's because I'm off kilter when untethered to the Earth. I envy rock climbers, pilots, and one friend who paraglides in rising thermals among circling eagles and hawks in the high Wallowa Mountains of northeast Oregon.

Gripping the phone tighter, I touch "voice memo" and whisper: "Solemnity. A state of grace. I sense wisdom, life, entanglement, and all we don't know. I'm so small up here, like a nuthatch tight against the trunk of this Douglas-fir." In the arms of this tree I feel a growing trust, even as my tongue touches the repaired front tooth chipped by a childhood fall.

I am eight years old and fearless as a squirrel. Shimmying up a leaning tree, crawling on hands and knees, or balancing with arms spread wide, MaryEllen and I play our game of Never Touch the Ground within the incense of redcedar, hemlock, and Douglas-fir. Spiderwebs trail from our flannel shirts. We do not think about landings. Doming the sky far above us is snowy Mount Rainier, rightfully Təqʷuʔməʔ (pronounced "Taquoma"), meaning mother of all waters in the language of the Puyallup people.

Sunlight strands through needled branches of young and elder trees, some straight and others crisscrossed in their falling. Close by, a newborn fawn curls up tight within a swale protected by sword ferns. Dark pooled eyes blinked. Cinnamon fur held a snowstorm of spots. On this summer day it is just MaryEllen of the long raven hair and me, then Debbie of the cropped short auburn hair and freckled nose. Nothing will divert us for hours. Or so we assume. Upright on a balance beam of a tree that had fallen and wedged between two tall Douglas-firs maybe five feet off the ground, I edge sideways across the span. Is it the startle of a Steller's Jay landing with a squawk and flash of cobalt blues and black crest? Or do I slip on slick lichen?

I remember flying forward and slamming headfirst into what ought to have been spongy moss, fern, sorrel, wild ginger, and decaying bark instead of unforgiving roots and stones. My teeth hurt. My eyes hurt. My whole face hurt. Warm blood trickled from my head and gushed from my nose. The raccoon eyes would fade. The chip in my front tooth would be permanent. I learned gravity is merciless. Balance is tenuous. But I did not stop climbing off the ground or wishing I had bird wings.

In contrast to sturdy and muscular Nina, I'm slight and small-boned, with the build of the long-distance runner I used to be until my lower back protested. When I took those first steps off the ground to climb Traverse, I spun in the air like a spider on her silken strand. Gradually, I took bigger air steps and pushed the hand ascender up the single rope with more confidence. About 20 feet off the ground, I paused to take in the enormity of tree trunks in all directions.

Close by, a western redcedar with shaggy soft bark held out her limbs bearing needlelike pressed ferns. Dark-eyed Juncos trilled from rhododendrons. Spiders seemed to twist sun rays into webs. At 60 feet off the ground, I reached the first branches—sturdy, shortened, and bearing a trove of papery, crusty lichens waiting for rain after a scorching weeklong heat wave.

Climbing slowed at 100 feet up as I navigated past limbs. Who lives in this Lilliputian world? So far, scientists have identified more than 3,100 invertebrate species alone in the Andrews Forest—from insects, spiders, mites, and beetles to millipedes, slugs, and snails.

I felt as If I'd slipped back into the great forests of hundreds of years ago, long before Euro-Americans arrived, a time when the Indigenous peoples knew their way well among forests and valleys, often lighting careful fires to nurture huckleberries and other foods on both sides of the Cascades. A time before the rampant logging that decimated more than 90 percent of the Pacific Northwest wild forests. A time when the Northern Spotted Owl was not on the brink of extinction, but was common.

Imagine. A Northern Spotted Owl flies on wings of silence among the misty columns of Douglas-firs and western hemlocks extending mile on mile, rising high in whorled layers of branches. Fringes on the trailing edge of flight feathers calm rough air. Comblike structures on the leading edge break up airflow. She glides, quickens her wingbeats, and glides on. Night-sky eyes are all-seeing. Hearing is keen—sounds collected in her disk-shaped face. There! A patter of feet. Hunger sharpens every sense. Sharp talons flex. She veers and strikes, then breaks the red tree vole's neck with her beak. Her call to a mate of seven years is a rising whistle.

Blink. I snap back to the present from Einstein's four dimensions of height, width, depth, and time. This day marks my third trek with Nina over the course of three months to attempt to climb a tall tree. I'd thought it would be as simple as walking up to a Douglas-fir, putting on a harness, clipping in, and ascending without a hitch. In June, I was stymied by rain. A month later, we hiked to the most massive of Nina's study trees, at six feet diameter, named Wolfy. There, I'd made it 15 feet up to spin in midair, but we were thwarted by the setup of the second rope, which jammed on a high limb. I also fumbled with the double-locking carabiners designed for safety. Confessing my difficulty with the maneuver, Nina handed me a carabiner.

"Now I know you're coming back, to return the carabiner and try again," she said. For the next month, I carried the D-shaped metal ring with the spring hinge in my jacket pocket. I'd close my eyes and practice the deft opening move to put the rope in and take it out. I was earning my right to unlock the door to safe climbing.

I'll never forget my scare alone with my foot no longer in the pulley or that moment of overcoming adversity. When the time came for us to rappel down, I found joy in the free fall of rappelling—more bird, less human.

At the tree's base, Nina's adviser Dr. Matthew (Matt) Betts of Oregon State University had waited for us, equipped with a hand radio for communication and safety. He had generously come along to help and to answer my questions for the story. I pictured him among the huckleberries, rhododendrons, and ferns seeking another thread to follow among endless ecological relationships. Perhaps he peeled back and then carefully replaced a strip of moist, fragrant redcedar to check for salamanders hiding in a nurse log, so-called for the fallen tree nursing new life.

An ornithologist, lead scientist, and head of Long-Term Ecological Research at the Andrews Forest, Matt has the lean physique of a cyclist. Sometimes he rides his bike the 100 miles from the university in Corvallis to the forest. He is the author and a co-author of several research publications in the Andrews connecting bird survival to the older forests offering cooling microclimates.

One of the birds is the Hermit Warbler, dazzling with a bright yellow head, a chickadeelike black bib, and a song finer than sugar. Nesting only in lush montane forests of northern California, Oregon, and Washington and wintering in Latin America, the warbler has a penchant for high canopies and for staying cool in hot weather. But how flexible is this bird in shifting down from the sunny canopy through the increasingly insulated layers to find respite from the heat?

As temperatures climb, climate-sensitive songbirds that stick to territories they defend for food, space, and nesting could be in trouble if conditions become unbearable. If flexible, they might find respite from heat. To know their vertical world takes being as birdlike as possible. After several years of craning his head to hear melodies of Hermit Warblers hundreds of feet overhead, Matt had a dream project in mind—to study forest songbirds in their vertical habitats to find out whether and where different species could find climate refugia. He faced a dilemma. What graduate student could take on long physically demanding days of climbing colossal trees in a temperate rainforest known for mists, showers, storms, winds, and mosquitos? No one had ever attempted a study of birds like the one he envisioned.

When Matt met Nina, a rock climber, he broached the subject. She said yes without hesitation. Little did Nina know that her studies would evolve from a master's degree project to a doctoral dissertation. After graduating from University of Vermont in 2016, Nina had tracked birds for field studies in remote northern Maine, Mount St. Helens, and the Sierra Nevada before pursuing her master's degree. She chose Oregon State University because of her admiration for Matt's work and a desire to research in the famed Andrews Forest.

Growing up with scientist parents, Nina had that enviable childhood where a muddy face and hair tangled in leaves marked a good day. Her mother worked as a volcanologist for the US Geological Survey, and her father as a plankton biologist for the Smithsonian Institution. "I was the kid who'd put a slug on her face," she said when we'd hiked into the forest in July. As a small girl in northern Virginia, she'd pull her bright red Radio Flyer wagon down the street collecting caterpillars and bringing them home. Once, her bedroom reeked from collecting jars jammed full of dead cicadas. That's when her mother put her foot down.

Despite Matt's confidence, he had a few qualms. "I was excited, but sending someone up a tree close to 300 feet tall made me nervous, too."

Nina learned tree-climbing skills from the legendary Dr. Eric Forsman, whose Northern Spotted Owl studies in the Andrews Forest in the 1970s showed the birds were threatened with extinction from the widespread logging of old-growth forests. Protecting owls under the Endangered Species Act led to protections of threatened forests. Now in his seventies and an expert trainer of research climbers, Forsman also tailored specific gear for Nina's unique task.

Andrews Forest director Mark Schulze took Nina under his wing, too. Together, they rigged the chosen trees for climbing and fastened the audio recording units and temperature loggers to the trunks. That task was far from easy, like putting a belt around an elephant. The tree I climbed was dubbed Traverse for a tricky maneuver that Mark had to make—crossing over from another tree to position the top rope. Mark has climbed tall trees for decades and studies cone phenology (timing of ripening) in a warming climate.

While Nina's ascents are mostly solo, she has at least one person on the ground for safety and to help lug heavy packs over trailless, steep forests with downed trees and thickets. I shouldered a pack with ropes more than once, only to slip and scrabble for footing. I wanted to pull my weight. Admiring her capabilities, I had asked Nina how she managed. "I'm super comfortable in the outdoors, but there's a physicality to this project," she said. "I remind myself I'm right for this study for other reasons. I work around my lack of brute force as a problem to solve."

Good advice for living, I think. Birds do this, too, through evolution to find their solutions to challenges and live in community—each with their own workarounds, like the Red Crossbills cruising the canopies of older forests seeking cones. These brilliant red finches with songs like chips of sunshine freed from clouds have crossed bills for extricating seeds from under the scales of cones. Over time, at least eleven types of crossbills further specialized, each with a finely adapted beak, such as a small crossed bill for petite western hemlock cones. Birders are recording their flight calls, which are distinctive for each kind of crossbill. I'm reminded to listen anew to every bird.

In 1958 (the year I was born), Robert MacArthur changed the course of ecology with his classic study of five eastern warblers—Cape May, Yellow-rumped, Black-throated Green, Blackburnian, and Bay-breasted Warblers.[1] Prior to his research in a northeastern conifer forest, scientists assumed the warblers flew randomly about tree crowns seeking insects. For his PhD dissertation, the twenty-eight-year-old budding ecologist studied whether this premise was true by documenting where the warblers liked to dine. The shorter spruce trees allowed him to watch warblers from the ground.

He discovered that warblers are choosy. Cape May Warblers hunted for insects on the outer tips of branches at the top. Bay-breasted Warblers gleaned the needled twigs in the middle of lower limbs. The birds specialized, too, in their capture techniques—from upside down foraging to hovering and hawking (snatching flying insects in the air). Called "niche partitioning," this apportioning of a forest canopy assures there's enough food to go around without competition.

One of the founders of evolutionary ecology, Robert MacArthur sadly died at forty-two from cancer. In a tribute to him, esteemed biologist E. O. Wilson and Evelyn Hutchinson praised his originality, imagination, and rigorous scientific method as a mathematician-naturalist.

Until Nina's studies, no one had tried to replicate vertical studies of birds in a Pacific Northwest forest across multiple conifer trees. The sheer height of the Douglas-firs, western hemlocks, and redcedars alone obscures the view from the ground. One distinct advantage today is LiDAR (light detection and ranging), a technology applying lasers to generate three-dimensional maps, now available for the entirety of the Andrews Forest. That means Nina does not have to describe the unique layered branches of every tree as part of her fieldwork.

A series of questions inform her quest to find out whether Pacific Northwest birds share or do not share vertical spaces as temperatures vary throughout the day at differing levels of the canopy. She compares the stratified older forests with simplified second-growth stands. Are the birds like high-rise apartment dwellers sticking to their given addresses? Or do they act in the way of Goldilocks seeking a chair that is just right? In an emergency, what options will they have to move? Will they compete or cooperate? Can birds adapt quickly enough during rapid climate change to take advantage of cool microclimates that are unique to the ancient forest? Where are those cool pockets located within the secretive recesses of a forest replete in branches, limbs, trunks of almost infinite variety?

When I rappelled down in bursts of free fall, controlled by braking, I felt something far different from the rock climbing I'd attempted in my early thirties. Here, a living tree limb held the rope. Close to the trunk, I tried to be butterfly-light and avoid harming lichens, ferns, moss, and insects clinging to the hardy bark. As I lowered myself from overstory to midstory to understory through the pockets, scarves, and buttons of a forest glowing in green light and layered in shelter, I awakened to the wild forest the birds know. Soon after, I would dive deeply into birds as pilots revealing the multistoried climate refugia of wild trees. The way of the feathered forest is a constant looping, circling, and connecting of old and young, life and death.

TWO

Feathers

An unearthly shriek pierced the glass window where I wrote at my desk at my home south of Bend, Oregon. Jumping up for a better view, I saw the source. A male Northern Flicker, upside down in the snow, beat his wings like flames fanning fire. A Cooper's Hawk mantled her quarry with wings spread and lowered to shield her prize from escape. Talons punctured the flicker's downy breast feathers. The wounded bird's cries cut through stillness like shards of ice. The hawk jabbed her hooked beak into the flicker's chest. Plucked feathers misted away. So patient, this slow killing of a woodpecker almost as big as the accipiter—a blue-gray forest hawk with speckled reddish barring on her chest, a banded long tail, and rounded wings for quick turns around trees.

Opening the front door a few inches at a time, I stepped outside with camera in hand. The hawk noticed. She picked up the flicker and lumbered with her burden to land below a plum tree. Her grip loosened. The flicker escaped. Struggling into the air, the injured bird flapped toward me like a smoking plane with a pilot clinging to controls. He cleared my head by inches and flew over our fence. Half his orange and black tail feathers were missing. The hawk closed the distance. From the neighbor's forested yard, I heard one more cacophonous cry. Then silence.

Kneeling in the snow among scattered feathers like fire and ash, I felt sorrow and acceptance. One life quelled. A hawk nourished. Dark-eyed Juncos returned to our feeders. As they flew in, their tails flared wide like piano keys—white, black, and white—feather music.

I couldn't keep the flicker feathers, but I brought a few inside. The Migratory Bird Treaty Act prohibits possessing feathers of native North American birds without a permit, excepting feathers from legally hunted game birds (like ducks, geese, and quail) and for cultural use by Indigenous peoples. My investigations were temporary.

Picking up a primary wing feather, I spun the apricot-orange quill between my right thumb and index finger. The quill is the calamus, the hollow part of the feather shaft that attaches to a bird's skin. Above that are the soft vanes extending on both sides of the shaft. Running a left finger from the top to the bottom of a vane, the feather tattered. Then, like magic, with one upward glide of my finger, the feather interlocked.

Seamless is a wild forest remaking herself in a windstorm. Trees fall to feed the earth as fungi, beetles, and all who work on the wood help the process of decay. New life grows from old. Seamless are birds that guide to all that interlaces, interacts, and creates refugia. Seamless is a feather holding secrets to flight. Made of keratin that is akin to our finger and toenails, a feather is a far more evolved structure.

With a handheld magnifier, I studied the wing feather's vane. Hundreds of pairs of barbs branch from the shaft. Each barb is lined with barbules that hook barb to barb in a herringbone pattern. Even tinier are the barbicels, specialized hooklets allowing barbules to slide over each other. The barbs, barbules, and barbicels working in unison lend flexibility and strength.

If a feather were a conifer tree, the trunk would be the shaft and branches the vanes with twigs and needles as barbs and barbules. When wind sifts through a tree's version of feathers, the sounds vary depending on the shapes of needles that may be stiff, spiny, scaled, flat, soft, or brushy. A centuries-old Douglas-fir may have 65 million needles photosynthesizing, converting sun to sugars, and capturing carbon. Like a feather, a Douglas-fir needle exposes secrets when magnified. While the needles appear to zip and unzip in a breeze, they don't interlock. But they do have stomata, pores on the needles that open to drink sunlight and transpire water from roots.

Feathers with barbs and barbules are flat and called pennaceous. The whisper of songbird wings, the whoosh of a raven, or the startle of a grouse are the sounds of air gushing over flight feathers. In contrast, the silence of a flying owl comes from combs on feather edges that disrupt rough air into tiny micro-turbulences.

Down feathers are plumulaceous, with barbs that are free to twist and trap air for insulation. Curly down feathers keep birds warm. In winter, birds can fluff up even more to trap air. When it's hot, birds compress the air pockets by pressing feathers close to their bodies.

If a bird were a forest, the equivalent of down feathers would be the places that create air pockets, among needles, twigs, lichens, and more. I dream on a pillow stuffed with goose down under a down comforter. My old puffy jacket leaks down feathers through the weakening seams. Still, I reach for the stained moss-green Patagonia coat, grateful for the company's practice of free repairs, even sewing in new baffles (or pockets) so the down spreads evenly and does not clump. Feathers growing on a bird act like baffles, too, forming air pockets. Designers of down coats look to birds to achieve maximum loft for warmth. Patagonia tries to emulate nature, where there are no throwaways, no dumps, landfills, or plastics breaking into micro-pieces of toxicity.

Showering us with lessons of efficiency, feathers can also be lavish, ornamental, and copious. A snow goose may have 20,000 feathers and a flicker about 2,000. Birds spend much of their day preening—smoothing the vanes between beaks, cleaning and oiling them by dipping beaks into uropygial (oil) glands at the base of their tails. A wild forest preens, too. Predators and parasites keep prey in check and prevent major insect and disease outbreaks. Decomposers, from fungi to bacteria and insects, break down fallen leaves, needles, trees, bones, and feathers to become soil.

Just as the sturdiest of socks wear out, so do feathers. Birds replace them through molting and then regrowing new ones. The trick is to do so in ways that least impair a bird's ability to fly. Ducks molt all at once after breeding season and find safety on the water until ready for liftoff. Most birds drop a few feathers at a time. Before breeding season, male songbirds like orioles and tanagers replace duller feathers with snazzy courtship plumage.

Every tree has a way of molting. Western larch tree needles in autumn turn flaming yellow, dulling to embers before falling to the ground, leaving a tree bare until spring—a complete molt. Evergreens drop individual needles to replace them in a partial molt. Squirrels cut cones along with needles in late summer, another way of shedding. Like feathers, the fallen leaves and needles never go to waste, chewed by mites and other insects and broken down by fungi and bacteria.

A discarded songbird feather might be nabbed by a Dark-eyed Junco to line a cup nest under an Oregon grape plant, or ferried up a tree by a Douglas squirrel into a messy leaf nest called a drey. When a high-rise tree draws up sap to the canopy and needles transpire moisture into the air, the droplets that seed the clouds are filled with minute particles from the soil, including what's left of feathers.

Taste a raindrop. Taste a feather. Know, too, the way of flying—bird and forest each in their own way. To fly, a bird's primary feathers are lightweight, waterproof, insulating, aerodynamic, asymmetrical, and synchronized for lift, flap, glide, and landing. Overlapping contour feathers are like armor plates, from fingernail-sized head feathers to shielding flank feathers. The vanes are symmetric around the shaft or rachis. Many vanes include afterfeathers, petite downy feathers near the calamus (hollow lower shaft) for a bit more insulation. A Great Horned Owl's ear tufts are afterfeathers. The twiglike tufts are not ears but camouflage for blending into a tree.

Flight wing feathers are stiffest, largest, and have asymmetric vanes. The leading edge is thinner to better stabilize wings under pressure of air currents. The ten outer primary feathers of a bird wing are rigid and pointed. Secondary flight feathers of the inner wing are a bit curved and broader, with a rounded tip. Wings also have an alula (or thumb) of three to five tiny feathers at the center of the front edge of the wing. Like a flap on an airplane wing, an alula helps with lift and prevents stalls when landing.

When winds flutter through the canopy of a wild forest, I'm reminded of wings flapping, every feather in unison. In the upper tree realm of Red Crossbills, Hermit Warblers, and soaring hawks are squadrons of bacteria and fungivorous creatures grazing on lichens and converting nitrogen, essential to the forest's growth. The way of lichen and lichen eaters is of hook and hooklet sustaining the forest.

As a child living in Mount Rainier National Park, I first heard on a ranger walk the story of algae and fungi taking a "lichen" to each other. Algae photosynthesizes and fungi provide the structure for lichen, I'd learned. Interlocking. In 2018, I found out differently when I interviewed Toby Spribille and John McCutcheon for a University of Montana research magazine. Their discovery upended 150 years of science by finding a second fungi essential to the process. An algae, a fungi, and a fungi took a lichen to each other. When the scientists showed a simple diagram to school children, the kids pointed to three parts. When lichenologists looked at it, they only counted two. Sometimes, we need fresh eyes to see what we've overlooked or fresh perspectives for a known subject, like bird migration.

Feather DNA is revolutionizing the field of tracking migratory birds. Every feather has a genetic marker that a bird passes on to offspring. Those markers reflect the regions where birds live. Examining the DNA from 1,600 tail feather samples of Wilson's Warblers caught at monitoring stations across North and Central America, ornithologist Kristen Ruegg in 2014 distinguished six populations with overlapping migratory routes and separate wintering areas.[1]

Ruegg is co-director of the Bird Genoscape Project, with a mission of mapping migration routes, wintering, and breeding areas of 100 North American bird species in decline. The maps pinpoint habitats to protect in an ever-more-developed landscape.

On their miraculous peregrinations, and in everyday flight, birds rely on more than wings. Tails are essential for takeoffs and landings, balance, stability, and precise steering. Typically, the fan-shaped tail consists of six pairs of feathers that become more asymmetrical toward the outer pairs. Some birds have fewer and others far more tail feathers.

Crest feathers, filoplumes, semiplumes, bristles, and powder down add to a bird's repertoire. Colors aid camouflage or showy displays—from muted browns and blacks to iridescent greens and purples and scarlets, lazuli, and sunflower yellows. They may be spotted, banded, barred, and streaked. The origins of colors can be pigments or in structure, like the blues of a Steller's Jay or bluebird that are drab or stunning depending on the sunlight.

From protecting a bird's skin from sunburn to soaking up water to cool a bird down, feathers are multipurpose and even create sounds, like the winnowing of a Wilson's Snipe in a courtship dive as wind rushes through special spread tail feathers. They can be snowshoes for ptarmigan and ruffed grouse, or act as oiled sealskin for dippers that fly underwater in fast-flowing forest streams.

Tough and flexible, a feather vane's name comes from the old English "fana," which translates to flag. Picture an American flag raised high on a pole in the wind and not tearing. Before the invention of synthetic material, flag-makers chose naturally resistant fibers like wool, cotton, linen, hemp, and silk from cocoons.

Holding a vane like a piece of paper between thumb and forefinger, I give it a slight tug with my other hand. The barbs and barbules stretch but do not break apart. Filling a dropper with water, I squeeze the rubber tube, and a droplet balances on the vane. Waterproof. A vane is also called a web, which I puzzled over until heading outside to examine an orb web strung between stems of a sunflower and mock orange. When I focused on each spoke (called a radial thread) in the wheel, I saw the vanes. A spoke is like a feather shaft. The fine strands crossing through the spokes that form the concentric rings are like barbs. Unlike barbules, however, the silken strands crossing the vanes are sticky to catch insects.

A spiderweb must resist rain and wind and be strong enough to withstand the impact of an incoming fly and for the spider to snare and wrap her prey. On a far larger scale, an ecological web is composed of predator and prey, competition, cooperation, and cycles of life, decay, death, and rebirth. To study a single feather is to go beyond structure to examine life upon life.

Through a microscope, I might spot the ultimate hitchhikers. Feather mites live on at least 2,000 species of birds in thirty-three families. Living within the spaces between the barbs, their eight specialized feet clasp barbules to stay put even when their bird host is flying in turbulence. Most feed on skin scales, feather debris, and oil from preening glands. There are even quill mites snuggled within the base of the calamus or even piercing the wall to feed on hosts.

Called ectosymbionts, the vagabonding mites cling to feathers like barnacles on whales. Far from being a problem for birds, the mites clean feathers as they gain food. Birds bearing feathers bearing mites also lead to uncharted territory of life upon life and life within life. Feather mites are also reminders of the "Linnean Shortfall"—the gap between the number of species that have been described and the number that actually exist on our planet, even as extinction rates accelerate.

Like a Russian doll opening to disclose ever smaller dolls, this is what complexity looks like. Once I interviewed a microbiologist who studied cicadas for the bacteria that lived within their cells, and in turn learned those bacteria split into two species living within a single cell. I wonder what lives within the cells of a feather mite?

After my tall tree climb in the Andrews Forest with Nina Ferrari, I yearned for wings. I am not sure when I first desired to be a bird—hollow bones, wings, and feathers. It might have been when I was nine, after my family moved from Mount Rainier to the eastern Washington town of Coulee Dam, by the Columbia River, when my father, Dave Richie, was superintendent of Lake Roosevelt National Recreation Area. On one hike, we climbed Steamboat Rock in the dry mesa country of sagebrush and rattlesnakes. Summiting the mesa, we saw a Golden Eagle launch from the rim. The sun on back neck feathers glinted with all the riches in the world. I held my arms out and imagined soaring for miles.

At nineteen, as a freshman at the University of Oregon, I flew a seaplane for a few ecstatic minutes. Earlier that day, I'd met the dashing pilot at a youth environmental conference in Seattle. Likely ten years my senior, he asked me to join him on a flight to the Olympic Peninsula, assuring me I'd be back by day's end. I said yes. That's the way I was then. Naive. Lucky. Why not fly in a seaplane like a gull skimming a cerulean sky? He promised a picnic on a beach with friends on the Olympic Peninsula.

The taxiing takeoff from Lake Washington was a roar of gull scatter into the skim of sky. The Seattle skyline receded. I noticed his capable steering hands. We flew in bright blinding sun. I was giddy. When we landed on the calm ocean waves, his two friends were waving on the beach. We had the picnic. Flying back, as we approached Seattle heading toward the Space Needle, he turned to me and said, "Why don't you give it a try?" Following his directions, I steered from the copilot seat. I was flying like a swooping bird—at last free from gravity.

I've never "flown" a plane since, but in that glimmer I understood the light in my father's golden eyes when he told stories of his jet pilot days as a Marine in his early twenties. He took off and landed on carriers in the ocean, flew in tight formations, and reveled in cloud formations. He'd found his passion for birds as a boy. I never asked whether birds led him to piloting jets in an interval of peace between the Korean and Vietnam Wars.

There's danger in the bird way. The flying way. The Northern Flicker feathers drifting away and weathering tell the story of the Cooper's Hawk even months later in summer. More flickers come to our home yard to drum on trees, call, eat, and drink. A mother feeds two fuzzy fledglings, begging with raised and quivering wings. She stuffs suet from our feeder into the scimitar-shaped beaks they would learn to use for hammering trees and stirring up anthills.

In flight, a Northern Flicker's underwings flare like fire or the rising sun, depending on whether the woodpecker is the western or eastern subspecies. Tail feathers mirror the colors. From above, there's a telltale white rump patch above the tail. The primary wing feathers beam sunset orange or yellow shafts against the darker browns, while the secondary wing feathers are scalloped. The smaller coverts higher on the wings leading up to the neck are flannel gray, with necklaces of dotted black. Black polka dots sprinkle an ashy breast below a black neck bib.

A male sports a red feather whisker if red-shafted (western) or black if yellow-shafted (eastern). Females lack the whisker, but the yellow-shafted variety bears a red spot on the nape, the back of the head. The hybrids I see can be a mix. Some have both the red nape and red whisker. Some have yellow tail feathers and a red whisker. Their differences remind me to go beyond the "oh, that's a flicker" to look more deeply at the bird. Once I study a bird, I'm also learning more of the individual. No bird is the same as another.

Besides the feeders, there are two to four bird baths close to the house. Slowly, my husband Wes and I are rewilding the front third of an acre with wildflowers, bunchgrasses, manzanitas, bitterbrush, and currants, all rimmed in ponderosas. Asters, goldenrods, and sunflowers blooming in fall straggle upward to heights of three, four, five feet or more. While I prefer the natives that in turn support a compendium of insects, the trees holding feeders are a lilac and an ornamental plum planted in 1999 when the simple ranch house was built.

A Hairy Woodpecker arrives with a sharp *pik pik* call. A Spotted Towhee scruffs through needles and leaves close to a manzanita. A covey of California Quail parades across the ground—always with a stunning male in topknot and finely patterned feathers keeping guard from a rock as the others feed.

As I write, our 15-foot-tall unruly lilac flurries with chickadees, goldfinches, nuthatches, and siskins. A Rufous Hummingbird is poised on a vertical dead branch. With windows open, I hear the shuffle of feathers. A Pygmy Nuthatch lands on the water bath for a quick sip. In the ponderosas, the nuthatches flock through the midstory. They nest in woodpecker holes in dead trees and in winter will pack tight together in a cavity for warmth. Relationships are reciprocal, with birds eating, storing, and planting seeds, and keeping insects in check. The birds at home are my touchstones to the roadless wilds.

A single feather is a miracle. Chickasaw poet Linda Hogan, in her book *Dwellings: A Spiritual History of the Living World*, wrote of feathers in her opening chapter:

> There is something alive in a feather. The power of it is perhaps in its dream of sky, currents of air, and the silence of its creation. It knows the insides of clouds. It carries our needs and desires, the stories of our brokenness. It rises and falls down elemental space, one part of the elaborate world of life where fish swim against gravity, where eels turn silver as moon to breed.[2]

Viewing the entirety of the forest through the lens of interwoven feathers, the shapes appear in the fronds of fern, the curl of moss, and the wing of a redcedar branch. A creek feathers around a rock in silvery splashes. Leaves unfold into featherlike venations. Diaphanous spiderwebs catch the dew. The feathered way. The flight way. Sunlight feathers through the canopy in shafts, plumes, and vanes. An arrow has a feathered shaft. Lightning feathers the sky. I'm ready to follow the flight of the arrow deep into the heart of climate refugia.

THREE

Refugia

Swainson's Thrush melody encircles a tall riverside spruce from roots to a pinnacle top redolent in cones. A trio of Vaux's Swifts arrow above wild waters in this far northeastern Oregon refugia. Their name rhymes with foxes and their wings remind me of the fast beats of bats. A Belted Kingfisher wings by with her telltale rattle and flash of red belt. Her wings scoop so low to the whitewater, the glinting flecks become her dazzle too. Now a Yellow-rumped Warbler flashes goldenrod hues. Threading willow to a lofty western larch tree in a cross-current flight, his song rolls like the Imnaha River.

I'm sitting with bare feet dipping in and out of frigid water, the kind that hurts after a few seconds. Tucked under a willow, I'm like all shade-seekers, as temperatures climb on this July day into triple digits. Close by are muddy hoof tracks from elk wandering through belly-high grasses and blooming corn lilies. In the doldrums, they've slipped into the density of unlogged conifers, where temperatures may drop ten degrees. Elk, black bear, mule deer, and marten rest in their refugia.

On a too-hot July day, a battered Chinook salmon rests in a deep cold pool created by a centuries-old tree falling into the waters. Guided by the scent of her birth river, she swam 560 miles from the ocean, up the Columbia and Snake past eight dams to this natal river. Three feet long, she is olive with black speckles. Like bird feathers, her scales are overlapping, protective, bright or subdued in color, streamlined to assure a laminar flow of water rather than air. Now they are flaking away, their job completed.

Soon the salmon will thrash her ragged tail to create a hollow among clean stones where the river is shallow and fast-flowing to better oxygenate the eggs she will lay in her nest, called a redd. A male with a telltale hooked jaw will fertilize the eggs. Both will die and renew the forest with their bodies. The fish live on within the trees. However, extinction is not far off unless people act to take down the four lower Snake River dams. Every year, the reservoirs grow hotter, and more salmon die. Every year, fewer come home.

On this day, warbler and salmon alike could have no better place to be than on the Imnaha Wild and Scenic River. Lucent waters swirl over rounded stones like jewels of jade, malachite, topaz, and garnet. Racing from headwaters in the Eagle Cap Wilderness for 73 miles, the Imnaha enters the Snake River in Hells Canyon, deepest gorge in North America.

In my journeys seeking climate refugia, from the Pacific Ocean to the Cascades to the Imnaha within the Blue Mountains, I am tracing birds to ancient forests by rivers, streams, ridges, valleys, mountainsides, and coastlines to understand what makes a wild forest whole—a forest that can "fly" in the way of a fully feathered bird.

I want to know the world as birds know it—to be like Alice in Wonderland, able to telescope down to be very small and then very tall—wandering about with a piece of mushroom in each hand, nibbling just enough to shrink or expand to fit within all the niches, to know the meaning of climate refugia.

Closing my eyes, I listen to the river speaking in tongues of all the creeks that merged with her currents. For thousands of years, Imnaha has ground, rolled, and polished stones. Trees fall. Beavers dam backwaters. The first wolves to enter Oregon from Idaho drank from her waters. Her free flow gives life to meadows and forests. I hear the *wheep wheep wheep* of a Spotted Sandpiper, the one I'd accidentally scared up from an exposed nest on a rocky beach just past a log jam. Flies buzz but do not bite.

It's the first night after leaving Missoula at the end of June of 2015. I'm camping on the free-flowing Salmon River of Idaho, not far from Challis. Common Nighthawks slice the sunset.

The river whispers my new name . . . Marina. I'd shed Deborah unofficially for my great-grandmother's name. From now on, all who met me would know me in my new yet same self. Popping open a can of Big Sky IPA, I toast the *hoo-h'HOO-hoo-hoo* of a Great Horned Owl. By the river's edge, I write the first entry for a new blog, *Kingfisher Journey*. "The end of June marked the beginning of a roving naturalist life. I don't live in a house anymore."

There by the river of the first night I felt supremely alive. I'd held a garage sale, stored memorabilia, and packed up my pickup truck with the compact four-wheel camper on top that I'd bought the year before. My son Ian had graduated high school and soon would leave for college. Sadness and elation twinned my days before departure. I would miss my friends, community, and kingfishers on Rattlesnake Creek. Perhaps because of my peripatetic childhood, I was like a migratory bird answering an ancestral call.

Following a year of peregrinations, I settled first in La Grande, in northeast Oregon. I felt a return to my younger environmentalist self, speaking up to save wilderness, as well as the maturity of a writer determined to finish her first adult book. "Keep growing new rings," Ursula K. Le Guin had penned to me so long ago. It was time to take more risks. I'd started following Belted Kingfishers in 2009. The book came into the world in 2022. By then, I was in Bend and happily married to Wes, a mellow, guitar-playing elementary schoolteacher.

Adjacent to a beaver dam just upriver, a huge living Douglas-fir fell across a river channel of the Imnaha. Sleeping in the small pop-up camper on our truck, Wes and I had jolted awake at dawn. Like firecrackers, the roots popped as the weight of the leaning tree broke loose from the riverbank undercut by floods. Then came a great rushing sound and reverberating thud. When we found the tree, we waded across the river using chewed beaver sticks for balance on slick polished stones of green, golds, and purples. There, we could peer into the mass of upper canopy branches that used to be 80 feet aboveground. Expecting a bird's nest, I saw instead delicate black hooves, stretched brown fur, and a skull—all that was left of an elk calf draped over a branch. Likely, a cougar had killed the calf and climbed the tree to protect the meal from scavengers. A tree is elk. A tree is salmon. You never know what you might find if lucky and curious.

Imnaha sprays fountains, slips over boulders, eddies, and, a few miles up from my camp and two miles into the wilderness, the river narrows through a great cleft in the earth. There, her clear waters deepen to form the Blue Hole, where I first saw Chinook salmon resting back in the 1980s when researching my environmental investigative thesis centered on Hells Canyon and the surrounding wilds.

There, by the Imnaha River parting around a heart-shaped island, I felt the possibility of reconnecting what's broken and protecting what's whole. Salmon risked impossible perils to come home to this refugia holding her secrets, sometimes in the treetops. The linkages are still there.

Barry Lopez defined "refugium" in his book *Home Ground: Language for an American Landscape*, in ways that suggest certain places on this planet are best left alone. He wrote,

> The myths and folklore of traditional people the world over are replete with descriptions and even geographic designations of refugia, the inviolable strongholds of animals and plants of which the storyteller and her people steer clear, places like Western Society's Eden, missing only the human, and holding out promise for a less tumultuous future.[1]

I value the places we do not go and respect the legacy of Indigenous peoples practicing careful prescribed burning, gathering roots and berries, hunting, and leaving certain places untouched, too. In this era some scientists proclaim as the Anthropocene, humans are meddling with the very climate and messing up the natural world's dynamic balance. A map of the globe tracking the human footprint of cities and development shows few places left that are not degraded.

Ecologists liken climate refugia for species as places for life in the slow lane. Chances of avoiding a wreck are far better there than in the fast lane. In our time of rapid heating of the planet, the ancient forests offer incomparable coolness. In a 2016 study of old growth within the Andrews Forest, researcher Sarah Frey, with Matt Betts, found the lower levels of tall, multilayered forests were 4.5 degrees (F) cooler in summer than in nearby shorter and even-aged sixty-to-eighty-year-old Douglas-fir plantations.[2]

The older forests are wealthy in giant fallen trees sponging up water, lowering the temperatures of their surroundings, and nursing new life. The more complexity and structure it holds, the more a forest can stay naturally air-conditioned on hot days. Nina Ferrari's bird studies are unveiling a hidden vertical world of climate refugia closely tied to old growth.

To find climate refugia, I look for the roadless areas—the glorious blank spots on maps free of roads. Some are permanently protected as wilderness areas, the gold standard of the 1964 Wilderness Act. Across North America, the roadless wilds are often where birds show up that had been thought to be extinct but survived.

In the southeast, a few Ivory-billed Woodpeckers appeared to survive in the refugium of the Big Woods of southeast Arkansas. A single woodpecker was sighted in 2004, about a century after the last known sighting. The culprit for the birds' demise was not shooting, but logging of bottomland hardwood forests, including cypress trees more than two thousand years old. Although the Ivory-billed was never spotted again after extensive searches, perhaps this largest of all woodpeckers still lingers in a place beyond our knowing.

Marbled Murrelets baffled scientists seeking the tiny seabirds' nests until 1974, when a tree trimmer found a plump robin-sized bird on a high mossy platform limb of a redwood tree in northern California. Where news of protecting biodiversity is mostly discouraging, I'm encouraged by reports of "lost birds" still existing, although often hanging on by the slightest of threads.

In Brazil's Amazon, arguably the most endangered bird in South America is the Belem Curassow, a turkey-sized black bird with a banana-yellow bill and a crest like twisted yarn. Decimated by deforestation and poaching, the bird was not seen in the wild after 1978. Forty years later, the Pirahã peoples helped scientists find the *mytunxi* (in the Tupi language) in pristine headwaters of their lands that are also threatened by illegal logging and poaching. The *mytunxi* finding drew attention to a rainforest to save and a culture wherein knowledge of plants, animals, and their behaviors is an essential part of survival.

A rare Northern Spotted Owl or a Marbled Murrelet can take us deeper into refugia's biodiversity. Charismatic megafauna open our eyes to enigmatic minifauna. The little things that run the world depend on their flashy ambassadors to save them. The Endangered Species Act of 1973, which passed the US Senate unanimously and the US House by 390–12, was signed into law by President Nixon. People cared about preventing species from going extinct, and that required saving their homes. Endangered Spotted Owls and Threatened Marbled Murrelets have become the champions for protecting wild, ancient forest habitats across the Pacific Northwest.

In Scotland, when people found out that a baby red panda named Roxie in an Edinburgh zoo had died from the stress of fireworks, a million people signed a 2024 petition calling for tighter restrictions on pyrotechnics. The tragic story of a beloved panda led to an outpouring of advocacy that, if successful, could lead to visually spectacular fireworks without the explosions causing distress for pets and wildlife alike. I'm pondering the power of personality and naming as another avenue toward erasing our separation from nature and enlisting activists.

In Melbourne, Australia, the city has given email addresses to seventy thousand trees in the city.[3] You simply go to a map, click on a tree, and up pops the name of the tree, sometimes information about the age, and the address. Across the world, people have written emails to the trees and some are answered by the arborists. I decided to give it a try:

> Dear Crow's Nest Poplar,
> Do you have a crow nesting? Are your branches hosting birds? Are you strong? I live far away in Oregon in the USA and have never been under your shade, but I see you are "semi-mature"—I hope you live long and people care for your roots. I've just learned a lot about tree roots and the dangers of city streets, pavement, and covering the drip lines. I hope to hear from you,
> Marina, a human, in Bend, Oregon

A few weeks later, I was thrilled to see my response:

> Hi Marina,
> Did you know the term Crow's Nest comes from the lookout station built onto the middle to the upper portion of the main mast of a ship. However, the term has come to mean a small, raised, auxiliary perch used for just about anything from spying, hiding, or looking out. So I suppose you humans think my branches make suitable perching spots for spying and hiding and hence my name. I do host birds from time to time, as well as many insects and other critters that call the city home. Thanks for reaching out to me. If you do ever make it here to visit, be sure to say hi, and I'll know to wave my branches at you.
> Your friend the Crow's Nest Poplar

Maybe we ought to write more letters to trees. Like the Crow's Nest in the ship mast and a tree's branches as perches for "spying, hiding, or looking out," refugia invite us to climb up, hang on, and perch. We also could simply be in conversation with a life-filled tree. I'd have that chance a few months later on the Oregon Coast, where I camped alone at Cape Lookout State Park for two weeks of wandering and writing. It's one of my favorite campgrounds on the Oregon coast, far away from busy Highway 101 and squeezed between ocean and bay on a narrow spit of land. I always choose a site among lush spruce enticing Pacific Wrens to come close.

In late October, I was glad for the pop-up camper on the truck when coastal storms struck and rain pounded hard. Always there were interludes with sun and clouds. Walking the long stretch of beach south, I could turn inland to hike the trail through old-growth forests leading to the tip of the cape with dizzying cliff drop-offs. Ten miles to the north is Cape Meares, haven to Oregon's champion Sitka Spruce. I came more than once to linger and listen. Writing back at the camper, I found it natural to address the spruce as "you." Perhaps I was writing a letter to a tree—a long one with a response I'd have to learn over time spent at the foot of the tree.

Ponderings with Climate Guardian Spruce

I will stay here like a banana slug among the moss on Cape Meares, a protected promontory of the north central coast of Oregon. It's not enough to gawk at your immensity and walk away. You who do not know that you were proclaimed the champion Sitka Spruce of Oregon in 2008, after the Klootchy Spruce of Seaside split in half in a winter storm. The sign names you Big Spruce. I will call you Climate Guardian Spruce. The engraved wood sign proclaims you as 144 feet tall, 48 feet in circumference, and 15½ feet in diameter, estimated to be between 750 and 800 years old.

You are more than the tally of your dimensions. You were taller before your top broke off in a Pacific storm. Your crown is blue-whale wide, or 93 feet, as humans say. Sometimes this largest of all mammals spouts offshore. Here in this Cape Meares National Wildlife Refuge on Oregon's north coast, you stand some 800 feet above the sea, ringed in western hemlocks and more spruce beyond.

Common Raven circles your tousled top on wings black as the seastacks harboring seabirds and sea lions. The gruff call is the breaking wave on pebbles. *Kraah! Kraah!* Raven has come—creator of sun, moon, and tides, trickster and shape shifter. The stories are many in the coastal tribal cultures of Cascadia, from the Tlingit to Haida to Quileute—all to the north. Your world is storied by the Clatsop, Chinook, Cathlamet, Nehalem, Nestucca, Salmon River, Tillamook, Siletz and Grand Ronde tribes. This is their homeland.

Within your trunk, branches, and roots you store half the surrounding forest's carbon. Your gathering and storing ability are exponential with your girth. Scientists have calculated that a two-and-a-half-foot-diameter tree stores 1.7 tons of carbon, and a five-foot-wide tree 19.2 tons. Measurements fail to encompass your grandeur.

Gazing up at your whale of a crown, I imagine a leviathan offshore spouting and diving. It seems improbable, but a blue whale stores seventeen tons of carbon over a lifetime by eating tiny krill and other carbon-rich small organisms that in turn feed on oxygen-making phytoplankton.

Can I tell you, great Sitka, that I'm scared of what people have done and won't stop doing? On this day in October of 2024, our thin fragile atmosphere registers 422.12 parts per million (ppm) of carbon—far beyond what's considered a safe level of 350 ppm. You must think humans are crazy in their scramble to invent carbon capturing technology instead of changing our ways and protecting nature. I'm sorry.

The bigger the whale and the more gigantic the tree, the greater are their abilities to gather and store carbon. When a whale dies and sinks, the carbon sinks, too. When a huge tree falls, the nurse tree stores carbon, too, while the agents of decay will very slowly over time return the tree to soil and release carbon.

The Earth's ability to store carbon is highest in the ancient forests and in the "blue carbon" of marine ecosystems, from salt marshes to kelp forests, and in the bodies of marine mammals. These superlatives may not concern you who have survived so much and for so long, but trees like you have become a rarity after the fierce logging of Pacific Northwest coasts.

You seem so comfortable in your roots. You do not know the words greed, more, and take. If I were to become a tree, it might be tempting to choose your kind. Sitka spruce are among the top six of all trees for record height. The trees are resistant to salt spray, and dwell within a coastal band from Kodiak, Alaska, to Mendocino, California. Up the coast from you in the Queets River Valley of Olympic National Park is the largest of all, at 55 feet around. The growth rings are wide, and the tree adds a foot to the circumference every thirty-five years. How long would I have to lean against you to feel you putting on your new rings?

I am here to thank you for far more than saving our atmosphere the best you can. You are not some carbon capture machine, but a sentient being in relationship with multitudes, from northern flying squirrels gliding in moonlight to spiders binding your twigs.

Here in the somnolent air of your breathing as fog opens to sun, I can almost forget the dangerous reports of a warming ocean storing far less carbon and fueling Category 5 hurricanes in the Atlantic. Time is short, yet time feels slowed down in your presence.

Within your branches, you hold micro-refugia of mossy gardens on high platforms that in turn support gardens where salamanders wander and huckleberries bloom. Younger trees cannot rival your sheltering crown that takes hundreds of years to form, shaped by storms and your strength to grow new trunks or "leaders."

When your top spire broke, you gathered strength to respond. More limbs sprouted from your trunk. Scientists call them epicormic branches that spring from dormant buds ready to awaken with more light. Tilting my head back, I can see that one of your high branches grows outward from the trunk. Thick as a wine barrel, this treelike bole takes a sharp 90-degree turn upward—as if you were showing off your muscled arm. You teach us to rise from what's broken, stronger than before.

I would guess that Marbled Murrelets have nested in your platform limbs so many times, you've lost count. The robin-sized seabirds fly at dusk to nest only in the ancient trees, like you with your ample branches mattressed in moss. As you have lost your brethren, the forest around you becomes too small to offer safety to murrelets from predators. Still, you are stalwart.

Pine Siskins, Red Crossbills, and Chestnut-backed Chickadees have flown with your seeds to carry you far away to new places. How many birds have nested, rested, fed, perched, hooted, warbled, and chattered right here over all those centuries?

On this October day, the migratory songbirds like Hermit Warblers, Townsend's Warblers, and Western Flycatchers have flown south. Still, I hear the wind chimes of Golden-crowned Kinglets calling among needles and branches. Kinglets with crowns in your great crown of branches know you in ways I can never rival. I might as well be a kinglet in size, small enough for you to hold me in your hand. That's how I feel next to you—humble and in my rightful place.

Writing about the Sitka Spruce back at my camper, everything has changed. It's not the dawn breaking wet and foggy, in the way of the coastal rainforest—it's the box. At my feet is a Western Grebe in a bulky cardboard box. I resist peeking in, knowing that darkness and stillness is best. Soon, she will be headed to Astoria, two hours north to the Wildlife Center of the North Coast.

With a wild living bird inches away, my fingers fly across the laptop keyboard in unexpected directions. My tapping is matched with the insistent tapping of a slender bill that is razor sharp. I'm comforted by the foot flaps and feather rustles. There is still strength. I want to soothe her, and tell her she will soon be helped by wildlife rehabilitators.

Western Grebes do not like high surf and whitecaps on the ocean. They are waterfowl far more comfortable on the bay side of Cape Lookout. For some reason, this one had braved the Pacific and washed up on the beach. With legs set far back on a body build for diving, a grebe cannot take off from land. The bird was stranded.

When I came upon the bird at midday, every feather was sandy and soaked. Western Gulls circled and gathered—considering whether they might take a chance with that sharp bill. A young couple watching in horror looked as stressed as the bird with bright red eyes. Soon we had a plan, with the help of the state park ranger who provided the box. The couple planned to drive to Astoria the next day and would take the bird to the rehabilitation center.

For now, the bird is in the box with a clean dry towel. The night before, I'd climbed up into the platform bed above the truck cab as rain drummed hard on the roof. We settled down. I worried. I desperately wanted the grebe to live, return to the bay, and find kin.

Sipping coffee and listening to feathery rustles, I'm contemplating human nature. We are cut out for rescuing individual birds and other animals.

Confronted with an ocean, forest, or other ecosystem in trouble, how can we throw our arms around the entirety of something so vast? When I held the suffering grebe, I felt intimately linked to the bird and her home. This grebe's future is dependent on our actions to stop burning fossil fuels, to stop using plastic that ends up in the ocean and within seabirds, to stop overfishing, and to live with simplicity. To feel the grebe's heartbeat and to sit at the foot of the Sitka spruce is to connect the dots. When I step into their world, I find magic. And why would anyone want to end magic on this planet?

On a walk through another ancient forest of the North Trail of Cape Lookout State Park, a few hours before the grebe saga ensued, I'd paused for the tintinnabulations of kinglets and only then noticed a crane fly landing on the underneath side of a salmonberry leaf. On long slender legs, the fly swayed back and forth in a hypnotic trance of translucent wings, with a light-green abdomen almost touching the serrated surface, backlit by a glance of sun after rain. The kinglets took me to the crane fly adult, which lives only long enough to mate and lay eggs, little more than a week. All is in relationship—plants to insects to birds to trees.

From the forest, I walked the beach to stumble upon the Western Grebe. To write now with a wild bird at my feet is taking me into a dream place, where I am feathered with a sharp beak. This grebe is meant to dive deep into waters to chase fish, run on the water to take off, and perform courtship dances—erect in the water with wings raised and neck arced to face a potential mate. Their arcing slender necks together form the shape of a heart. I hope the grebe will live long enough to dance with others.

Soon, the grebe will leave my camper. I opened the box and added some paper towels to cover the green, brown, and white liquid excrement. The box does not seem too wet, and the grebe has moved onto the soft towel. The bird seems so weak, yet still preens the overlapping and damp gray-black contour feathers covering the back. Grasping a feather at the base with the spear-like beak, the bird pulls it through to the end, and then moves to the next.

Sheltered in this box with a towel and a bit of heat from the propane, the grebe has the energy to do what's most important. Feather care. A wild forest is all about the equivalent of feather care—always renewing, never staying still. I send a silent message to the grebe. Travel safe to the North Coast

Wildlife Center, where you will be tended and attended and returned to join other grebes in a safe bay. You will find refuge.

Return to Spruce

Hello Climate Guardian. I'm thinking about your way of becoming old. You appear to grow at a glacial pace, but that's deceiving. You are a living, expanding pillar or column, words with Greek origins so not right for you. The word pillar, however, can also be a fundamental precept. You are the pillar of the community, the wise one. I have much to learn here, as tiny as an ant at your toes.

I must go deeper than a Varied Thrush flipping twigs and leaves from the soil. Go deeper than a salamander burrowing into decaying wet wood of a fallen nurse tree. Go with the voles and their tunnels to follow the roots threaded in mycelium. You do more than exchange nutrients. You communicate danger, too, all underground. This, too, is climate refugia—where the forest connections are still as interlaced as well-preened feathers.

Lounging below as fog lifts and shadows pattern your scaled bark lightly furred in lichen, I consider who brushed by you long ago when you were a thumb-sized sapling back in the early 1300s. Your history is with the people who knew the vast coastal forests, with countless trees the size of you—rocked by storms breaking off tops and in places sculpted by fires from lightning and from cultural burning.

Forty miles to the south, I've climbed the steep slopes of Cascade Head, where the Nechesne people of the Salmon River long set fire to create and renew meadows flowing in butterflies and wildflowers. Their descendants, including the Confederated Tribes of Grande Ronde and Confederated Tribes of the Siletz Indians, light fires again as controlled burns with The Nature Conservancy, managers of the preserve. "The grasses remember the nights they were consumed by fire, lighting the way back with a conflagration of love between species," wrote Robin Wall Kimmerer in "Burning Cascade Head," of *Braiding Sweetgrass.*

Here with you, Climate Spruce, I wonder, if I stayed long enough if I might transcend time, whisked on your memories to know your way of loving while rooted in place.

Today, few wild forests remain in coastal Cascadia, hit the hardest by logging because the trees were enormous and accessible by ship. Cape Meares and Cape Lookout (11 miles to the south) were spared, because of lighthouses. Cape Meares became a national wildlife refuge in 1938 and Cape Lookout a state park in 1935, a donation of 975 acres from the then US Lighthouse Service. The park would expand over time with more acquisitions. Cape Meares, while designated as a breeding headland for seabirds, protected a premier old-growth forest—a Research Natural Area as of 1987.

When I first walked up to the sign signifying your champion status, two men turned around to walk the short trek back to the parking lot and seemed relieved to see me there. They looked puzzled.

"How do you get to the lighthouse?"

"The lighthouse is down the road, but you did find the biggest remaining Sitka Spruce in Oregon."

They nodded and then hustled on to their destination, which also has a record as the shortest lighthouse in Oregon. Hunkered on the tip of Cape Meares, the lighthouse is an appealing historic structure with a red glass center light, one that served ships for seventy-three years by alerting them to the rocks at night or in fog. Lighthouses have a dark history, too, for their role in attracting migrating birds at night that collide into the glass. I'd take you, Sitka Spruce, over a lighthouse every time.

I stretch, say my farewells, and decide I will walk to the lighthouse. Mostly I want to look for Peregrine Falcons, seabirds, and marine mammals from the overlooks. And I like to check on the interpretive signs scattered around the park. As part of another hat I wear as a writer, I was part of a team (artist, designer, ecologist, sign producer, and writer) that created an award-winning series for the Oregon Islands National Wildlife Refuge along the 300-mile coastline. The signs draw attention to the rocky islands hosting more than a million nesting seabirds. Together, the rocks form one refuge and are also the smallest designated wilderness area in the country, at 300 acres.

The funding came as part of the mitigation for a tragedy. On February 4, 1999, a 640-foot freighter, the *New Carissa*, went aground in a winter storm with 400,000 gallons of fuel oil and diesel onboard. A few days later, the ship broke in half. As much as 140,000 gallons entered the sea—deadly oil that coated the feathers of birds. The Fish and Wildlife Service estimated that more than three thousand seabirds and shorebirds died or were injured. Those included at least 262 Marbled Murrelets, seabirds nesting in ancient forests and already at risk.[4]

A premier part of the sign project (completed in 2018) is at Cape Meares and includes a panel about the lighthouse from the point of view of birds. I wrote of flocks of birds that crashed into lighthouses, and how technological advances have helped with quick flashing beams at lower light intensities that alert birds at night to veer away. Our team tied the message to the importance of people steering clear of the sea stacks and rocks that are seabird nesting homes and keeping lights out at night in all buildings. In almost all the sixty-seven panels, we included an "Ocean Alert," such as "lights out for seabirds," to give people a tangible way to help protect the birds.

Down the winding road to the south is the tiny town of Netarts, a name that in the Tillamook language was Ne ta ats, translating to "near the water" or the "big water." A local historian put together a timeline that reads like a straight line to losses, beginning with Sir Francis Drake sailing the Oregon coast in 1579. Captain John Meares, an English explorer, sailed to the bay in 1778—hence the Cape Meares name. Indigenous people never named places for humans. Fast forward to 1853–1859, when the US government forced the tribes to cede their lands from Tillamook Bay to the California border with treaties never ratified. The lands were stolen. The year 1890 marked the building of the Cape Meares lighthouse and a decade since the first sawmill in Netarts.

In 1901, naturalists William Finley and Tom Bohlman drew attention to the rampant shooting of nesting seabirds on the Three Arch Rocks, just off the cape. As naturalists, photographers, and adventurers who climbed the steep sea stacks, their publicity for the wonder and plight of birds attracted the attention of President Theodore Roosevelt, who created the Three Arch Rocks National Wildlife Refuge in 1907.

The year 1911 was the beginning of the end for the great forests, when a railroad was built to the town of Tillamook just to the north and, in 1917, a second mill was built at Whiskey Creek—of Netarts—a mill that would be running full tilt with great spruce trees cut down for World War I biplanes. Then automobiles showed up in the 1920s. The roads led to logging the great forests of the east slope of Netarts Bay. In the 1930s, electric power arrived. But it wasn't until 1957, when a new road to Cape Lookout State Park opened, that log trucks could roar into this country and commence clear-cutting—a practice that has not ended. Visible from both capes are logged hillsides, some recently scalped and others growing a monoculture of even-aged Douglas-firs. These are no longer forests but tree farms, growing on lands poisoned by herbicides.

I'm grateful for this protected cape. After walking the loop trail and drinking in my fill of cliffs, breaking waves, shorebirds, and vast ocean views. I return to resume my time with the Climate Guardian. I have a question.

Are you lonely from the loss of the great forests or are you cocooned and unknowing? No matter what, you are quietly giving to all this Earth in trouble. I think you understand deep time far more than any human and are capable of feats none of our technology can rival. Your crown is like a solar panel, except far more sophisticated. You photosynthesize—something people have never figured out how to replicate. As your needles drink sunshine, they separate molecules to make sugar and to store the carbon in every part of you, for a very long time.

In this era, with our fossil fuels desecrating our precious atmosphere with carbon dioxide at levels not seen since the Permian Period, 252 million years ago, people are scrambling to find ways to capture excess carbon, applying expensive technology that fails every test that a tree passes. You are here to tell us the solution is simple. Just look up.

I circle your mighty circumference, noticing how different you appear in perspectives, even from my antlike view. From one side, I can see that you have a slight lean, and on another there's that broken top, and now the forest garden. Two twin burls the size of brown bear cubs protrude from your base—a sign of recovering from an injury, the way of growing over, the way of your individuality. The raven returns for another convolution.

The fog is rolling back in. I think of a story I learned in Alaska of the Dena'ina people who lived for thousands of years where Anchorage is today. Fog Woman and Sunshine Man fell in love, but when they were together only fog prevailed and the people suffered without sunshine, that was also essential for the caribou that they hunted. The lovers parted in great sadness. The world needed fog for moisture and sun for plants to grow and feed the caribou and the people. The story served as a lesson for the Dena'ina, who thrived by being unselfish.

What are we willing to give up now for this planet? What do we part with? As I stand in the drift of fog and sun, I believe the two lovers of the story can still dance together, to love, and intermingle—just not for too long and too close. I will return to visit you with your great branch wings outstretched to welcome the raven.

Spruce, when I gaze up into your immensity, I feel your sentient ways. What is the secret to your longevity? Where do you store your memories?

The Western Grebe is recovering at the North Coast Wildlife Center in Astoria. She is female, with a beak a bit shorter and stubbier than the male. All the sand deprived her feathers of critical oils and left her waterlogged. The volunteers are putting her in a warm water tub for short periods for her to swim and wash more sand from her feathers. After a day, she's better but not yet eating on her own. When healthy, they will take her back south to release in the calm bay right across from where she washed in on rough waves. I'd like to be there with the grebe for the release.

I feel attached. Walking on the beach and finding a washed-up dead young Western Gull, I am sad but not emotionally connected. I accept that death as part of nature. How different it was to hear the grebe tapping on the box as we both listened to the hard rain pinging off the camper.

When I see the horrendous clear-cuts on the inland ridge beyond the state park I am horrified, but not as distraught as I would be if someone cut down Climate Guardian spruce. How can affection for one extend to action for many? The lesson of Fog Woman and Sunshine man resonates. What will we give up, so others may live in the future? Still, this is the best of who we are as humans, when we are moved to care for the wounded, elderly, and helpless.

Save one grebe. Save one great tree. Feel the sorrow of loss. Grow from what is ruptured into something stronger. Give to others in a community. Riding my bike from the campground at Cape Lookout the six miles to the town of Netarts, I spotted a wooly bear caterpillar crossing the road. I stopped, got off my bike, checked for oncoming cars, cupped the caterpillar in my hand and carried this determined little being to safety on the other side.

FOUR

Understory

Insulating as Down Feathers

Rambling in June by lower Lookout Creek in the Andrews Forest among bigleaf maples and western redcedars, I pause. A meadow spills over with clover-sized oxalis (redwood sorrels) folding their shamrock leaves like butterflies at rest in sunny gaps. In the shadows of great trees, leaves open wide. The plants are moving in response to the sun. I drift into sunlight and then into shade.

This is understory. Refugium on a sweltering day. The world is emerald light. The creek a hushed constancy. Looking up into the tallness of trees interlacing winged branches, I know climate refugia like the downy feathers of birds. The plants and roots belowground form a living tapestry. In the rich humus are truffles, fruits of fungi in relationship with root tips and dependent on flying squirrels and voles to eat and spread their spores that will power the forest.

I've stepped into a community of the low-down denizens. Varied Thrush, Hermit Thrush, Pacific Wren, and Wilson's Warbler. Clambering up, I balance on the wide belly of a nurse log festooned in moss, lichens, and sapling western hemlocks. If a western redcedar, the tree may have fallen a thousand years ago. That's how long this species may take to fully decompose. I'm not sure where to step from here. It's like walking in the intertidal zone among mussels, anemones, sea stars, and barnacles—seeking the bare ground to avoid crushing life in miniature.

I try to make every footstep light, but my 120 pounds are dangerous. Tentatively, I tiptoe to an enormous redcedar by an equally gargantuan

Douglas-fir above a steep drop-off. Below is a translucent pool. Quick-footed water striders speed across the surface. Their shadows are dancing dots on the bottom.

Water infuses my being until I'm in the thrall of the forest, listening to what she tells me: Put your cheek on the flaky felt of redcedar trunk and your hand on the neighboring moss-enveloped maple. Become one with redcedar and maple.

Buffered by layers of forest above me, I am cushioned and safe. All children should know this way of beginning—their lives an understory sheltered by a village of parents, grandparents, godparents, teachers, cousins, friends, and kin. Contrast this refreshing refugia on a hot day with a logged forest with little shade. Bereft of elders, what community remains suffers.

In my understory of childhood, I had the luck of growing up with parents who took care of us well, and yet trusted us to be independent. My two brothers and I were feral, running wild with other kids and called to dinner by my mother ringing a cowbell. Not long ago I found these words my dad had written about me and my mother, Catherine. I have a fuzzy memory of the trail and what it was to be small and close to the little things underfoot:

> Catherine and I still marvel at the vivid mental image we retain of Deborah not yet two, plodding steadily up the steep slope of Hawksbill Mountain the highest peak in Shenandoah National Park. She reached the top, as she has done many times since, without our help.

They were protectors, but never hovering. Around that same time, my parents left my brother David and I with our aunt and uncle in Princeton, New Jersey, for most of the summer while they drove their baby blue VW bug to western national parks, from the Tetons to Glacier. Once, my dad (ever the jet pilot from his prior years in the Marines) took a turn too fast and rolled the VW on the way into Yellowstone National Park, scarily close to the Yellowstone River in Gallatin Canyon. Shaken and bruised, my parents were rescued by a local sheriff who lectured my father for speeding, but did not give him a ticket.

After that national park loop, my dad felt the pull of the West, but he would not land a position in the National Park Service until I turned seven. Then, with three children in the backseat (no seat belts) my parents loaded up a white

Chevy 2 station wagon for a cross-country drive to our new home in Longmire in the heart of Mount Rainier National Park. On our way, we stopped in Frankfort, Kentucky, to leave our cocker spaniel Cindy with my grandparents. There could be no pets in a national park.

Our family moved about every two years. By the time I graduated from high school, we'd lived in nine houses. It wasn't easy, but we adapted like a flexing forest enduring wind, flood, landslide, and wildfire. We were a bit like migratory birds following flyways. Rather than the typical north–south–north, our flight lines went east to west and west to east.

When I look back at the childhood understory from my vantage point today, it's impossible not to mix in memories from who I would become later. Dipping into the understory, I begin with the American Dipper of fast streams that nurture forests, including this one by Lookout Creek.

FIVE

American Dipper

Currents Carry the Forest

Constellations of American Dipper song star the rippling Metolius River curling around a boulder. A robin-sized, plump bird, gray as a storm cloud with a wrenlike cocked tail is dipping and dipping on the slick rock. The silvery white eyelid blinks and blinks. Listening to whistling cheery riffs, *chrrrs* and *trills* wrapping my winter heart, I am swept away like a spun leaf.

Dippers, also known as water ouzels, are inextricably linked to the feathered forest. The birds' understory is the lively river or stream, overhung by shrubs and trees that are drinking the cold oxygenated water through their roots and giving back to the fresh water that in turn gives to us. Their quarry dwells below the surface. Where caddisfly, mayfly, and stonefly larvae abound, the food web is healthy for riverine and terrestrial life alike.

The Metolius River of central Oregon, an hour northwest from my home in Bend, reflects centuries-old ponderosa pine, incense-cedar, western larch, Douglas-fir, and grand fir. Sepia trunks waver across dark swift waters lined in snow. With my mittened hand touching the spongy burnished red bark of an incense-cedar, I watch a second dipper from upriver land near the first, perching like a tossed stone on a mossy, ferny rug. As their twinned songs skirl into the forest, I wonder if they are mates, since both male and female are equally talented vocalists. They sing in every season, their notes at once frolicking and mellifluous as the river. Dippers may pair up for multiple years. Perhaps couples are like sandhill cranes that dance and bow to renew their bonds beyond the spring season of typical courtship for birds.

On another day in July, I'm hiking a trail within Eagle Cap Wilderness by the West Fork of the Wallowa River in northeast Oregon when startled by quick phrases of notes. A dipper calls from a slick smooth boulder parting the fast currents. The bell-like calls ricochet off Douglas-firs, grand firs, Engelmann spruce, and ponderosas leaning over waters born among granite peaks rising to elevations of 10,000 feet.

Then quiet. The dipper plops into an eddy whirling below the boulder, vanishes below the surface, and hops back up on the boulder. A quick shake and pearled droplets fly from feathers. More bobbing up and down in place like a person doing a vigorous set of squats—who knows why a dipper dips?

As North America's only aquatic songbird, the American Dipper flies underwater with wings like paddles and walks on shallow stream bottoms. Wading or swimming on the surface, a dipper often peers below the surface to spot aquatic insects hiding in the interstices of stones that are free of sediments.

Joining four other species worldwide in the family Cinclidae (meaning dipping or bobbing), the American has much in common with the White-capped, Rufous-throated, White-throated, and Brown Dipper. All live in the splash and spray of lively streams or rivers. Europe's White-throated Dipper wears a splotch of snowy feathers like a bib. The Brown and American share similar habitats of whitewater mountain creeks—the Brown Dipper above 5,000 feet in the Himalayas and the American Dipper in a wide range of elevations. They know how to read water and not be swept into the washing machine of whirlpools below eddies.

Right out of college, I almost drowned on the Blackfoot River, east of Missoula, Montana. It happened so fast. My friends and I were paddling a rented raft from Army Navy. It was late summer. The river was low. We drank cheap beer from cans. Aiming for a boulder that promised a small roller-coaster ride below, I reached forward to stroke hard, but hit only air as we went over the lip. Over I went headfirst and laughing. Popping up in the eddy's whirlpool, I opened my mouth to breathe, only to be sucked back under. No air. Lungs filled with water. Frantic, I kicked and spun my arms. Popped up. Dragged under. How many times before I was tossed out of the spinning hole like some bit of detritus? Then, strong arms gripped me. One of my companions pulled me to shore. I gasped, coughed water, and lay there shaking. We put on our life jackets. Sober, somber, and chagrined, we drifted downriver.

I've navigated the Blackfoot in a canoe or raft many times since then and always I wear a life jacket, knowing there's danger even in calm waters. On that same river, I've floated by dippers, kingfishers, swallows, mergansers, and waxwings within the shadowy forest corridors.

While the Blackfoot has suffered from logging and mining, the river has many lovers restoring the wildness, especially in the removal of the Milltown Dam that blocked the confluence with the Clark Fork River eight miles above town. On March 28, 2009, I joined hundreds of people on a bluff cheering at the moment of breaching, a plan a decade in the making that included cleaning a Superfund site of toxic mining wastes in the soil of the reservoir. "For the first time in a hundred years, let her run!" shouted Governor Brian Schweitzer. A woman in an excavator lowered the bucket, pulled out the plug, and we went wild at a trickle, a current, and at last a roar as the freed river found her way home.

In contrast to my poor preparation for rafting the Blackfoot River, the American Dipper is well equipped. Layers of waterproof contour feathers arranged like roof shingles insulate and repel water. With no exposed skin between feather tracts, the body stays warmer. The dipper's oil gland for waterproofing is ten times bigger than that of a comparable-sized landbird. Add a flap over nostrils, and this river diver is prepared for the iciest of waters.

But how does a buoyant bird keep from floating up when underwater? Turning to my feather motif of barbs and barbules as interlocking as the forest, I take a dive into the physics of water interacting with a dipper feather. The barbs (extending from the rachis or quill horizontally) are spaced perfectly for droplets to bridge the gap and bead up. Water drops adhere to materials (like feather keratin) but not to air. When a drop of water strikes the feather, it hits the tiny spaces between and doesn't squeeze through. While all feathers have this quality, some are more repellant than others. To counter air bubbles that do form on feathers, the bird has sturdy gripping toes to walk on stony bottoms. When diving about, a dipper uses short round wings like paddles and never stays down for long.

Walking in the rain in feathered forests, I am shielded under umbrella branches. To feel the full strength of soaking rain, I step into an American

Dipper's world. In meanders near rivers and creeks from the Pacific Coast across the Cascades and into the Northern Rockies of Montana, I've found their woven mossy nest balls glued under rocky overhangs on midriver boulders, snugged among log jams, and even stuck to the bottom of small bridges.

A denizen of the West's fast-flowing mountainous creeks and rivers, the dipper is a guide to the reciprocity of flowing waters and wild forests. River quenches tree thirst. Roots anchor, filter, and clean waters. Drifting leaves from riparian alders, maples, and willows feed insects that feed dippers as well as fish that in turn feed kingfishers. When leaves stack up behind logs and rocks, they become lively islands of life. The streams are of the forest, gathering up all that falls or blows into the currents. Lichens, moss, sticks, twigs, needles, leaves wash into the water to be colonized by microscopic fungi and algae that form a slimy biofilm underpinning freshwater food webs.

Conifers year round and deciduous trees seasonally shade and cool waters. Natural log jams slow currents, form deep pools on the downriver sides for resting trout and salmon, and release nutrients. Beavers cut saplings of alders, aspen, and birch to construct dams that store and spread subsurface water to be drawn up in the roots of thirsty trees far away.

In spring and summer, swallows, nighthawks, tanagers, flycatchers, waxwings, hummingbirds, warblers, and bats nip winged mayflies, caddis, and stoneflies hatching from the free flow. Some insects escape to court, mate, lay eggs, and, sometimes, fly a surprising distance into forests to foster new life and bind one stream community to another. The forest and the river are like partners in a swing dance.

In my seven seasons of observing Belted Kingfishers by Rattlesnake Creek in Missoula, Montana, I developed a fondness for dippers. In contrast to my skittish kingfisher quarry, they ignored my presence, except for the one unlucky bird that bounced off my camouflaged blind. Only two bends of the creek down from the kingfisher nest hole, a pair of dippers raised four or five chicks in a basketball-sized moss nest fastened to a rocky promontory overhanging the creek. Every creek has her rhythms of bird life.

Returning to Missoula in January of 2025 during an arctic spell with temperatures in the single digits, I bundled up in a billowy down parka with a hood, a scarf wound around my face, heated gloves, and insulated boots. No other person was out by Rattlesnake Creek. Fluffed-up Black-capped Chickadees flitted among ponderosa pines and Douglas-firs. Chickadees are equipped with a denser layer of feathers to keep them warmer than comparably sized songbirds. At night when individuals snuggle into tree cavities, they can drop their body temperatures to enter a state of torpor and conserve energy.

I kept close to the creek edge following the snowy yet beaten path and paused often to survey snow-domed rocks and slabs of broken ice with waters racing over round stones. There! Below willows and alders jeweled in frost, I heard a flamboyance of singing. A dipper crouched on the ice and blinked. The melody spun from a thin bill as the bird looked left and right. I could see neck feathers puffing in and out with the music. The creek glinted in hues of obsidian and ice. I forgot to be cold. The dipper stopped and began to preen. The eyelid flashed like a bright silver coin.

Straightening to show pink sturdy legs, this polar plunger warmed up with a few swift knee bends and then belly-flopped in, with wings held high. A few seconds later, the dipper bobbed up like a cork and leaped up on an iced-over rock for a quick breath, a flutter of wings, and then a jump in, swim in a circle, and up again. Next a quick-step walk across the thick ice with water pouring around. Peer in. Leap. This time with a bit more of a headfirst arc. Propelled by stubby wings, the dipper's forays were swift and sure. In sunlight, I could see the cocked flicking tail better as the bird pinged between water and air.

Then, I heard sweet arias flowing my way from downstream. I scanned thin ice, the frosty outlines of willows, and there, where the water dribbled from ice, was the second dipper. Were they duetting? They appeared to pay little attention to each other. I have no idea why dippers carol on an 8-degree morning among ice and sunshine and forest and crisp blue sky. But I know that both the male and the female are sweet singers, even if I can't tell them apart by their plumage.

On another freezing day, I went looking for a long-established dipper nest about two turns of creek below the kingfisher nest bank. Crunching through foot-deep snow tracked by white-tailed deer, ducking under low-hanging alder branches and climbing over a black cottonwood log, I parted the maroon-hued limbs of red osier dogwoods. Something had changed. A Douglas-fir had crashed down from this east side of the creek and into the water, almost all the way across to the sedimentary cliff.

Obscured by the branches, the familiar mossy dome rested on a slatelike ledge, tucked under an arched roof of light gray rock. A dark golf-ball-sized entry hole dotted the middle. Whitewash on the stones below suggested the dippers had nested there last season. With a little sprucing up, the nest would be ready for spring.

I've watched a pair of dippers dunking moss chunks in water first, before flying up to a nest in need of a bit of refurbishing. Dippers give thanks to mosses in the way of Robin Wall Kimmerer's book, *Gathering Moss*. More than a thousand species of moss dwell in Cascadia, extending from the Pacific Northwest into western Montana, too. Moss adds precious humidity to the air. Moss shares with songbirds, chipmunks, and often rims their nests and dens.

Dippers weave moss with grasses, leaves, and soft bark to form an inner dome and then compose the outer dome of mosses that shield, protect, absorb moisture, and keep the inside warm or cool. If I could shrink to squeeze inside a dipper nest, as beckoning as a hobbit hole, I know I would feel as coddled as a baby.

On that same January visit, my son Ian and I skied to a different Rattlesnake Creek cliff, forming a cavern above the gentle stretch of clear creek, anticipating finding a dipper nest I'd known since 1986 when I moved to Missoula for graduate school. I had not anticipated that we'd pass a new beaver dam. Festooned in icicles and snows, the crisscrossed branches and saplings formed a lattice spanning the creek. Water like clear brown tea percolated through the lower edges of the dam. Ice glassed over half the pond above, where Douglas-firs greened the sky on one side and leafless cottonwoods and alders formed a silvery thicket on the other.

Ian, who had just graduated from University of Montana in math and philosophy, pondered the dam that formed a branched hedge almost four feet tall. Often, his mind works in ways that I find boggling. He's a deep thinker, but on this day, he asked a simple question: "How do the fish get through?"

There's a saying among fisheries biologists, "Beavers taught salmon to jump." That's true for bull trout, cutthroat, and rainbow of Rattlesnake Creek's cold water refugia, too. Beavers have co-evolved with native fish. Smaller fish can slip through the sticks where water trickles through the branches. If the large fish can't leap over, the restless, free-flowing creek is an ally. When snows melt in spring, the rising creek overflows the dams and fish head right through. Dams also break and need repairs. The ponds behind dams serve as nurseries for young fish and favored fishing pools for kingfishers. Meanwhile, the beavers were likely cozy in a hidden lodge of sticks with an entry from below in the woodland, dry on the inside.

Skiing on to our destination, I saw not one but six dipper nests in this prime spot where faulted rock forms protective lips about 10 feet above deep slow waters. A mated pair will choose only one nest each season. Flat lichens the color of sage and curry painted the overhang. We waited but did not see or hear a dipper.

Wherever I am in the presence of a dipper, I enter the fluidity of springs, headwaters, tributaries, confluences, rain, of cold filtered water splashed on my face, and refugia of moss storing life-giving moisture and hosting water-loving insects. Forests sprinkle their magic of needles, leaves, and insects into the water from above. Mayflies and other adults hatching from streams fly out into the forests to enter a food web far beyond the channel.

Where dippers share streams and rivers with salmon, the birds are healthier—twenty times more likely to nest twice in a season and female chicks grow larger—the conclusions of a dipper study after the removal of the Elwha River dams on the Olympic Peninsula. The marine-derived nitrogen and carbon fatten up the aquatic insects that the dippers dive for. Everywhere I turn is interdependence.

"Life rhymes at every scale," wrote Ferris Jabr in *Becoming Earth, How Our Planet Came to Life*. "The planet is the largest known living system—the confluence of all other systems—with structures, rhythms, and self-regulating processes that resemble those of its smaller constituent life forms."[1]

Birds are poets of the rhyme. Dipper song is an alliteration of the rhyming creek. Slipping below the surface, the seal-bird plunges into a freshwater ecosystem that is the river continuum from headwaters to the mouth, where communities of life respond, adjust, and navigate the plummets, wave trains, falls, and pools. In turn, those communities are shaped by topography, influenced by tributaries and the seasons of flood and drought.

Ancient forests assure the rhyming with water showering down through the canopies, entering deep soils, and renewing groundwater so the deep roots of the big and old trees can pull the water up to the surface in summer to quench their thirst and the younger trees around them.

When I climbed Traverse, I could hear Lookout Creek purling far below me where dippers plunged. Focusing on the canopy birds—Red Crossbills, Western Flycatchers, and Hermit Warblers—I was only faintly aware of the transfer of water from creek, moss, and dipper to roots to crown and atmosphere. When trees transpire through the pores on needles and leaves, they release all that has come up through the soil and roots—fungal spores, pollen, and bacteria. Those particles are the key to atmospheric moisture condensing to become rain. The wide-spreading crowns of these oldest and tallest Douglas-firs offer far more needles to the sun to photosynthesize and to transpire moisture to the air. Half of a great tree's weight is water. A person is more than half water. We have much in common.

From the mountains, springs trickle into creeks entering larger streams and rivers shaped by topography, gradient, width, depth, and structure. In turn, aquatic life is as fluid as moving water, yet selective, too.

The Lookout Fire of 2023 burned across two-thirds of the Andrews Forest, with some of the highest intensity within the old growth. Scientists shifted from grieving to studying the aftermath, armed with decades of stream and wildlife data. The opportunities for understanding fire before and after are unparalleled. The great trees are like water towers, and the fallen trees are water tanks. Standing trees (burned or green) and fallen trees anchor soils and prevent erosion. Ash from fires carries nutrients into the water.

To rhyme at every scale is to cherish entire watersheds and the interstitial spaces between stones in a small stream. I put my hands in the clear water and remember how it felt to be eleven years old and saving a creek.

I'm with my sixth-grade class at Westtown Friends School, an hour west of Philadelphia. Wading in Chester Creek with nets, we sample aquatic life and fill vials with water to test the chemistry. The video camera is running. We're making a movie. I have the best teacher ever in Peg Lippincott (called Teacher Peg in Quaker tradition). Week after week, we gather more footage.

When not filming, sampling, and testing, I'm climbing maples and oaks with the boys. I don't pay enough attention until the day our vials revealed something awful. In one stretch, the water was fine, but downstream the results showed a sudden influx of pollutants. We returned on high alert as detectives scouring the stream banks until we found the illegal pipe spewing foul chemicals. The cameras rolled. We had our film and our proof. The newspapers covered our story. We exposed the culprit company and rescued Chester Creek.

There at Chester Creek I learned a pivotal lesson. Eleven-year-olds can wield power. It was 1970, the year of the first Earth Day. Our family had moved to Pennsylvania the year before from Coulee Dam, Washington. It proved to be a two-year hiatus from the National Park Service for my dad to teach history. After an awkward entry (like wearing saddle shoes instead of penny loafers), I'd found my stride by sixth grade—braces off and hair growing in thick, curly, and past my shoulders after years of forced pixie cuts. I was at once a "tomboy" and a flirt with more than one boyfriend. We held hands and once there was a quick kiss.

I did have quieter moments at Friends Meetings at school and on Sundays, a silent worship without a minister and an emphasis on the "light within." While not practicing today, I dip back to Meetings and appreciate my Quaker heritage of pacifism. The Richies have a long legacy at Westtown, a school dating to 1799. My father attended as a boarding student, and his parents had met and fallen in love there years before.

At Westtown, I was free, wild, and learning from nature. Teacher Peg also set us loose in the school's arboretum to create leaf collections. My mother helped me iron the leaves between wax paper, and I wrote handwritten descriptions for fifty trees. At the end of the school year, I forgot to bring home my book. The custodian threw it away. I was devastated, but the imprint remained.

Decades later, in 2002, when my dad knew he had only a short time left to live with late-stage colon cancer, he suggested we place some of his ashes under a tree within the Westtown Arboretum. We gravitated to a tall deodar cedar, struck by the soft textures of bluish-green needles and the winglike sway of weeping branches. Native to the western Himalayas, the tree held female cones shaped like smooth beehives growing upright on the tips of upper branches. Nearby was a much younger tree. Digging small holes near the trunks of the large and small deodar cedars, our family sprinkled ashes as an offering to the trees. I keep a lemon-sized cone on my bureau, the seeds sealed tight within.

Returning for a visit in February of 2025, I wandered the 600-acre campus with my brother and sister-in-law and niece Anna as chevrons of honking Canada Geese crossed a pewter sky above leafless treetops of oak, maple, beech, hickory, black walnut, and perhaps ash. We found the cedars—the one I remember with pendulous limbs draping low to the ground and the young sapling now about 40 feet tall, half the height of the elder. Touching soft short needles growing in starry bundles on twigs, I imagine trekking through high-elevation forests of the Himalayas, where Hindus worship deodar cedars as divine.

Walking by Westtown Lake, I could close my eyes and visualize ice skating with the boys in long glides and twirls, and knowing another way of being birdlike. I looked up the long walkway descending to the lake and remembered rocketing down on glare ice, hands gripping the steering handle of a Flexible Flyer sled. (My great-grandfather was one of the inventors).

On the campus "Granolithic"—the main wide sidewalk—I could almost hear Crosby, Stills, and Nash turned up loud from the dorms then in the height of the Vietnam War. I remembered my "big brother" Adam from the upper school who taught me how to take photos and develop film. In the outdoor amphitheater with the stone seats, I was again Helena in *A Midsummer Night's Dream*.

Always there were birds and my father guiding us to see spectacles, like trips to Hawk Mountain to count migrating raptors in fall. Thanks to my mother saving old school relics, I have my fifth-grade science fair project in a manila folder with the title where I'd traced each capital letter in red, "OBSERVING BIRDS FEEDING HABITS." I wrote entries such as "The White Throated Sparrows were quite numerous and every morning rain or shine the whole bunch showed up." In my ten-year-old way I tended to add adjectives freely—"handsome English Sparrow," "Pretty yellow Goldfinches," and the "bright red cardinal certainly brightened up our drab picnic table as he stopped in for his breakfast."

Going back to childhood homes can be risky in a fast-developing world. My brother Rob and I could not find the two-story white clapboard farmhouse off campus where we lived as a family of five. We walked up to the familiar stone mansion and red barn, but not our humble tenant house. In a serendipitous meeting with the owner of the house next door, we learned of the demise, which began with new owners. The wife found our house creepy. The husband hired local Amish workers to move our old home out of her view. They did, but the city then denied a permit to hook up electric and sewer. The husband then cut a big door into the house and stored his boat there. The demise was well under way, and eventually the house was torn down.

Where was the maple tree that held me up for hours every day as I read *The Hobbit* and *Lord of the Rings* in summer? No trace. But we could find a stone wall with a row of Norway spruce trees—the very ones I used to ladder up to the tippy top in the wind.

The house and the maple tree where I read are gone. My childhood bird report is my window into that lonely girl then freshly moved from Coulee Dam. This was my refuge—that project, the trees, our family farmhouse.

Thanks to teacher Peg and the Chester Creek Project, I found out even kids can change the world—at least a corner of it. Today, I am like an older tree with thicker bark, scars, and the ability to shelter others in ways I could not do as a sapling.

In my home in Oregon, I seek the streams and rivers interlacing wild forests. The dippers singing in every season are reminders to dip into the wilds no matter what the temperature. Their notes are the cascades of waters, trees, and birds as one. I listen and feel the water within my body as a watershed fed by tributaries. I no longer see a linear chronology. Instead, there are confluences throughout.

The longer I spend in the feathered forest, the more I'm yielding to free-flow. Sometimes I dream of sleeping on a deep bed of moss by restless waters. Perhaps a dipper might pluck a curly strand from under my fingertips and fly off to her nest behind a waterfall.

SIX

Pacific Wren

Tangled Roots and Mossy Springs

Tucked low in the contours dwells the rain bird, Pacific Wren. Spicing up fern-laced creeks in jazz riffs and nutmeg feathers, the tiny cedar-hued bird knows the wettest pockets. Alert, fast, and hard for a predator to catch, the wren maps a thicketed, shadowy maze. No other wren species is so closely tied to ancient forests—if they are clear-cut, the wren's song fades away. Highly sensitive to fragmentation, the breaking up of habitat, this species relies on complex structures within understories. Where the wren thrives, so does a secretive community.

When a 200-foot-tall tree cracks, shatters, splits, and crashes down, a wall of roots invites wrens to sing from the root tops and to nest within the exposed lattice. In turn, the tipped-over tree exposes loamy soil like a vertical garden bed. Pools may form in the hole where the tree once stood and invite salamanders, newts, frogs, and other aquatic life. Sunlight funnels down in the gap, where blooming plants invite bees, butterflies, and hummingbirds to sip nectar or gather pollen.

Tip-up trees are a signal to scan for signs of the bird with black barring on a cinnamon tail that's often upturned, too. Like an exclamation mark, the wren's tail accentuates an excitable life. Tail flicking in many songbirds—sparrows, juncos, and other wrens—also sends a message to predators. "I'm alert, quick, and hard to catch."

In early October, I heard an emphatic *chup-chup* in our central Oregon yard. A lone Pacific Wren had found our unruly sunflower stalks, goldenrod, and asters to hide among and glean insects. Wrens that live higher in forested mountains fly to lower elevations in late fall after the critical times of summer nesting and raising chicks. How far they travel and the details of their behavior outside of breeding season remains a mystery.

To find Pacific Wrens in Oregon reliably, I seek them west of the Cascades and often near springs. However, on a July day hike under a penstemon sky up the West Fork of the Wallowa River within the Eagle Cap Wilderness of northeast Oregon, I heard a Pacific Wren and a Swainson's Thrush singing in piccolo trill and flute ascension. Did they intentionally duet or was that morning too irresistible for singing? Their music sprang from a native honeysuckle thicket, flowers matching the blustery oranges and yellows of a Western Tanager on a ponderosa pine limb overhead. The wren and thrush reminded me of how verdant and wet are certain forests of the Blue Mountains.

Farther up, the trail zigged away from the rushing river to zag past the aftermath of a microburst, caused by downdraft winds in a thunderstorm. Among the standing Douglas-firs were dozens of fallen comrades that had stood for more than a century. Listening to a jubilance of wren song among the downfall, I felt a rush of relief. Here, in the protected wilderness, there would be no logging, no meddling with nature's dynamism.

On another day in early spring, I wandered the Old Growth Trail within the McDonald Research Forest of Oregon State University above Corvallis in the rain-soaked Willamette Valley. One male wren after another spun love songs and proclaimed territories. Ferns scarved the trailside. Lichen boutonnieres festooned Douglas-fir branches. Watching a fluffed-up bird with trembling wings open his beak and pitch arias into the sky, I heard the collective voice of a community bustling in biodiversity. The male's lower bill rose and fell like a sewing machine on high speed.

A male Pacific Wren is all about dazzling a female. When he perches on a twig above her, he sings with his whole body—a mini-Elvis shaking his booty as his tail pings back and forth. He lures her to a nest he's built in anticipation, inviting her to dive into the hole. Why stop at one? He might lead her to two or even three for her choosing. How about this one in the creekbank behind a moss curtain? Or the free-standing moss dome, woven from the base to the top with feltlike bark, rootlets, feathers, and deer fur? Or perhaps she will fall for his masterpiece—a spherical dome of moss swaying from the limb of a great spruce, with a neatly twigged entry hole.

If the female approves, she will line one nest with downy feathers before she lays up to nine tiny white freckled eggs. Only she will incubate, while the male serenades. Singing and nest building are his best skill sets. And yes, he will carry insect treats to his beloved as she warms the eggs for about two and half weeks. Then, the featherless chicks will chip through shells. Together, the parents will hunt for flies and beetles, with the male taking the most interest as the chicks grow closer to fledging. A little over two weeks after hatching, the chicks take their first flights. The family groups stick together in summer.

Occasionally, I've come within arm's reach of young wrens still learning to be fearful of strangers. In their presence, I've thought of times in my youth when I was most vulnerable.

Monkeying up a favorite maple tree, I settle into a crook and reach for a book from my daypack—a steamy romance novel set in the 1800s. The knot in my stomach loosens. My aching jaw unclenches. There, enfolded in leaves and among robins, cardinals, chickadees, titmice, and nuthatches, I am at once cocooned and exhilarated to be 25 feet off the ground.

I'd survived another miserable day at Williamsburg Junior High School in Arlington, Virginia. It's October 1972—not long after our family moved from Westtown School. In gym class, the teacher barked at me for shrinking from a volleyball instead of pounding it across the net. In the locker room, two girls wearing matching hoop earrings shoved and pushed each other. One grabbed the other's earring and yanked it right through her earlobe. In history class, the teacher assigned us a textbook claiming enslaved people were happy on plantations. The woods behind our family's two-story house on North Twenty-Sixth Street are my sanctuary. I count the hours until the last bell rings, the bus drops me off, and I can grab a snack and book to take the woods trail leading to a monastery where monks in long robes chant and bells ring.

One warm October afternoon along the trail of fallen oak, maple, and beech leaves I notice a gray squirrel leaping with an acorn clenched between teeth, a wooly bear caterpillar, a cat-faced spider in an orb web, a lone box turtle, and a garter snake. I avoid poison ivy. Robins, titmice, and cardinals call from my destination—a native oak tree with an ample trunk and horizontal limbs low enough to grab with two hands to swing up to safety.

The second year at Williamsburg Junior High leads to a few friendships. I wear hip-hugger jeans with a wide belt and ruffly peasant blouses. My then-frizzy hair at last tumbles halfway to my waist. My mother and I march in the 1973

Nixon counter-inaugural parade. Among 60,000 gathered at the Washington Monument, we watch Congresswoman Bella Abzug stride up to the stage wearing one of her classic hats. She grabs a microphone: "Richard Nixon just finished his speech . . . and not once did he mention the word Vietnam. We are not going to stop protesting until he takes all forces out of Vietnam."[1]

Her bold voice rings out across the crowd. I might still crave hiding places in a forest, but on this day with my feminist mother, I find my voice.

Wrens may be tiny, but they can sing freshets of music that would fill a piano book. In the McDonald Forest back in 1970, ornithologist Donald Kroodsma, author of *The Singing Life of Birds*, stunned the bird world with his findings. Perhaps one of the males I listened to spinning arias was descended from a wren he recorded back in that same heady era of antiwar protests and of the first Earth Day.

Kroodsma observed that one male performed 441 unique songs in three hours, with each tune lasting about five to ten seconds. Graphing the variations later that day, he noticed most songs began with the same introductory notes. It's in the second half that a male "unleashes his creative bent." Over two mornings, he recorded 831 songs with 67 variations. The problem with wren song is the high speed. It's like watching a hummingbird hover. All is a blur. But slow a recording down to quarter time, and trills become mellifluous whistles.

Kroodsma praised the singer as producing the "pinnacle" of bird song: "His songs are so expressive, ranging from the loud and vehement to soft warbles, to whispers of sibilant notes that might be audible only a few inches from the bird. Perhaps only if I were a wren for a day would I know all he is saying and thinking."[2]

To be a wren for a day. Feeling that yearning, I decided to vary my way of hiking from upright, occasionally scrunching down and peering up instead of looking down on leaves and ferns. Scientist Matt Betts in his Landscape Ecology Lab at Oregon State University stresses the importance of research from a "species-eye" view, because every kind of bird perceives the forest differently. He also speculates that Pacific Wrens may position themselves within concave topographies to amplify their songs, in the way of musicians playing in amphitheaters.[3]

When we take an animal point of view, we begin to "see" forest inhabitants in ways that help close the gap of our separation. Sometimes that takes ecological studies requiring scientists to wade, crawl, kneel, scramble, and, yes, swing up high into trees.

On November 5, 2024, on a fateful presidential election day, I found respite from worry by hiking a forested trail following cliffs of Cape Arago, a favorite haunt on the southern Oregon coast I've known since attending the Oregon Institute of Marine Biology in Charleston, a small fishing town near Coos Bay. While not ancient forest, it still contains many qualities key to wren happiness—10-foot-tall tipped up roots of Sitka spruce, hidden side streams, and dense thickets.

As ocean rollers crested and struck cliffs to shoot frothing whitewater 60 feet high, I channeled my inner wren. Crouching under sword ferns, I looked up through their laddered symmetry like feather barbs. I noted golden-brown spores forming dotted lines on the outer sides of each pearled water droplet. Behind the fronds, I could see a backlit translucence I'd missed before in leathery salal leaves, each oval big enough to be a roof over a wren and some bearing the chew marks of insects. Parting a hedge of salal and evergreen huckleberry, I stuck my head through a small opening to a Lilliputian world with hundreds of twigs, forks and mini-perches.

Where a fallen tree spawned lichens, moss, mushrooms, and new saplings, I touched spongy wet wood becoming earth. Spiderwebs swung in root recesses. A bonnet mushroom the size of a thimble shone on a long stem above moss and hemlock needles. Lichen like snow patches encircled more moss. A raised root formed a wren window. Rootlets from new trees draped from the nurse log out into the open, each one encased in fungi. Fairy parachute mushrooms lined twigs like moon jellies of the nearby ocean.

To enter a wren's world is to crawl on hands and knees in wonder of all we miss in our two-legged upright way. If only I had feathers, I'd come closer to the tiny bird of bravado.

In Thor Hanson's book, *Feathers*, he described plucking, counting, and sorting all the feathers on a roadkilled Winter Wren, the species to the east of Cascadia and ranging to New England, with a lighter chestnut plumage than a Pacific Wren. Until recently, the Pacific and Winter Wren were lumped together as one species, the Winter Wren. After scientists noted differing songs, plumage, and genetics, they split them into two kinds.

After two hours with tweezers, Hanson's feather piles added up to more than 1,200: 208 per wing; 12 tail; 375 belly, breast, and back; and 400-plus delicate feathers on the neck, head, and face. He described face bristles, and "down from the belly, so soft their touch was like the faintest brush of air, less a sensation than an anticipation." While each feather seems weightless, together they are twice as heavy as a wren's skeleton.[4]

More than the sum of its feathers, a Pacific Wren cannot be quantified any more than a great tree can be measured by diameter, circumference, height, and percentages of crown. Even the name Pacific Wren cannot contain all that is *wren*. Yet, I do like the moniker wren—from Middle English "wrenne," meaning little tail. The Latin name is *Troglodytes pacificus*. A Winter Wren is *Troglodytes hiemalis* (Latin for winter).

The genus name *Troglodytes* connotes a grumpy hermit unwilling to come out of a cave. If you say it with affection—"hey you little Troglodyte come on out of your crevice or hole"—the name can sound endearing, like in French saying, "mon petit chou," my little cabbage.

An older forest's "floor" is akin to wren feathers—layers of leaves, twigs, logs, bark, roots, moss, and lichen. The duff can feel as airy as downy fluff. Insects bore, tunnel, and munch in a circular rhythm of living, growing, dying, and renewing. The way of wrens seeking insect prey is like a naturalist with a hand lens. The birds peek into cracks and crannies, glean from leaves, and probe loosening bark and decaying wood seeking beetles, bugs, caterpillars, ants, flies, pseudoscorpions, millipedes, spiders, and daddy long-legs. They pluck bees, wasps, mites, and even ticks. Often wrens search within the panoply of lichens—more than 2,000 species in the Pacific Northwest, with their highest diversity and biomass found in ancient forests.

Wrens hunt insects that are grazers, fungivores, predators, and prey. Beetles are their top prey. Boring, tunneling, and munching, beetles are returning wood to cellulose to earth, with help from fungi. Of the million named insect species, 400,000 are beetles. I'm reminded of the famous quote attributed to the British evolutionary biologist J. B. S. Haldane (1892–1964): "If one could conclude as to the nature of the Creator from a study of creation it would appear that God has an inordinate fondness for stars and beetles."

Compared with beetles, the mites that wrens also glean are minuscule. In one square meter of leaf litter below a tree may be from 50,000 to 500,000 mites. Most are the width of two human hairs or sometimes a pencil tip. They scurry around on eight legs armed with stout shells and a bevy of defenses. Depending on the species, they raise hairs on their bodies, roll into balls, cover themselves in soil, or release toxins. Chewing away, they break down leaves into pieces that fungi and bacteria then decompose. Other mites directly eat fungi.

If wrens depended only on mites, they'd be hungry. Curious wrens are always sleuthing for clues. A rolled leaf hides a caterpillar or pupae. A chewed leaf is a clue to the presence of a camouflaged green sawfly larva. I found one of the fat sawfly grubs when studying a salmonberry bush in late fall, noticing the leaves of insect-chewed art.

Wrens also team up with other petite songbirds to find food. During my October stay of the grebe rescue, I often hiked the Cape Lookout State Park North trail. Coming to my favorite ravine with a swinging bridge over Cape Creek, I heard the *chup-chup* call notes of a Pacific Wren. A bird wave rolled through the salmonberry, salal, sword ferns, and red elderberry. The wren cavorted with several Golden-crowned Kinglets, a Ruby-crowned Kinglet (striking with a white eye ring), and a Brown Creeper. The creeper emerged from thickets to ascend a spruce trunk's shaggy scales of bark in quick upward hops and bill probes, only to drop down low to repeat the maneuver on an adjacent tree. Kinglets flitted in and out of view among salmonberry, salal, and sword ferns. Like birds in the tropics that feed in mixed-species flocks, they share prime feeding spots and warn of predators, like Pygmy Owls or Cooper's Hawks.

If I planted myself long enough, I might meet the hopping, slithering, and pattering inhabitants. A coastal-tailed frog morphs from chocolate to green to blend into the step pools of mossy stream. A garter snake with a red stripe swallows a rough-skinned newt, one of the few predators that is resistant to this salamander with an orange stomach proclaiming "I'm toxic!" A dusky shrew races among seepages, below fallen trees and among marshes, hunting beetles, snails, or pausing to take bites from a dead mouse. A slightly larger Pacific shrew twitches her nose and twitters to echolocate like a bat in the night. Lightning quick, she jumps into the air to snatch a passing dragonfly and pins her meal with her tiny forefeet, then bites off the head.

Crossing the bridge 20 feet above Cape Creek, I looked down into classic Pacific Wren habitat—impenetrable devil's club, salmonberry, sword fern, and fallen trees above redwood sorrels. Watching an American Dipper swimming in the rivulets in search of aquatic larvae, I'm reminded of what else this creek offers—spawning habitat for salmon. At the start of the North Trail, I'd crossed Jackson Creek, where coho salmon spawn in the fall and enter on high tides. These are the lucky ones returning within a protected forest. Beyond the state park are ragged clear-cuts on private lands, logged on tight rotations of about forty years.

How many Pacific Wrens improvised jazz in the Cascadia forests before logging? Some studies show their numbers are half of what they were before the time of logging. Statistics can't do justice to the loss. Of all artists, Emily Carr of Vancouver Island best depicted the wild forests of the early 1900s. Studying her watercolor, *Wood Interior*, from 1909, I wanted to step into the painting of numinous light streaming through a grove of giantess cedars. I'd be so very small. Emily also witnessed the tragedy of clear-cutting ancient western hemlocks, Sitka spruce, and western redcedars in the 1920s and 1930s. Pain emanated from the stumps she painted and called "amputations." In her published journal, she wrote,

> There's a torn and splintered ridge across the stumps I call "the screamers." These are the unsawn last bits, the cry of the tree's heart, wrenching and tearing apart just before she gives that sway and the dreadful groan of falling, that dreadful pause while her executioners step back with their saws and axes resting and watching.[5]

Today, less than 3 percent of British Columbia's great wild forests remain—and not all are protected. But within the Cape Lookout wild forest, I could lose myself.

In every walk in every wild forest small or large, I'm on alert for birds that are often secretive and tricky to spot. In contrast, on the open beach, I had a clear view of Brown Pelicans skimming the waves—a line of a dozen pterodactyl-like birds with wingtips curved slightly down as if to touch the cresting whitewater. Western Gulls stalked the incoming waves with barely a glance my way.

Among the inscrutable curtains of tree limbs, it's easy to be confused by the ventriloquism of calls. I'm reminded of the great Chilean poet and avid birder Pablo Neruda's poem, "Ode to Birdwatching." His praise of the singers among leaves shifted to curses when the birds eluded him.[6]

What if Neruda had access to the Merlin app? Launched in 2014 by Cornell Lab of Ornithology, the app records multiple bird songs and calls at once, identifying each one. A photo of the bird flashes when a sound is detected. Accuracy keeps improving. People are awakening to birds not just as background chirps and trills but as singing or calling sparrows, finches, woodpeckers, warblers, vireos, chickadees, and more. Merlin leads to more people adding bird checklists to eBird, the community-science project that has become essential to checking the pulse of birds, their numbers, where they're showing up, rarities, and more. Sometimes, it's okay to apply artificial intelligence, as long as we remember to put down our smartphones and take in the world around us without distraction.

When I try hard to see the moving birds, I pay more attention to the little things. Studying ferns, lichens, violet and saxifrage, and twigs on the ground, I notice a banana slug at trail's edge and the scurry of a shiny black beetle. Hiking higher up the North Trail to intersect the parking lot for the main trail to the tip of Cape Lookout, I heard cars on the road and saw clear-cuts in the distance. Then, I came around a bend and into the calm of a mothering spruce above elderberry, salmonberry, and ferns. Sure enough, two wrens hopped among the shrubbery. And right then, one wren whistled up a song like a tumble of miracles.

When professional whistler Molly Lewis was asked about the why of her art form, which draws crowds swooning over her birdlike arias, her answer was as sure as her tone: "To communicate, to create, to gesture. For sadness and for joy. It is an instrument unlike any other . . . a beautiful form of breathing."[7]

Across the world are more than eighty whistled languages that communicate with less reverberation and harm to vocal cords than shouting over long distances in thick forests and rugged terrain. On remote St. Lawrence Island, Alaska, in the Bering Sea, Yupik children learn their whistled names early. Listening to a National Public Radio story on Yupik whistled conversations, I was stunned at the birdlike inflections and purity of pitches.

Whistle on, wrens. Whistle up beetles, caterpillars, ants, mites, ticks, millipedes, flies, and bees. Whistle nests lined in feathers, rootlets, moss, and animal hair, and nestled into the roots of fallen trees.

In the center of all that is wild and wet, Pacific Wren sprays odes to rain filling creeks and rivers that eddy, pool, shimmer, glimmer, spark, and plume. Sweeten every waterfall in song, Pacific Wren. I will dip my hands in the cold clear waters. I will crawl on hands and knees to the feet of a fallen five-hundred-year-old tree and whistle.

SEVEN

Varied Thrush

Arias for a Hidden World

A Varied Thrush sings two chords, the first a higher pitch than the second and with a pause between the burry whistles. The music braids the redwoods into a ballad for the tallest trees on the planet. The thrush is tuned to life in the shady interiors deep down low. Leaning back with hands on hips in the Rockefeller Grove, I hear a second male singing in counterpoint from farther away.

The birds give voice to the redwoods, from cones to seeds to saplings to soaring giants to snags to nurse logs to soil. Like polyphonic thrush song, the forests sing many notes in one harmonic chord of renewal, decay, and death, and of fire, wind, rain, and fog. The scientific species name for the coastal redwood is fitting—*Sequoia sempervirens.* Ever living.

The music floats down from the midstory, because in spring the males perch on song posts on the tops of short snags or young hemlocks in the shadow of 300-foot trees. Like singing from an elevated stage, the sounds carry farther than if sung on the level. As birds keep teaching me, layers cannot be neatly divided. This thrush may never fly in the highest treetops, but multiple levels of verticality are essential for finding song posts, lush thickets, and animate soils.

Listening to embers of fading chords, I drop to my knees to study a trillium wildflower cupping snowy petals. Close by is Bull Creek hushing along like a lullaby. Alone within Humboldt Redwoods State Park in northern California, there can be only one word. Sanctum.

As April unfolds in crisp air perfumed in new leaves and flowers, my breath joins a collective inhale and exhale of redwoods growing impossibly tall and wide with individuals weighing more than a million pounds. In a remote corner of Redwood National Park is Hyperion, the tallest living tree on the planet today at 380 feet tall.

At the base of a redwood that must be 25 feet across, I caress plaits of reddish-brown bark, the same hues as thrush plumage. Their feathers remind me of a campfire—burnt orange, sooty black, and ash-white. A dashing eyebrow (called a supercilium) flames across charcoal head feathers and a shiny black eye. A ruffly black breast band drapes down a breast the color of glowing coals. The back and tail are blue-black, and wings spark orange flecks on black. A female's feathers are softer browns and paler oranges. In silhouette, a Varied Thrush might be mistaken for an American Robin, which is also a thrush.

Tassels of sunlight trace the path of singing down to the soils where miniature lives are in motion. Varied Thrushes join Hermit and Swainson's Thrushes, also understory lovers. A Hermit's haunting aria is the shape of a wave, while a Swainson's is a twining vine of blooming song. All have large eyes to see better in dim light, an advantage for singing early and late in the day.

Of Cascadia songbirds, Varied Thrushes are likely the most dependent on older forests dripping in moss and lichens. They avoid forest patches of under 40 acres and edges where predators (from feral cats to Cooper's Hawks) can detect their nests. The territories set by males can be up to a half mile apart.

The name "varied" refers to the patterns that may help with camouflage in dappled light. The Latin name *Ixoreus naevius* translates to a mountain mistletoe berry-eater, with *Ixoreus* referring to favored foods of a European thrush and *naevius* meaning spotted.

In the northern range, the Yupik tribe of the lower Yukon call the thrush *ciitaarayul*, "the bird that's really good at squashing something."[1] When kicking both feet forward at high speed to stir up the soil to then pluck some juicy larvae with a beak, a thrush clamps down hard and definitely squashes the prey. Naming comes from close observation of behavior of birds nesting in the spruce forests. In winter, the *ciitaarayul* flies south across the border, except for birds living on the benign coastline.

The music of thrushes gives voice to the redwood elders as if the very trees played flutes with twigged fingers pressed on keys. Chords reverberate like spiderwebs suspended between maidenhair ferns. In David George Haskell's book, *Sounds Wild and Broken*, he described the difficulty of transcribing bird music flowing through the space of forests and other wild places that would require "six-dimensional music paper to record variations across frequency, loudness, time, and the three axes of space."[2]

Envision an orchestra with musicians perched like birds on song posts at vertical intervals from floor to the high ceiling of a symphony hall and spaced throughout and overhead. The more intricate a forest, the more niches there are for birds to sing where sound carries to claim territory or proclaim love without overlap and competition.

A Varied Thrush's spaced chords carry through deep shady forest where trunks, branches, and leaves soak up, reflect, and dampen sound. Haskell wrote of this phenomenon of birds tending to sing more slurred and slow notes within forests. In windy prairies, grasshopper sparrows sing in buzzes, trills, and staccato to be heard above the turbulence. That's true, too, for the rattling call of a kingfisher reverberating above whitewater.

When singing is not enough to define territories, male thrushes will lower their wings and cock their tails to confront a rival. Taking it up a notch, two males may even lock bills and fan wings and tails. If all else fails, comes a real chase with reckless flights down through bushes and small trees, even striking branches along the way. But singing is far easier and sweeter to all who are there to listen.

All bird song emanates from the syrinx, a structure that, like feathers, is unique to birds. Shaped like an upside down and hollow Y, the syrinx rests where the trachea (the breathing tube) forks. A bird sings or calls by breathing in through lungs and tightening syrinx muscles that in turn cause membranes to vibrate. The more elaborate the notes, the more highly evolved is the syrinx. The chordlike music of the Varied Thrush comes from an elegant ability to squeeze the two parts of the hollow Y separately or in unison at will. This is the way, too, of the Hermit and Swainson's Thrushes. Two notes sung at the same time at a different pitch give a richness to the fluting whistle.

As a teenage flutist, I played duets with a friend, trading lead and accompaniment. When alone, I put on a record from the Music Minus One series and desperately tried to keep pace with Bach, Faure, or Mozart, often rushing to the turntable to lift the needle and begin again. I noticed that, with effort, my hearing sharpened to hear the other part and synchronize.

Entranced by the music of dippers, wrens, and thrushes, I'm picking up my flute after years of neglect. I almost began again in 2014. My friend Sandra and

I were driving across Oregon and stopped for gas on the sleepy main street of my long-ago home community of Prairie City. I noticed the attendant looked vaguely familiar. Our eyes locked. She spoke first. "We planted trees together. You played your flute at every break."

The puzzle piece snapped in place. I remembered the weight of pine saplings wrapped in wet burlap. Paid fifty dollars a day to drop to my knees and tamp soil around a straggled root, my ears rang from the whining blare as muscled young men dug holes with chainsaw augers. Steadying a canvas bag stuffed full of tender trees, I'd get up to walk ten feet to the next drilled hole. Wiping dirt from my face, my steps would become a stagger.

The woman I spoke to at the gas station, I remember as tireless and unflappable. In the blessed silence of rest in the shade, she would urge me to lift my flute. I'd open my case and put together the three pieces to play arpeggios of daisy chains—nectar notes pattering down on sweat-stained, long-sleeved cotton shirts, sap-sticky blue jeans, and Redwing work boots. Our crew guzzled lukewarm water from plastic jugs.

At the gas station, I noticed her cropped, deer-brown hair was streaked in gray and her step quick as a fox. Her lips parted, "Do you still play?"

I wish I could tell her I have started to play again. I lift my flute to horizontal, cover the open holes with my fingers, tighten my lips, and blow across the opening. Gradually, my tone is less breathy. I'm extending my range to reach the high and low notes, but I'm rusty. Next up is to mimic bird song.

In my early twenties, I risked taking my flute on a raft trip down the Grand Canyon. I'd hike up to a high ledge and perch like a Canyon Wren, fluting that long waterfall of notes into the Colorado River.

My father gave me my silver flute with open holes on my fourteenth birthday. I'd learned on cheap school rentals with closed holes. To play with open holes means your finger position must be precise to cover each hole at every speed. The tones are purer and the open holes also lead to versatility for birdlike warbling notes. There is precision in the patterns of a wild forest, too, as scrupulous as fingers on open holes.

Varied Thrush song crosses Cascadia landscapes where forests are wet and feathered. I've heard the fluting held notes at midday when clouds blocked the sun before rainfall, at dusk in the Selway-Bitterroot Wilderness straddling the Montana-Idaho divide, in Glacier National Park, the Blue Mountains, Cascades, Coast Range, and redwoods.

A female Varied Thrush is not a singer (so far as scientists know), but she listens with a keen ear to a potential paramour. Joining in calls shared by both genders, she churrs, cherts, and trills when alarmed or in defense. Once paired up, she builds the nest, typically below 12 feet and close to a trunk of a small conifer, lashed to a fork of a sturdy shrub, or even on top of one or more old nests. In Alaska, females often choose the south side of trees as a protective microclimate.

Like a forest divided into three vertical layers, a thrush nest is a trio of horizontal layers—outer, middle, and inner. Breaking off twigs (often fir, hemlock, spruce, or alder) with her bill, a female flies to her chosen crook to begin. Her rough platform is the base of the basket she will weave with supple bark. Redwood and redcedar are favorites. Lichen forms a tough outer layer. The dense middle layer is coarse moss and spongy decaying wood that will harden. For the downy inner layer to cup three to four pale blue eggs, she chooses velvety mosses, grasses, and leaves. For the finale, she adorns the outside in moss.

A female designs and builds a miniature refugia for her chicks—sturdy and insulating from cold and heat. The camouflaging moss soaks up moisture to keep the humidity of the nest at the right levels for her eggs. The shells have microscopic pores shaped like trumpets and can dry out if she's not careful. A finished nest is the size of a soup bowl. There, the female settles in to incubate for about twelve days before the featherless chicks crack open their shells. Then, the male steps up to help for two weeks before fledging.

To keep up with the chicks' insatiable appetites, the parents forage in a frenzy of tossing of leaves, cones, and needles to yank caterpillars from comfy naps or snap up a scuttling beetle. Thrushes lead to the living soil. The chicks grow strong on high-protein insects, while their parents add variety to their diets when huckleberries, thimbleberries, and salmonberries ripen, as soon as early June in the California redwoods. As summer heats up, the high forests above cosset the birds in coolness.

In winter, Alaskan Varied Thrushes shift south into the Lower 48, to Washington, Oregon, or California—sometimes leapfrogging farther south. Oregon's coastal forest thrushes may remain in place or fly short distances to populated valleys and people's yards where they can find hiding cover, berries, seeds, and nuts. Cascade mountain thrushes may fly into central Oregon, and a few come to my home yard in Bend—in ones, twos, or threes—and if I'm lucky, a small flock of six or so. They hide under the manzanitas and rush out into the open in the way of Spotted Towhees to hop and rough up the ground for seeds under leaves.

Away from their wild forest homes, Varied Thrushes face dangers from car collisions and window strikes. Buildings with first-story, large glass windows pose the greatest risk, because they reflect vegetation attractive to thrushes as well as towhees, since both feed and find shelter low to the ground. Outdoor cats, too, are a prowling threat for all birds within reach of their claws. At our one-story, cat-free home, we have a simple and cheap solution that reduces collisions—hanging white parachute cords spaced four and a half inches apart on the outside of our windows. If wider apart, the birds could still hit windows. We've had success, except when a Cooper's or Sharp-shinned Hawk chases birds, sending them flailing in every direction.

Once in the fall, while visiting friends in Missoula, I sat outside a café with a large reflective window. As I sipped a latte at a small round table, I heard a thud and a scream. The bird fell right onto the neighboring table where two women stared in horror. I rushed to pick up the female Western Tanager with the broken neck—still warm. Later, my son and I would place the tanager under a tree near the river and show our respect. This was the fate of one bird, yet the collisions across the country for bird life are monumental. The American Bird Conservancy estimates there are a billion fatal collisions with glass each year.

Here in the Rockefeller Grove, I can listen to the thrushes without worry, knowing they likely stay in the vicinity. When I hear their spectral music, I'm like a tree holding up my leaves to be soaked in life-giving rains. The stratospheric redwoods are rainmakers. Their leaves soak up and condense fog into raindrops and release terpenes into the air to condense moisture into clouds.

Examining a featherlike spray of slender flat needlelike leaves, I would need a microscope to see one of the secrets to redwood survival. Like all tree leaves or needles, they have stomata that open to photosynthesize and close to conserve water. But redwoods are special when it comes to their leaves. They have two kinds. One gathers light for food and the other absorbs water. On this rainy North Coast, the water drinkers grow low on the trees and the light eaters are high in the crown to catch as much sun as possible. But to the south, where it's sunnier, the positions are reversed to drink as much water as possible. One redwood may have a million leaves.

These remarkable adaptations, found only in 2022, suggest redwoods may adapt to challenging climate, if there's enough fog.[3] When the frigid, protein-rich waters meet warmer air, they create the source of a third of the moisture of redwoods annually. High canopies gather the drifting fog. Droplets filter downward to brighten mosses green, turn lichens from crisp to rubbery, to soothe the backs of newts, and enter the streams. Ongoing fog studies are still murky for predicting the future, but scientists worry. A warming planet is lessening the daily hours of fog and shortening the summer season.

What I do know from walking in foggy redwoods is a sense of dissolving into the before times. Once, millions of ancient redwoods breathed within the ocean fog belt from Monterey, California, 450 miles north to southern Oregon. Some lived to be four thousand years old. The size of Yellowstone National Park, at just over two million acres, the range of redwoods was home to Indigenous people for more than ten thousand years. Always, they respected the ways of water, fire, wind, and flood shaping all.

The ancient redwoods rooted in place are knowledge keepers, like tribal elders passing down wisdom of their ancestors, despite near genocide and attempts to eliminate Indigenous cultures rooted in forests, rivers, and ocean.

The Yurok know the great trees as sacred guardians and call them *keehl.* Only from fallen redwoods did their ancestors craft homes and sweathouses. Today, the tribe is reintroducing endangered California Condors to once again nest in the hollows of voluminous redwood trees. The word for condor is *prey-go-neesh,* a sacred bird prominent in the Yurok origin story.

The Tolowa named the redwood *k'vsh-chn*, and traditionally wove roots into ceremonial baskets, gathered needles for medicine, and created dugout canoes from trees that naturally crashed to the ground. *Keel. K'vsh-chen.* Pursuing tribal words for redwoods, I found a range map with twenty-four corresponding names from many cultural groups, part of a volunteer-run project called the Decolonial Atlas. The Turtle Island Decolonized project resulted from consulting hundreds of Indigenous elders and language keepers. Looking at a map of the groups from north to south, I read more names that include Hupa *qawh-kyoh*, Sinkyone *gaashchow*, Lassik *kahsch cho*, Central Pomo *q'a siil*, Coast Miwok *lume*, and Chocenyo *summen.*

Each name stems from thousands of years of relationship. In 1981, Minni Reeves, an elder and spiritual leader of the Chilula people, shared a warning that rings true today: "Destroy these trees and you destroy the Creator's love. And if you destroy that which the Creator loves so much, you will eventually destroy mankind."[4] Earlier in a 1976 interview at Hupa Reservation, Reeves said the Chilula people are "from within the redwood tree."[5]

Then came the Euro-Americans. Serious logging started in the 1880s. With crosscut saws and double-bitted axes, it could take a week for men to fell one four-thousand-year-old giant. Loggers swarmed to the redwoods. The pace accelerated with unrelenting chainsaws until 95 percent of the great redwoods had vanished.

How many songs of Varied Thrushes fell silent forever? How many California Condors lost their nests within high hollows of standing snags? How many Marbled Murrelets flew from the sea to seek high mossy platform branches for nesting and found only decimation? How many red tree voles, flying squirrels, and salamanders lay crushed in the aftermath as Spotted Owls fled—only to have their next homes destroyed?

There are still those who want to cut the last trees. Forty miles to the north of the Rockefeller Grove is the Headwaters Forest Reserve, saved in 1999 only after a decade of activists putting their lives at risk. They climbed high trees, erected platforms, and sat in stunning redwoods for days and months, confronted by violent threats, bulldozers revving, and glaring spotlights turned on them at night. We owe them gratitude.

The Rockefeller Forest, at 10,000 acres, is the largest contiguous redwood stand remaining, safeguarding more 350-foot-tall trees than any other protected area. In 1926, there was no big clash of loggers and environmentalists directly but—instead?—a picnic. With logging imminent, Save the Redwood League's first executive director, Newton Drury, threw a Hail Mary pass. He invited the philanthropist John D. Rockefeller and family to dine right in the heart of the threatened forest. And that made all the difference.

Rockefeller's initial funding and then further assistance helped the league buy more than 9,000 acres. Despite Rockefeller's wish to remain anonymous, in 1952 the grove officially became the Rockefeller Forest. The family continued to give generously for additions to Prairie Creek Redwoods, Calaveras Big Trees State Park, and Redwood National Park. Save the Redwoods League is still purchasing lands, creating parks, studying, and restoring forests.

When I was a child, redwood lumber from centuries-old and thousands-of-years-old trees was cheap and common—converted into decks, fences, doors, siding, veneer, furniture, posts, stakes, shingles, bridge timbers, beams, and planks. I never put the two words together. There was red wood and the glorious redwoods. In 1963, a National Park Service study concluded all unprotected stands and their bird-filled ecosystems would be gone by the year 2000.[6] That terrifying projection factored into President Lyndon Johnson signing the Redwood National Park into law in 1968.

New threats to redwoods and thrushes include megafires (fires larger than 100,000 acres) driven by climate change. Varied Thrushes, like Pacific Wrens, are not birds of fire. However, they do have an intriguing relationship. Even hot, stand-replacing fires tend to skip and dance, driven by winds. The result is a mosaic of black burned trees and green living ones. The birds will reside in the refuge of green islands. From there, thrushes can hop out into recent burns to scratch for insects in exposed soils free of plants. Wildfires stimulate many plants to grow back with vigor, including bushes with berries for thrushes to crush in their beaks and savor syrupy delights.

Fire seems improbable in the coastal redwoods. The ancient trees teach us otherwise. They could not be better prepared for fires touched off by lightning and Indigenous burning. Tannins within the bark are natural fire retardants and lend the reddish color. The bark acts like a foot-thick, water-laden protective jacket. The sheer height and high limbs of older trees help prevent flames from laddering up to the crowns, where the fog-capturing needles hold moisture into hot summers.

Will the relict redwoods experiencing record temperatures survive today's extreme fires? Scientists discovered something startling and a bit hopeful after 97 percent of the Big Basin Redwoods State Park's 18,000 acres burned in the Santa Cruz Mountains fire of 2020. When tree crowns more than 295 feet high lost all their needles, the trees did not die as expected. Instead, they resprouted needles by tapping into their impressive carbon reserves stored for more than half a century, a phenomenon discovered only by studying the postfire trees, some more than 1,500 years old. The research team recorded the new growth with phenology cameras high in the canopies to show the remarkable return from red burned needles to new green.[7]

Sempervirens. May thrush song be ever living. May the true names guard thrush and redwood. May the braided chords of Varied Thrushes in the dusk forever bind the redwoods tight like a nest with supple bark, lichen, and moss.

Picking up a redwood branch broken off in the wind and on the ground, I notice cones the size of marbles on their tips. If I were a hungry thrush, I'd hop backward, then swipe my bill to clear needles and cones to uncover a tasty prize below the surface.

EIGHT

Truffle

Food of the Forest

A few inches below the surface, a ripe truffle is sending an alluring aroma that translates—"Eat me!" My hand is in a shallow hole dug by Dante and Lucca, Italian truffle dogs with perspicacious noses adept at picking up the ambrosia that can range from tropical to garlicky. The dogs have sniffed out a single truffle, but my inexperienced fingers aren't detecting the prize. Their damp noses try to show me. I feel only the rich dark humus of decomposition.

Charles Lefevre comes to my aid. In a nanosecond, he grasps a truffle the size of a rabbit pellet, explaining how he can feel a certain sponginess, shape, and size that can be as big as a lumpy small potato. I feel like I'm with an elfin Green Man, the mythic figure of folklore in Britain, celebrated in pageantry by people dressed head to toe in moss, leaves, and ferns and linked to the seasonal rounds of life, death, and renewal. He's actually a mycologist (a fungi biologist), founder of New World Truffieres, a leader in cultivating edible truffles in pastoral settings with planted trees, and a bit famous, too. Merlin Sheldrake wrote about him in his astonishing book, *Entangled Life: How Fungi Make Our Worlds, Change Our Minds, and Shape Our Future.*

Charles is one of only two mycologists with truffle dogs surveying ancient forests to find, identify, and record rarities. While some are edible to humans, many are not. By documenting diversity, he hopes to save older trees from logging that would endanger sensitive species that in turn indicate a rich and rare ecosystem.

So much of birding is observing—but this? I grope with my hands among the duff of crumbly cones, needles, fern bits, and leaves turning to soil. Half the soil volume is air. In the oxygenated pockets live minuscule life forms, from microbes to insects, as well as roots. The loose soil absorbs and stores water, too. My fingers touch what I cannot see—bacteria, fungi, protozoa, mites, spiders, nematodes, and more—all cycling nutrients. Some fix nitrogen, others recycle plants, and still others loosen and improve the soil. Truffles are the fruits of mycorrhizal fungi living on tree rootlets in the topsoil below the duff.

It's mid-November in an unprotected chunk of older Douglas-fir forest less than an hour from Eugene, Oregon, and close to the Hardesty Mountain Roadless Area. Golden-crowned Kinglets patrol Douglas-firs and redcedar limbs just above eye level. Their plinking calls are like raindrops.

Our hike on the upper Eagle's Rest trail is a meander yielding prizes buried in the soil several inches down—the ones that the dogs sniff and uncover. I'm with a group of eight from the Eugene Natural History Society. We are bundled in raingear, hats, and gloves in hypothermia weather at 40 degrees Fahrenheit. Clouds somber the sky. Ferns and mosses cast a viridescent light. There must be Varied Thrushes here, but they are like ghosts today. Instead of birds, I'm focused on the dogs sniffing for truffles, finding them often by the decaying mossy fallen trees.

Several of the giant Douglas-firs show the blackening of past fires at the base of their well-protected trunks. So craggy is their thick insulating bark that small bats often roost within the fissures. Mingled among them are smaller western redcedars and madrone trees. Red alders and bigleaf maples chase the sun in a gap created from a single tree falling. Sword ferns like swashbuckling feathered tails are waist high. Oregon grapes with parallel leaves shine with moisture. We pass a cut log where someone has carved "400 yrs. Carbon Bank."

Charles and his two Lagotto Romagnolo dogs share striking similarities. His curly gray-brown hair is a match for their wavy poodlelike fur. He's compact and agile like the medium-sized dogs bred to sniff out truffles. Dante is the grandfather of Lucca. Training took only a few hours of hiding truffles in his backyard and rewarding each find with a dog treat.

Once, I was the only one in the group to race after Charles through rhododendrons and up and over a rotund nurse log. Where Dante and Lucca pawed as their noses snuffled the earth, I saw the way he attended to dogs and truffles—one hand pulling up the truffle like a hidden Easter egg and the other reaching for kibbles from the bag around his neck for the reward. If he's too slow in catching up with the dogs, one might gobble the prize.

Two people emerge from the trail with empty mushroom baskets. They're surprised to hear of our riches, thanks to the dogs. While not in search of edible truffles, we soon would know the delicacy of a black truffle or the Oregon truffle, also named Kalapuya for the native peoples in this region. When Charles slices one open and holds it in his palm for us to sniff, we murmur scent comparisons and settle on spicy pineapple.

Truffles are the food of the forest, Charles tells us. Their scents are deliberate attractants to all who will spread their spores—from voles and flying squirrels to deer. Some of the truffles he cuts open look like vanilla ice cream marbled with chocolate, while others are a pumpkin hue. Some smack of garlic and woodsmoke, and others are too subtle for our unpracticed human noses.

After cutting the truffle in two and showing us, Charles places the unpretentious earthy fruit in a plastic bag with a special card he will fill out later. He documents the location with a photo, also recording the geolocation. On return, he identifies each species, placed under a microscope. Some he sends to a Michigan State University research project investigating the microbiomes within truffles.

Truffles are the mysterious underground fruit of certain fungi living in a symbiotic relationship with trees. While related to mushrooms, truffles never grow aboveground. If that were not intriguing enough, to know they host a community of bacteria, yeast, filamentous fungi, and viruses adds a twist of science fiction to their tale. Microbiomes live within us, too. We often refer to one of our microbiomes as gut bacteria. Treat them poorly—like antagonizing our digestive system with processed food overloaded with sugar—and our bodies suffer.

A 2025 study published in the journal *Nature* found that a single tree hosts about one trillion bacteria as microbial communities in the sapwood and heartwood.[1] The communities differ from each other sharply, with oxygen-requiring microbes in the sapwood only. Every kind of tree has a unique microbiome. Like us, keeping microbiomes healthy and happy is important. We are not so different from trees and truffles—expanding the meaning of kin.

Certain truffles are considered sensitive or even endangered. Those, Charles reports to the Forest Service or the Bureau of Land Management—and that in turn should lead to protection of an acre or two, he tells us. It's far from enough, but it's good and important work if the agencies and politicians heed the science. After the day with Charles, I'm considering the value of fragrance to save wild places. Charles sent this summary to our group:

> We found 13 separate collections on our outing, only two of which were duplicates, so we collected 11 different truffle species over a span of a few hundred yards and about 90 minutes. To put this in context, truffles are so hard to find that there are probably only two or three fungal herbaria that have more than a few hundred specimens in their collections. At the rate we were finding them on Saturday, it wouldn't take long to have one of the largest collections on the planet.

Later in our correspondence, Charles relayed that different kinds of truffles grow far and wide yet are always associated with a tree host—from the harsh Arctic tundra under willow shrubs no higher than mowed grass to pastoral Oregon farms under planted hazelnut trees. Only in the ancient forest does the highest diversity reign. More than 350 truffle species are known in Pacific Northwest forests.

Within the leaf litter are unseen fungi decomposing organic matter into nutrient-rich soil. So specialized are the truffles that one kind grows on a Douglas-fir cone, another on the needles, and still another on a maple leaf. Just as birds partition food sources, so do fungi, assuring every plant part will become part of the forest and no fungus will go hungry.

There in the wild forest with Charles, I'd also picked up ruffly lettucelike *Lobaria* lichens, nitrogen-fixing canopy epiphytes (plants, lichens, and mosses that grow on other plants). Nitrogen is essential to life; 80 percent of the air we breathe is nitrogen. However, the gaseous form is impossible for a forest to gather into herself. Enter *Lobaria*, with the ability to capture and then convert the gas to forms that fungi and other plants can process into compounds for growth, from proteins to amino acids and DNA.

When *Lobaria* drift down to the ground, set free from a loose grip on a high branch or riding to the forest floor when a limb breaks, the lichens bear nitrogen for mycorrhizal fungi to uptake and transfer to tree roots, which in turn give fungi their sugar and carbon. Only in forests growing for five centuries or more does *Lobaria* thrive, and only where the air is clean and safe from pollution. The species *Lobaria oregana* is highly associated with old-growth Douglas-firs in lush forests west of the Cascades, from Alaska to northern California. As light as lettuce, this *Lobaria* swathes so many tree branches that the weight per acre exceeds one ton.

A truffle is possible because of a lichen fixing nitrogen hundreds of vertical feet above the truffle. Trees form relationships with mycorrhizal fungi that produce truffles that in turn must be eaten for their spores to spread and inoculate roots of forests. Every species of truffle has an aromatic profile, one that intensifies as the spores mature so the truffle is not eaten too soon. Those scents range from pineapple to smoky garlic, strong cheeses, sausage, and certain nose-wrinkling smells, too. The scents aren't meant for us, but for a host of wildlife of day, night, and of every level.

California red-backed voles are tightly tied to ancient forests. The tiny mycophagists (animals that eat mushrooms) rely on the elder trees in perhaps the most important phase of the tree's life after death, fallen to the earth to decay and offering the perfect micro-refugia for mushrooms above and truffles below. Living within or below the soil-leaf interface, the voles have fragile, dainty teeth susceptible to breaking. They live almost solely on truffles in California, mostly on truffles in Oregon's Coast Range, and, in the higher Cascades, more than half their diet comprises the soft spongy delights. The milder the climate, the more truffles are available. The voles find alternatives in lichens and tender green plants their teeth can handle. While one truffle would fill up the teensy vole, this fine diner will nip pieces of a dozen species, each one with certain nutritional qualities.

As night falls, a northern flying squirrel sails down in pursuit of the scent of a truffle, digging only as far as needed to extract the prize. This denizen of older forests dwells in Douglas-fir-dominated forests on the west side, and in the mixed conifers of surprisingly lush forests in northeastern Oregon. More casual eaters of the gourmet truffles include elk, deer, black bears, fishers, deer mice, shrews, chipmunks, and squirrels. All are mammals with keen noses for sniffing truffle aromas whorling up from belowground.

I wonder where birds fit? Oregon mycologist Jim Trappe noticed an Eastern Yellow Robin following him as he collected truffles in Australia. Curious to see what the bird would do, he flipped a truffle toward the bird. The robin flew down and ate it. He fed the bird five more—each met with enthusiasm. He surmised a robin couldn't dig up a truffle, but enjoyed the gourmet fare, as we do for certain edible delights.[2]

Like most things in a wild forest, pay close attention and assumptions fall away. Just as we now know far more female birds sing than previously thought, it's highly likely that a sense of smell is part of the repertoire of songbirds finding their way to food.

The life of Varied Thrushes is tightly crocheted with fungi and soil. We don't know that they might also be nibbling a truffle and spreading spores farther than any rodent. There's a common adage that most birds have little or no sense of smell. Because of that, scientists have not looked for truffle spores in bird poop within Cascadia yet. That might change as scientists study birds' ability to sense aromas. Dark-eyed Juncos can distinguish different preen oil odors. Male European Starlings detect and choose certain aromatic leaves of a plant called milfoil to thread into nests, creating a chrysanthemum-like perfume that females find irresistible.

Far to the south in Patagonia, Argentina, bird biologist Matthew Smith of University of Florida and colleagues tracked a wrenlike Chucao Tapaculo and a thrushlike Black-throated Huet-Huet. In 2018 and '19 they collected 169 fecal samples (bird poop) along a 435-mile transect and found that a third or more contained many intact truffle spores.[3] There, truffles applied a different strategy. They had no scent, yet many were like bright ripe berries in the soils—just what birds would like. In Patagonia, there are fewer mammals to spread the spores, so it makes sense to employ birds. But given truffle intelligence, I wouldn't put it past them to expand their spore-carrying allies to birds in the Pacific Northwest. Until we know more, the question floats on the wind.

If Varied Thrush chords carried forest aromas, as tall trees carry molecules of duff to release into the atmosphere, I'd select wild ginger—sweet and spicy with a linger of resin. When asked on our field trip his favorite way of preparing truffles to eat, Charles was unhesitating. He loves shaving thin slices of fresh truffle over hot macaroni and cheese. Fat releases the truffle aroma, he explained. No wonder I like French fries with truffle oil, or pizza with fresh mozzarella and truffle. The tastes are smoky, earthy, and even erotic in the way of deep green moss beds where thrushes serenade.

Within the truffles are proteins, amino acids, carbohydrates, fats, vitamins, and minerals. Fresh truffles are also filled with water and, for some small mammals, provide their main source, rather than drinking from pools or streams. Douglas squirrels, western gray squirrels, and woodrats will hang truffles and other mushrooms on branches or place them in the sun, then stuff their larders with them for later. The dried fungi contain vitamin D, making up for a shortage of sunshine. Favorite pantries are hollow logs and woodpecker holes. Sometimes Steller's Jays raid the stores to eat truffles and mushrooms, maybe seeking a dose of vitamin D, too.

It takes a menagerie of truffle species for animals to satisfy their dietary needs and in turn spread truffle spores through their scat. The spores will colonize roots of certain trees. Without the truffle movers, trees are sickly. All is connected. Trees drop leaves and needles that tiny organisms feed on to release nutrients to mycorrhizal fungi that return them to the trees. The trees are energized by carbon, nitrogen, and water made available by fungi. Underground fungi are tapping cryptic messages traveling through the mycelial network, sharing nutrients to trees in need and warning of insect attacks.

The trees with the greatest ability to communicate are the biggest and oldest, described by Canadian forest ecologist Suzanne Simard in her consequential book, *Finding the Mother Tree: Discovering the Wisdom of the Forest.* From her introduction,

> When Mother Trees—the majestic hubs at the center of forest communication, protection, and sentience—die, they pass their wisdom to their kin, generation after generation, sharing the knowledge of what helps and what harms, who is friend or foe, and how to adapt and survive in an ever-changing landscape. It's what all parents do.[4]

High in the canopy, squirrels feeding on truffles are prey for Northern Spotted Owls that transfer the spores through their pellets farther than a small mammal would travel. Great trees falling to the forest floor are soon engulfed in all that helps the wood decay and soak in moisture, forming the right microclimate for trees to root and truffle-making mycorrhizal fungi to grow and feed the next generation of trees. Weaken a link and the loop frays. Remove a link and the loop breaks.

A Varied Thrush's scratching toes take my attention downward into soil and upward into song that showers happiness on my thirsty spirit. Being among truffles and thrushes reminds me to welcome soil under my fingernails, breathe in musky ferns, and lie down for an eye-level view of trillium and sorrels.

We are of the forest, too. Run fingers through good earth that transfers infection-fighting bacteria and ups the anti-inflammatory molecules in our blood. Before my son could walk, he'd crawl among our native plant yard (then in Montana) and eat dirt. His pediatrician approved. He's building up his immune system, he told me. The question then circles back. What do we give back? We could begin by respecting the soil as a lively ecosystem that will perpetuate forests only if treated with care. The life of the soil is the strength of the forest.

Take off my shoes. Place bare feet on soil. Connect with the mycelial network. Feel the tapping of reciprocity and community. Through the complexity of it all comes the euphonious chimes of Varied Thrushes humming through a forest scented in truffles, textured in lichens, tangy sweet with salmonberries, and hugged by Mother Trees.

NINE

Midstory

Bustling Layers of Life

A Bald Eagle flaps by. Sunlight gloves my cold hands. When darkness falls on our Metolius River campsite, with a fire blazing in the snow, I listen to the muffled hoots of a Great Horned Owl coming from the forest midstory.

Who calls the winter forest home? California myotis bats hibernate within the safety of a large ponderosa snag. American martens scramble up leaning trees into the canopy to hunt for tree voles. By river's edge, a Northern Goshawk pursues a Belted Kingfisher swerving around trunks of multiple heights, species, widths, and stages of life and decay. Like a bird with the fluffiest chest feathers, the more layers clothe the forest between the overstory and the understory, the better for withstanding bad weather.

Shade and sunlight exchange glances among needled branches of the midstory. Like feathers, the midstory is far from uniform—rather a mélange of trees of different heights, kinds, and stages. Some are shade-lovers, such as incense-cedars and western redcedars and western hemlocks, while Douglas-firs incline toward partial shade and ponderosas are sunseekers. Nothing is static. A tree may fall partway, only to be caught on another in a precarious lean. Most defy any rule we would put on them. The birds delight in every twist and turn, each finding their niche.

I ponder, too, my own midstory in multiple dimensions. Midlife is typically from age forty to sixty. We're supposed to have our act together, to be industrious, providing, and contributing to society. And yet our bodies are showing some wear and tear. We are questioning where we've landed. Where midstory begins and ends depends on the depth of the middle. For my purposes, I'll stretch the accordion to include earlier parts of my life—not a nestling or a fledgling but starting with adolescence and a shift away from the protective wings of parents.

More chickadee than flycatcher, I'm shaped by a life of moving, adaptation, and reaching out to make new friends. In my early midstory of adolescence, I stumbled through awkward times, taking refuge by climbing trees and hiding. At every step into my becoming, I learned from mentors and wise elders. To cross from youth to adolescence is akin to ascending the lower parts of the midstory.

If the midstory chronology of my life followed my ascent of Traverse, it might look like this. Climbing above the understory—a 30-foot sea of rhododendrons, huckleberries, and Pacific yew trees—I'm thirteen and paddling a canoe in a Maine wilderness camp for six weeks with nine other girls. I learn silence and solitude, pitching in to help, and navigating rapids. Sixty feet up Traverse and within an arm's reach of needled branches of redcedars and western hemlocks, I head west for the University of Oregon to run, to join environmentalists, and come alive to fieldwork and lab work at the Oregon Institute of Marine Biology.

Higher still on the rope of my twenties, I'm living in northeast Oregon, lobbying for the Oregon Wilderness bill, working seasonally for the Forest Service, and reporting for the weekly newspaper. That led to leaving for graduate school in journalism at the University of Montana and to heartbreak when my relationship did not survive the long distance.

And still, I have yet to reach that midlife definition beginning at forty. A few more steps up, and I'm in my thirties, working for Montana Fish, Wildlife & Parks as a watchable wildlife specialist in Helena, the state's capital city. There's a marriage, divorce, another marriage, and, at thirty-nine, my first and only child.

In those higher levels of midstory, life speeds up, just as trees grow faster instead of slower with age. In my forties, I'm raising my son, losing my father to cancer, and writing for a living as a freelancer. In my fifties, my marriage falls apart. I follow kingfishers and come to know the wild neighborhood of Rattlesnake Creek. My son graduates from high school, and I branch out for solo adventures in my pop-up camper that will lead me back to Oregon. As I grow older, I find my stride—first marathon, a joyful marriage, leadership within an environmental group, and the publication of my book on kingfishers. I also lose my mother, who was my friend and confidante.

At every turn in our lives, we miss unseen dimensions—the ones that birds know in their vertical flights. Birds lead me to the places of interconnectedness. A feathered forest community flourishes with entangled diversity, unlike a city park, with trees spaced apart and branches pruned of any sign of dying, malformation, disease, or tangle. A manicured park may appeal to aesthetics of orderly beauty, but far fewer birds, animals, and insects can live there. A wild forest is not a park, not a planted garden to weed, thin, and yank out all the parts whose functions we don't understand or value.

Similarly, creativity blooms with free exchanges of ideas and a flowering of the arts. Birds flying in the midstory teach us to break out of molds. Be adventurous. The midstory is a three-dimensional maze without wrong turns.

TEN

Great Gray Owl

Silent Flights and Dense Forests

Plowing feet first into pillowed snow, a Great Gray Owl flew up with a vole plucked from the subnivean world. Flapping away on muffled wings, the spectral bird vaporized into the midstory of a dusk-dark forest. After our collective gasp, we tromped through knee-deep snow to touch the imprint of fringed feathers.

It was winter in the early 1990s in Yellowstone National Park. Only minutes before, our bird guide had pulled the van over. A meadow like this one would be ideal for spotting a hunting Great Gray, he said, turning around to address our small group. Within minutes, the owl struck the snow.

From a perch on a lodgepole pines, the owl had listened to a vole's rustle under snow some 50 feet away. Wisps of telltale sounds funneled into the bird's facial disk, a bowl-shaped ruff of filamentous feathers, acting like a satellite dish directing signals to a TV. Faint digging noises entered one ear a fraction before the other. Mere slits protected by the outer rim of the disk, the asymmetric ears (one higher than the other) evolved for this locative purpose. Slowly rotating his or her head until the sound coalesced in both ears at once, the owl pinpointed the vole's position.

Lifting from the branch on velvety wide and round wings, the Great Gray flapped as sure as a Belted Kingfisher diving headfirst at an angle from a perch to scissor a fish from a pool. One hears and the other sees. Both are keen of senses and must navigate the trickiness of entering from one medium to the other. A kingfisher tracks a fleeing silvery fish with eyes able to focus close and wide at the same time to adjust for refracting light.

I don't recall a pause before the owl struck the snow in Yellowstone, but researchers in 2022 noted a Great Gray often will hover to overcome an acoustic mirage: sound waves from the vole bend up to 5 degrees in snow.[1] Directly above, the mirage is minimal. The owl's huge facial disk is ideal for gathering the low-frequency sounds coming up from snow.

Balling into a fist and muscling downward, the clenched black talons sifted through snow. Rotating one of three forward toes to face backward, the owl clamped down on the unsuspecting vole. Three toes in front with one back offers best balance for perching. Two in front and two behind is the ideal vice grip. Ospreys, too, have this ability to move a toe to hold a slippery fish, aided by spiny toe pads.

At close to three feet tall, with a wingspan of four feet, a Great Gray is one of the largest owls in the world and the lightest, relative to size. A Great Horned Owl's feathers exceed 12,000, including 4,000 on the facial disk, and the larger Great Gray has more. The fluffiness is deceiving for an owl that can break through icy crusts strong enough to support a 175-pound person.

Like most birds of prey, the female Great Gray is bigger than the male. Dwelling in boreal forests of North America, Europe, and Asia, the circumpolar range gives this owl an international flair, and other names: Spectral, Sooty, Spruce, Cinereous, Bearded, and Lapland.

Perched on a branch in midstory close to the trunk of a grand fir, the bird and the bark become one. The owl's silvery-ash-gray body plumage is flecked with whites, browns, charcoal, and faint barring. The gray face forms a pattern of concentric black tree rings. A white bowtie across the neck adds a dash of pizzazz. Brilliant yellow eyes and a yellow beak like a short downward-pointing knife seem ready to pierce a star glittering above a pinnacled treetop. Feathers shaped as two crescent moons line the inside edges of the eyes. How many moons do I miss while I sleep with a roof over my head? With their rod-packed eyes for night vision, owls see every phase in detail.

The owl's body feathers form the warmest of parkas. Even their legs and feet are heavily feathered. Chest and side feathers are long, at four to six inches. The Great Gray can be diurnal as well as nocturnal. Always when in owl country, I peer into the shadowy trees looking for motion and stillness. In daytime, Steller's Jays making a racket is a sign to look for a dozing owl suffering from the squawks of mobbing birds.

So cryptic is the plumage, I could picture a tree giving a deep hoot. How many enigmatic owls have I walked past when I'm in thickets of forests with meadows or bogs they prefer? Like a bull elk with six-point antlers stampeding through dense lodgepole pines, a Great Gray maneuvers on wide wings. The light weight combined with a five-foot wingspan results in low wing-loading to allow for slower flaps and glides, like Turkey Vultures and Red-tailed Hawks. When the owl's wings bat against branches inevitably in the way, the soft, flexible flight feathers prevent breakages.

Strix nebulosa, the scientific name of the Great Gray, places the owl among 22 species in the genus *Strix* (owls lacking ear tufts). Only the Great Gray nests in both the New and Old Worlds. North America's Barred and Spotted Owls are also in the genus. The word *strix* stems from a Greek myth of a vampire-worthy bird who drank the blood of humans and ate their flesh. Far gentler, the species name *nebulosa* means misty.

Great Gray Owls tend to be passive (except for being a predator) compared to strident Great Horned and Barred Owls that harass the much larger owls. If there's a root personality, what is *Homo sapiens?* If we dug deep, would we find our older tap root far kinder and connected to this Earth than it is today? I wish that to be true in this time of unrooting. I yearn for a softening of our touch, like the brush of owl feathers.

Great Gray Owls range southward from North America's boreal forests only in a few places. In Cascadia, they find mountainous homes in the Klamath Mountains, Cascades, and Blue Mountains of Oregon. In Washington, the owls are more elusive, with nest sightings in the far northeast corner. Some find conducive forests in California within the heart of Yosemite National Park and the western Sierras. While Yellowstone falls outside of Cascadia (as defined by rivers flowing west to the Pacific), it's part of the Northern Rockies ecosystem stretching from Yellowstone to Yukon, which is also the name of a nonprofit (Y2Y) dedicated to connecting wildlands that include northeast Oregon.

The drama in Yellowstone marked my first sighting of the Great Gray. Wing feathers etched in snow held the secret to stealth. Unlike other birds, most owls have eyelashlike combs on the leading edge of wing feathers to break up turbulent air. Fringes on the trailing edge and silky flight feathers further mute sounds. The silkiness comes from pennula, elongated hairlike extensions on the barbules (that hook barbs to barb). Of all owls, the Great Gray has the thickest velvet surface and the longest pinnula.

Silent flight also helps the owl hear a vole scurrying below the snow. In Yellowstone, montane voles are the prey. Plump, with a shorter tail than a deer mouse and small enough to fit in an adult's outstretched hand, the voles survive winter by nibbling stores of roots and tubers in chambers. Mothers give birth to up to four litters a year of two to ten young, breeding from February through November. Being fruitful is a necessity, since many offspring will become food for owls, coyotes, foxes, grizzly bears, and wolves in Yellowstone. Active day and night much of the year, voles escape summer heat by staying below ground in summer.

Since that day in Yellowstone, I've been fortunate to observe Great Gray Owls in Montana and in Oregon. So much about this owl is about silence and solitude. These, too, are qualities found only far from roads and mechanization.

Debbie Darrow and I are portaging a wood and canvas canoe from one lake to another in the wilds of Maine. We are thirteen years old and staggering under the hundred pounds on our shoulders. My legs trembled. We were the last of our fellow girl campers and the youngest. Our married counselors, Lisa and Peter, were not about to lend a hand. Instead, Lisa helped us count the steps between rests when we'd heave the canoe off and down to the ground without harming the boat, as we'd learned, only to lift it up again. Quitting wasn't an option. When we finally made it a mile to the next lake and put down the canoe for the last time, we felt as light as dragonflies helicoptering over ripples.

I can picture Debbie with her sturdy tanned frame, curly, sun-bleached, thick and curly below-the-shoulders hair beneath her ball cap. Daughter of the camp founders, George and Janie Darrow, she received no special favors. I was the scrawnier one, weighing not much more than the canoe. Over the camp's six weeks, we all grew strong and flexed our arm muscles for our group photo.

Only the first week did we stay in cabins on an island in the middle of the 22-square-mile West Grand Lake, long enough to learn paddle strokes of bow, cross-bow, back paddle, ferrying, and J-stroke for keeping the boat straight from the stern. By the second summer, I'd graduated to the stern to steer whitewater and call out commands to the camper in the bow. In both years, we left the calm lake for one wilderness river after another—the Machias, St. Johns, and St. Croix. We camped in tents for five weeks, and never stepped on pavement. We grew comfortable with quietude.

Every Sunday, we gathered for an outdoor Friends (Quaker) Meeting—sitting in a circle in silence among Common Loon tremolo, White-throated Sparrow *old-sam-peabody-peabody-peabody* melody, and the wash of waves on rocks. The Darrows were Quakers, like my family—the connection that led my father to find the camp.

Our light came from campfires and flashlights only. Under the darkest of skies, we learned constellations and the phases of the moon, leaned back in our sleeping bags and counted shootings stars. Our counselors taught us songs we sang as harmonies and rounds. Bull moose waded in waters with paddlelike antlers. Porcupines waddled by camp. River otters raced downstream. Beaver tails slapped a night marsh. There could have been a Great Gray Owl, rare in Maine but possible in our wild surroundings.

Right before the camp's end, we separated for twenty-four hours solo time on small islands or peninsulas of our choice. We had only a tarp, water, a little food, and matches. The first year, my tarp sagged in a rainstorm. Mosquitos kept me awake. And yet? I was in charge. I made every decision. Sitting cross-legged on my tiny island, I meditated. When the solo time ended, I walked a little taller, dreamed a little bigger.

I also got tougher. Maine is infamous for biting moose flies, mosquitoes, black flies, deer flies, and no-see-ums that squeezed through tent netting. We slathered ourselves in DEET, not thinking in 1972 about the toxin. We got used to welts and itches. Some days when rivers grew wide as lakes, we paddled into headwinds over waves crashing into our bows, making little progress. We spilled over in rapids, hit rocks, and duct-taped the torn canvas on canoe bottoms. We lugged heavy cans of food in wanagans (wooden crates) up trails to campsites.

We weren't always good. The braver teenagers smuggled in pornographic books and cans of snuff. We'd pinch the mint-scented tobacco, sniff it, sneeze, and feel dizzy and nauseous, then try it again. We longed to run into the boys from the camp, but George Darrow planned our trips to never overlap. My first year was the first to allow girls since the camp opened in 1957.

Spending six weeks in a rugged camp far from roads on wild rivers and lakes singing in loons changed me. When I returned to Arlington, Virginia, pavement felt unyielding and wrong underfoot. My ears hurt when a car engine roared, a lawn mower revved, or a jet split the clouds. Hiking with my parents and brothers, I bristled when conversations interrupted birdsong. In six weeks I'd shed some of that painful awkwardness of junior high, but still, I retreated to the trees and the forest for solitude. I'd become comfortable with human silence among nature's chorus. This is refugia as well, the places where our senses sharpen. And when we do speak or sing? Our voices feel more in communion than before. Our songs carry loon, sparrow, and cresting wave.

Rain fell steadily. The forest floor glowed green with silky pine grasses. Lupine leaves cupped jeweled droplets. I'd signed up for the Great Gray Owl field trip as part of the Ladd Marsh Bird Festival. Our group of ten swished along in rain pants among centuries-old western larches, ponderosas, and Douglas-firs. A recent wildfire at low severity had swept through the understory, renewing soils and plants. It was May of 2016 in the Blue Mountains, a half hour west of my then home in La Grande, a college town of 13,000 in northeast Oregon, where I lived for a year before moving to Bend.

Our leader Mark Penninger (then a Wallowa-Whitman National Forest biologist) knew the Spring Creek Great Gray Owl Management Area well. Up to eight pairs have nested within 4 square miles of this highly studied forest since 1982. While pairs seem willing to overlap territories, that's still a high number, owing likely to the wood nest boxes, 2 feet square, attached to large Douglas-firs and ponderosa pines in the midstory, about 30 to 50 feet up.

Not a nest builder, a Great Gray prefers an American Goshawk ready-made home. A female goshawk chooses a sturdy branch on a big tree in the midstory. She flies to seek the right-sized limbs and twigs to break off and carry back to create a crisscrossed scaffolding. The final touch is to line the inner bowl with pliable bark and greenery. For alternatives, she may build several more, as if in offering to the Great Grays. Logging of old growth and thinning of dense stands spells trouble for American Goshawks, dependent as they are on large nesting trees and forests with about 60 percent closed canopies (where crowns touch and overlap).

The boxes in Spring Creek replaced American Goshawk nests that fell apart over time. We did not see these largest of accipiters, forest hawks with rounded wings and long tails for a swerving chase through tree trunks. While Cooper's and Sharp-Shinned Hawks prey on birds, a goshawk may tackle a snowshoe hare. Their prey ranges from grouse to Pileated Woodpeckers, Steller's Jays, and Belted Kingfishers.

Our group of ten birders strolled onward, past ponderosas with glowing amber trunks among a few old stumps, signs of light logging in the 1970s that retained enough big trees for nests and dense stands of western larch, ponderosa, Douglas-fir, and grand fir for hiding and cover. Mark stopped short at a fresh-cut stump about three feet across, a former nest snag poached by firewood cutters. A mild man, he was clearly upset after we found several more. Old-growth snags are in short supply. With few forest guardians, protection takes an honor system. Without ethical birding and a moral compass, this critical owl habitat is at risk.

Outrage receded over the next couple hours in the thrill of finding not one but six Great Gray Owls. A mother owl tended three fuzzy nestlings peeking from a numbered nest box about halfway up a tall and wide ponderosa pine. Farther on, we spotted a lone owl and, a half mile away, another. While their camouflage was flawless against the gray, scaly bark of Douglas-firs, Mark knew where to look.

He also pointed us toward potential owl nests among balls of dwarf mistletoe, like knotted fishing ropes on branch. Excavate a clump on a tree, Mark told us, and you'll find bones where American martens have brought their meals for dining. Songbirds—from Gray Jays to Pine Siskins—may squeeze nests there, too. In winter, Ruffed and Dusky Grouse may roost there for thermal cover.

Cascadia's forests evolved with similar-appearing and host-specific dwarf mistletoes, all in the genus *Arceuthobium*. For example, one species (western dwarf mistletoe) is found only on ponderosa and Jeffrey pine and another is hosted by western larch and mountain hemlock. The parasite's shoots remind me of mustard-colored ocean corals. They cluster on branches or boles that have swelled slightly in response.

Varying in length from fingernail- to hand-sized depending on the species, they all have sticky seeds that hitchhike on bird beaks and feathers to new host trees. The berries are favorites of songbirds, from Evening Grosbeaks to American Robins and Western Bluebirds, which spread their seeds.

Their primary way of reproducing is dramatic. As berries ripen, water pressure triggers an explosive mechanism, launching seeds 50 feet. To increase chances of seeds landing on another tree's branch or trunk, the stems bend to 30 degrees in advance.

A mistletoe feeds from trees by plugging rootlike structures (called haustoria) into the tree's circulatory system. After a few years, the branch responds by twisting and knotting into a gnarl, nicknamed a witches'-broom. Not all, but most, dwarf mistletoe species cause trees to form gnarls. In the Turquoise Forest near my home, I visit a ponderosa not far from the Grandmother Tree that I call the Witches'-Broom Tree, which lives on with multiple whorls. One broom is low to the ground, massive, and when I give the twisted net of branches a gentle push, the whorl sways like a swing. For years, this weighed-down branch resists falling. How many birds have nestled there? On every walk, I marvel at the broom's perseverance.

Studies of western hemlock dwarf mistletoe illuminate a powerful connection to the structural diversity of ancient forests. Infected trees fall and create sunny canopy gaps. Branch swellings from infection invite heart rot fungi—a gift to woodpeckers and the vital processes of decay and renewal. After wildfire, mistletoe perseveres in unburned pockets of older forest refugia, often found within creek bottoms and benches collecting water. There, the parasite can hang out for decades until host trees grow back and birds plant their seeds in the renewing forests.[2] For Great Gray Owls, the same islands of refugia offer nesting.

Seeking owls, I'm taking more notice of mistletoe. I might blow a kiss their way, even if dwarf mistletoes are not the same kind as the leafy mistletoe pinned above doorways in a Christmas tradition that originated with Celtic Druids who revered the plant as sacred.

That holiday mistletoe of the genus *Phoradendron* does grow on Oregon white oaks of low-elevation forests and valleys, mostly west of the Cascades forests. Only a partial parasite, *Phoradendron villosum* benefits both from leaves photosynthesizing and from tapping into the tree host. As a result, mistletoe leaves are supercharged with more nutrients than tree leaves. The fallen leaves are key to the soil's renewal, acting as a natural fertilizer.

Like thousands of feathers on a Great Gray Owl, relationships multiply at every turn, with many yet to be named, counted, and teased apart.

South of where I live in Bend in the vicinity of Sunriver is another hot spot for Great Gray Owl seekers. Naturalists like Sevilla Rhoads keep their nest sites quiet. On a Christmas Bird Count in 2023, our small group saw a Great Gray misting up from a small meadow of dried bunchgrasses and leafless shrubs to fly mothlike into a permeable wall of lodgepole pines. We watched the perched bird swiveling a round head almost 360 degrees.

Adapted to higher elevations, lodgepoles are most comfortable in a crowd. They evolved with high-severity fires that snap open their serotinous cones, which require heat to open and shake free seeds. Burned trees that fall shelter new saplings. Wildfires rejuvenate meadows for a prosperity of voles—just what owls are looking for.

On a late March day in 2025, I joined Sevilla and her two naturalist children Ander and Chloe to look for a Great Gray Owl nest she'd documented in a ponderosa pine on the Deschutes National Forest, also by Sunriver. Her finding and reports to a biologist led to protecting the nest area from thinning, mowing, and prescribed burning during spring nesting that would have endangered the owlets. The project was one of thousands across national forests aimed at reducing wildfire risk. It's a shaky strategy, akin to trying to stop a hurricane. Far better is to shift focus to preventing home ignitions, as explained in detail by fire scientists in the must-see 2022 film, *Elemental: Reimagine Wildfire.*

Meanwhile, the heavy machinery damages or kills pollinator plants and compacts soils, a far cry from the natural beneficial role played by fires before heavy logging of the big resilient trees and a century of snuffing out flames. Clearing dense stands removes hiding cover for elk and nesting havens for birds.

Tall and lean, with straight dark brown hair below her shoulders, Sevilla is originally from rural England. Equipped with a long-lens camera, binoculars, and a pack with whistle dangling from a strap, she spends an enviable amount of time in the field. She's taught Ander and Chloe to navigate the forest and study nature since they were toddlers. In eighth grade, homeschooled Ander is pursuing his dream of becoming a wolf biologist—volunteering to set out trail cameras and record gray wolves returning to central Oregon.

A herd of Rocky Mountain elk raised their furry ears as we walked past them on a snowy riverside road. Chickadees, creepers, nuthatches, and juncos quivered in the trees. Sevilla shared an observation earned from long hours watching ponderosa pines in winter with Ander and Chloe that I couldn't resist recording:

> A winter flock will come in and first the chickadees arrive. They have different calls for different kinds of predators. When they give the all clear, suddenly like magic all the rest of the winter flock appears. You've got the Brown Creepers that work their way up the ponderosa and can get the bugs with their curved bills in the deep crevices. Then you watch the Red-breasted Nuthatches getting bugs at a different level, and the White-breasted Nuthatches at a different level. The Hairy Woodpeckers are usually with them and are going in at another level. And the Golden-crowned Kinglets are getting the bugs at the edges, like a hummingbird. It's a cleaning service for the ponderosa. You can imagine the tree with its arms out and the birds are getting all the bugs that emerged, readying the trees for spring.

Every forest bird's life history entangles with other birds and the trees if you look long enough and pay attention. As we walked, we scanned for a Great Gray Owl, often active on a winter's day. While our bird of desire eluded us, always there were rewards.

A male White-headed Woodpecker and two Hairy Woodpeckers circled up ponderosa trunks in momentary companionship, until a male Hairy chased off the White-headed Woodpecker. Closely related, the species overlap, sometimes compete, and divvy up their feeding. Hairy Woodpeckers tend to seek insects higher on tree trunks and branches in winter, and sometimes at different times of day. In northeast Oregon, researcher Evelyn Bull found White-headed Woodpeckers chose ponderosa pines and Hairy Woodpeckers fed on several tree species.[3]

Sevilla pointed to a tree-lined meadow across the river that looked ideal for hunting owls. Close to the river, the Forest Service had left the riparian area the way the Great Gray Owls like it, with broken branches, downed trees, saplings leaning like ramps on big firs, and woodpecker-chiseled snags. For owlets, mess is a necessity. When owls first leave the nest, they cannot fly for the first two weeks. Fluttering to the ground, their only way back up into a tree is to climb up nature's planks, ladders, and ramps. A thinned and tidied forest leaves the owlets helpless and stranded.

A feathered forest shields, insulates, hooks and unhooks, but can be far too easily plucked and frayed. Keep it wild. That's my mantra—for the wild forests and for our children who enter this world like Great Gray Owls, wide-eyed, vulnerable, and free of spirit.

Only Chloe glimpsed owl wings gliding through pines as she sat quietly on a rock waiting and watching with her back turned away. A wave of sadness washed over me, knowing she is inheriting an ever more diminished world. And yet, what if there were far more Chloes and Anders? Far more adults like Sevilla taking their children to the wilds and setting them free?

Defying the impossibility of flights through trees too close together for a wingspan of four feet, the owl offers many lessons. Trust feathers that flex. Know softness can be strong. Listen to forest silence for the faintest of whirs, clicks, hums, thrums, and creaks. Always be aware of surroundings. Do not fear the shadows, thickets, and dense forests sheltering life. Reach out to catch the drifting fringed feather.

ELEVEN

Chestnut-backed Chickadee

Insects at Every Level

Sitting on a wooden bench with the words "Let nature bring peace and tranquility to your soul" painted in white letters on the backrest, I hear Chestnut-backed Chickadees. Four spry birds seek insects along needled branches of a western hemlock about 30 feet above me. Their *dee-dee-dees* are light and quick.

Of all Cascadia's chickadees, this one is the ancient forest bird, sensitive to warming temperatures. Chestnut-backed Chickadee populations fell by more than half between 1966 and 2015. The decade following has not been kind, with scorching heat, erratic and extreme weather, intense wildfires, and logging.

I'd come to the south side of the coastal town of Newport, Oregon, during my two and a half weeks of house- and bird-sitting for friends who live a few miles inland. The Mike Miller Educational Park is barely big enough, at 45 acres, to host one pair of Varied Thrushes. However, the older Sitka Spruce, Douglas-firs, and hemlocks form an oasis among clear-cuts, roads, houses, and grazed meadows. Every protected patch matters for rewilding, reconnecting, and for the human-centered reason written on the backrest.

These acrobatic birds hunt for what sustains a songbird-filled forest—a cornucopia of arthropods, the largest phylum on the planet, encompassing the six-legged insects and eight-legged spiders, mites, and others. When one chickadee darts to another tree, I'm drawn to a skiff of sunlight overhead. Dainty winged insects rise and fall like a mayfly hatch over a trout stream. A loose strand of spider silk disappears like a passing thought. At eye level, a bumblebee buzzes on a salmonberry blossom the color of raspberry sherbet.

Tiny communities are cycling nutrients with every pounce, chew, tunnel, bore, and wound-up insect in a web. Bees, flies, wasps, beetles, and ants are pollinating along with butterflies and moths. In streams, young salmon grow fat on aquatic larvae that are in turn reliant on the forests. When herbivore insects devour plant leaves, the nibbling can stimulate the leaves to put more energy toward flowers and fruits.

In the ancient forests, predatory arthropods rule. In tree plantations and logged forests, there's a paucity. Predators keep the older forests far more resistant to outbreaks of leaf- and needle-devouring insects. Chickadees join other songbirds in eating spiders, wasps, and other predators along with their favorite juicy caterpillars. All is in relationship of eating and being eaten.

As birds find niches in the vertical canopy, so do arthropods. The more microhabitats the better among tree wounds, scars, broken limbs, sap, cavities, woodpecker and beetle holes, mistletoe, fungus, and sky gardens. Diversity sprouts from every nonconformity. The climate buffering that is key to chickadees finding refugia makes it possible for arthropods to reach astonishing numbers and variations and to dwell at every height. When I am in the old forests I feel my limbs bathed in what insects love—humidity, relief from heat, and shelter from cold.

Wedded to Cascadia's lush and wet conifer forests on the coast and Cascades, the Chestnut-backed Chickadee also finds home in the moist forests of mixed conifers in northeast Oregon, southwest Washington, northern Idaho, and northwest Montana. The overall range extends from southeast Alaska to central California. In the Wallowa Mountains, I've seen them mingling with Black-capped and Mountain Chickadees.

Perky, cheeky, and a favorite of bird feeders, all seven species of chickadees in North America are equally adorable. Sitting among a Mountain Chickadee family in late June in our yard one year, I held up my iPhone to take a photo, and a fledgling perched on the rim. I've held a sunflower seed in my palm for a spunky bird to eat. But no chickadee lives on seeds alone.

Keeping my focus on a single Chestnut-backed Chickadee, I lift my binoculars and bring the mini-whirlwind into focus. A pointy black bill skims the surfaces of twigs encrusted in lichen and moss. The chickadee is tweezering insects and spiders from foliage, even twirling upside down when a needled sprig droops. If you held two US quarters in your palm, that's the weight of this smallest of chickadees. From bill tip to tail tip, the bird is five quarters long.

Tarrying at the bench, I am there when Golden-crowned Kinglets join the loquacious chickadees. Sorting through hemlock cones like scaly marbles and thumb-sized spruce cones on the soft ground, I'm stirring invisible insects. Examining a leathery leaf of a salal bush, I read the chewed inscriptions. One makes a sickle cut, another a ragged hole in the center, and one more bit a ruffly chunk off the edge. There's room for every chewer to share one leaf. In a similar way, songbirds called "timber foliage insectivores" specialize in hunting techniques by hovering, hawking, gleaning, lunging, or flycatching.

A rumble of a logging truck's jake brakes on Highway 101 jars my naturalist meanderings. I'm snapped back to register a lurking feeling of unease. Oregon's Coast Range forests are some of the worst in Cascadia for repeated clear-cutting in watersheds vital to drinking water for coastal communities like Newport. With every gashing wound comes a round of herbicides to kill the native brush, harming birds, humans, and the forests. In clear-cuts sprayed and planted in Douglas-fir monocultures, you will not find a single Chestnut-backed Chickadee a decade later.

The best relict coastal ancient forests left in Oregon are a half-hour south of Newport and include Drift Creek, Cummins Creek, and Rock Creek Wilderness, all part of the 1984 Oregon Wilderness Act. Together, they add up to 23,000 acres of the Siuslaw National Forest's 630,000 acres. The Cape Perpetua National Scenic Area (also on the Siuslaw) gives a lesser level of protection to Gwynn Creek, one drainage over from Cummins and the finest of all. In the steep-sloped valley where Gwynn Creek runs two and half miles into the Pacific, many columnar trunks of Sitka spruce exceed four feet in diameter. After extensive wildfires burned through these coastal forests in the mid-1800s, the highest numbers of surviving ancient trees are here.

A few days later, I'm parking in a pullout by the Pacific Ocean. On Earth Day of April 22, 2025, the sun is bright. The waves are wind-tossed and white in the ocean where Marbled Murrelets have yet to make their inland flights for nesting here. Crossing Highway 101 to enter Gwynn Creek, I feel salty gusts funneling up the valley to slow among Sitka spruce and western hemlock that have stood for five centuries or more. The old ones have survived ocean tempests, wildfire, floods, landslides, and, so far, the perils of human-induced climate change. They grow fast in the thirst-quenching fog that often shrouds the coastline in summer.

Wilson's Warblers have just touched down in familiar thickets after a perilous migration from western Mexico or, farther south, from Central America.

The black cap of a male is chickadeelike, but the rest of the bird is dressed up for a party in goldfinch yellow. When a storm felled great trees on the far side of the creek from the trail, the openings were quickly filled in by the alder, maple, and red elderberry they prefer.

Like a slip of paper bearing a haiku, a white butterfly sways from sun into shadow. The trail curves in and out of glens, each with a humming creek. I'm on a south-facing slope, looking across to the other side. Below is a glimmer of Gwynn Creek, where salmon come to spawn. Her waters are a composite of all who enter—falling leaves of overhanging maples and alders, needles, branches, whole trees washed down after floods, and the fauna that find home here, from birds to voles to black bears, black-tailed deer, and Roosevelt elk.

A male Wilson's Warbler pops up like a yellow flower and then evanesces into an elderberry's blooming white-clustered petals. Listening to his song of repeated syllables, I hear *Yes Yes Yes Yes!* This forest is a yes for a warbler now designated as "a common bird in steep decline" by the bird conservation organization Partners in Flight. Facing a litany of troubles in breeding and wintering homes and along the migratory pathway from as far away as Central America, the bird is also sensitive to the heat that is the new normal of climate change. This refugia offers both the shrubby havens and chilly retreats of shadowy understory.

The earth is sequined in yellow violets, redwood sorrel, candy-striped flowers, and trillium with trios of petals and sepals. Each of the three leaves are the size of my hand spread wide, and I have long fingers. As in Alaska, everything seems more bodacious. The petals change colors like a flight of wines from white, rose, pinot noir, and then burgundy before curling up and putting energy into their seeds. A haphazard web guarded by a dime-sized spider with yellow and black stripes stretches between trillium leaves and pedestal. Golden pollen dusts the web. Nearby, a slightly larger spider crouches in the center of her dreamcatcher orb laced between salal leaves.

A mile in, I hear the airy rivulets of calling Chestnut-backed Chickadees. The birds are far above me in the midstory of spruce and hemlocks, now joined by Douglas-firs, bulky as grand pianos. Snags of all sizes become ever livelier with shrinkage as they decay and feed the forest. The sinuous trail snakes in and out of microclimates of springs, trickles, and streams enfolded in ferns, salmonberries, and thimbleberries unfurling maplelike leaves. Always there are Pacific Wrens' splashing fountain notes.

On this sidehill, I'm high enough to investigate the midstory of trees rooted far below. A mop of red huckleberry crowns the top of a two-story woodpecker snag. Chickadees and other songbirds eat their berries and plant seeds up high in huckleberry gardens that have become epiphytic.

Pressing my right cheek on the fine scales of a wise and wide Sitka spruce, I clamp my ear to the bark. Imagining I can hear the old one's heartbeat, I am startled by a Pacific Wren a few feet away among sword ferns and roots of a coiling stream. His short tail flicks, and he flings rapid notes like ticks of time. Close by, a Chestnut-backed Chickadee's notes are as effervescent as droplets jeweling needles.

Coming to a redcedar four feet across, I notice the branches curve like fishhooks and brush the ground. Looking across Gwynn Creek through the redcedar curtain, I have a strange sensation. Before I'd entered, I watched flocks of migrating sandpipers lifting from the beach in aerial synchrony. Here, the tossing branches in a breeze remind me of their flights, as if every limb senses the movement of the other.

I stop at one of the biggest Douglas-firs, to touch the spongy, thick bark with ruts and ridges, where spiders have strung webs like hammocks of rock climbers on a multiday ascent. High above, a brawny branch sprouts huckleberry plants from cradled soil. Could a Marbled Murrelet nest there?

Another spider has spun a dinner-plate-sized orb web. Studying the spokes in the wheel, I imagine spinning away from my human form to become a Chestnut-backed Chickadee swinging from twigs, a banana slug in a slow slide, a salmonberry bloom feeling the tick of bee feet, or a hummingbird twining my delicate teacup nest to salmonberry stems. The orb would roll again and I'd become vast—a belt of summer fog wrapping the forests, a storm hurling waves against cliffs.

In this ecstasy of light-stepping through my version of Ursula K. Le Guin's Immanent Grove, I'm flooded with euphoria. Watching bees on flowers, I'm reminded of the growing movement across yards, parks, towns, cities, and farms to save not just pollinator habitat, but havens for the full suite of biodiversity and that, in turn, has led to bird-friendly practices.

In Latin America where many of the warblers, hummingbirds, and tanagers of Gwynn Creek winter, certain families run coffee plantations certified as Smithsonian Bird Friendly, where shade-grown means a true native forest supporting not a handful of bird species but hundreds.

Each time I've joined the annual October gleaning day at Rainshadow Organics, a farm in Terrebonne (north of Bend), I've found lightness, too, as children raced the long rows tugging up carrots and taking sweet gritty bites. The farm honors the land as an ecosystem of native bees pollinating crops, swallows catching aerial insects, and songbirds tweezering caterpillars. When I go there, I slip back into memories of my farming summer at eighteen when our family lived in Concord, Massachusetts.

I'm bicycling home from working at Hutchins farm, after a run in the Harvard woods on trails wending past old stone walls. Side baskets overflow with the day's harvest. Carrot tops, lettuce, and chard wave as I speed downhill along the Concord River. It's July of 1977, before I would head west to University of Oregon to run for the cross-country and track team.

Soon, I'll be in the kitchen with my mother concocting another vegetarian dinner from the Moosewood Cookbook. Quiche or carrot loaf or ratatouille? I'm ravenous. Arms and shoulders ache from daily hoeing weeds between plants and lifting heavy baskets to carry uphill to the roadside stand.

The Bemis brothers, Johnny and Gordy, who run the 20-acre family organic farm, have refined the art of growing cabbages the size of basketballs, heirloom tomatoes, eggplants, corn, cauliflower, and melt-in-your-mouth strawberries. Gordy is often in the tractor dumping another load of chicken manure to feed the soil teeming in insects that are aerating, chewing, and renewing. Johnny is with the crew, teaching us how to plant, thin, hoe, and harvest. He is lean, bow-legged, tan, and his eyes are river sparkle.

What the brothers both know is that insects rule. Pollinators. Flowers are everywhere—wild and planted. They leave as many native plants as possible close to the others for the bees, butterflies, and hummingbirds to pollinate and for wasps and other predators to keep plant-chewing herbivores in check. The organic farm swoons in birds. Our days are filled with herons, waterfowl, blackbirds, kingfishers, and, yes, there are Black-capped Chickadees and many songbirds in the adjacent forests.

Home in the kitchen with my mother, we exclaim over the day's vegetables. Ratatouille is a winner with the ripe red and gold tomatoes and eggplant. Our family of five will feast—my parents, my two brothers, and me.

Looking back at that summer of 1977, I remember feeling wistful before boarding the plane from Boston to Eugene, Oregon. Part of me wanted to stay there with my fingers deep in the rich topsoil, laughing with the other young workers on breaks when we toss squashed tomatoes at each other. Dirty, stained, and, even for fair-skinned me, tanned.

We'd moved to Concord from Virginia when I was halfway through ninth grade. Our dad commuted by train from Concord to Boston to serve as assistant director for the National Parks Northeast Region, a job that would include managing the Appalachian Trail, a turning point in his career. After a bumpy entry into Concord-Carlisle Regional High School, I found my stride as a competitive runner and a nerdy nature romantic with Thoreau's journals often in hand. I had friends. I was happy and yet still I longed for the big wilds of the West. I graduated halfway through my senior year, visited Pacific Northwest colleges, and volunteered at what is now Chaco Culture National Historical Park in New Mexico. I'd returned for the summer committed to University of Oregon. I didn't anticipate roots tendriling into the deep and rich river soils of Hutchins Farm.

To separate my life cleanly into childhood, adolescence, and adulthood is as challenging as dividing the ancient forest into under-, mid-, and overstory. I placed the Chestnut-backed Chickadee in the midstory, but the birds have their own ideas. I've heard them high in the canopy, too.

After my coastal forays in the vicinity of Newport, I tracked down Tim Schowalter, a preeminent entomologist with a deep well of knowledge from his studies of the arthropod biomass of ancient forest canopies. I'd read his studies from the Andrews Forest and the Wind River Experimental Forest in the 1990s.[1] I wanted to hear his stories. I had questions.

On the phone, he could tell me like no science paper ever could what it was like to find soil-dwelling oribatid mites, so minuscule you could fit several on a pinhead, living hundreds of feet aboveground in the tree canopies. Because the older trees with their signature wide branches can develop soil in their crowns over time through the work of insects, they become aerial homes. The mites find microhabitats in crooks of trees, broken tops of old snags, and the sky gardens. There, they can merrily feed on fungi, bacteria, and leafy particles, which in turn builds soil. To find their way up, they hitchhike on bigger insects, birds, and mammals or can even be wafted up on winds.

From Tim, I also learned that Douglas-firs in old-growth forests host the bulk of arthropod diversity. That's likely to do with their ability to grow so tall, with more microhabitats. Before our call, I'd pictured chickadees snagging one caterpillar after another to feed their nestlings in spring. But it's not that easy, he told me. Even in the ancient forests, the juicy larvae typically make up about one in five arthropods.

In fact, 40 percent of what Tim sampled in the canopies were spiders—a reminder of the significance of predators and their ingenious hunting habits. While all spiders make silk, not all are web builders. Crab spiders crouch within blossoms and change colors to match the bloom. When a bee or small moth flies in, the spider ambushes the prey.

The drifting strands of silk that catch sunlight or dew in the forest are not all from spiders dangling and linking new webs. A spider knows how to drift to new realms when ready—a feat called ballooning. Often, the young ones disperse to colonize new places. The trick is to scramble up to a high spot, stand on tiptoes, release a long silk filament, and take off on the breeze. Sometimes, meadows can be filled with gossamer when there's a mass migration. Spiders even balloon away after wildfires.

Spiders have another quality. They contain an amino acid called taurine, also found in a mother's breast milk and known to help premature babies develop. Kathryn Arnold, ornithologist at University of Glasgow, had wondered why Blue Tits (chickadeelike birds in the same family) fed their hatchlings high doses of spiders. She found out that spider-fed chicks learned faster and were bolder. Chestnut-backed Chickadees thrive on a diet that's 65 percent arthropods—with many spiders.[2]

As cavity nesters, chickadees prefer holes below 10 feet, but may raise their chicks as high as 70 feet up, either in a woodpecker hole or one they dig in the pliable wood of a highly decayed snag. While a male appears to choose the site, the female is the decider. For an existing hole, she enters first and then accepts deliveries from the male of moss, soft bark, fur, feathers, and grass.

After a week, she lays a clutch of up to eleven eggs, white with reddish spots and as small as jellybeans. While the female incubates, the attentive male feeds her. After the featherless chicks hatch, the frenzy of feeding them high-protein arthropods begins. Brain-food spiders are definitely on the menu.

Chickadees remind me to be alert, dedicated, and chipper, too, when called to act. I will protect the sylvan way of feathery moss, fiddlehead ferns, and spider silk radiant in sunlight filtered by conifer needles. I will defend a pair of Chestnut-backed Chickadees gleaning twigs for juicy insects in the shimmer of evergreen as they fly back and forth from their nest hole in a standing dead tree.

On another coastal day during my house-sitting stay, I'd observed three Chestnut-backed Chickadees feeding among a straggled line of Douglas-firs between a rural paved road and a marsh. The trees were less than a century old and perhaps 60 feet tall. They could not offer safety on their own, but the chickadees had found a bonanza of insects. Hopping on a branch to the tip, a chickadee leaped onto a cone that swung wildly as the bird probed between the scales. In the next tree over, another chickadee dangled upside down. Jotting notes of their rapid motions in my field notebook, I scrawled "hop up, hop down, down, peck, probe, and flutter to a higher branch. Scour a lichen on the side of a branch. Pause on a lichen frill and glean. On to the next chickadee-sized cone."

A chip truck from the nearby Toledo mill roared by. Deafening. How do the birds handle this? My ears hurt. From the ensuing silence, a Song Sparrow whistled up a tasty brew. Nearby Pine Siskins joined in with their *zeeeeet* calls. The chickadees kept up with their methodical inspections in between looking up, down, and sideways for perils. A breeze flicked the higher branches. Low down, it was still, reminding me that even this small band of trees offers some food and shelter.

Within Douglas-fir cones (before or after opening) are insects that co-evolved with this tree. There might be Douglas-fir cone moth larvae, Douglas-fir cone gall midges, Douglas-fir seed chalcid wasps, or Douglas-fir coneworms. Each insect has a unique life history paired with the life of birds and other insects preying on them.

Chickadees lead me to arthropods whose future hinges on the fate of intact forests, also the source of our very drinking water. The birds remind me, too, that it's not enough to observe. We could all use more gleaning in our lives to connect us to the source of our food and to good earth.

Below in the airy soil are the secrets to living not for one but for seven generations. All we must do is join the cycle. When I die I want a green burial. When my spirit wings away with birds and forests, my body will become soil. Maybe I'd end up high in the canopy, transported by a chickadee that had come to the forest floor for a seed or a bug.

TWELVE

Kelp Forest Interlude

The Ocean's Wild Trees

I've taken a break from house- and bird-sitting seven miles inland from the Oregon coast. Rarely do I want to leave my friends' four-acre sanctuary where wood ducks glide the curvaceous slough. There, I write with a rescued Amazon parrot outside her cage on a perch a few feet away. I've learned to slowly raise one hand up to Esme and, if she bows, to stroke her head feathers of tropic greens and periwinkles. Often, she purrs in pleasure.

When I do emerge, it's to head to the ocean and Newport, one of my favorite coastal towns, with a historic waterfront on Yaquina Bay where sea lions haul out on docks, and home to the Hatfield Marine Science Center of Oregon State University and the Oregon Coast Aquarium.

Gray whales feed on krill (shrimplike crustaceans feeding on plankton) that hide in nearshore underwater forests of bull kelp, brown algae anchored to rocks on the ocean floor by holdfasts. But kelp can grow as much as 10 inches a day to reach heights of 60 feet at the surface, where hollow bulbs with blades float. South of Oregon, in California, giant kelp can grow a foot a day and to heights of 175 feet.

When I was eight and nine, my parents took us for spring vacations from our Washington homes (Mount Rainier followed by Coulee Dam) to Yachats, a half hour south of Newport. There, we'd stay at a modest motel, chosen for the warmth of a heated indoor pool after wading in the frigid Pacific. Whenever we'd spot bull kelp washed up on the beach, we'd sprint over to jump on the round bulbs that make that terrific popping sound. Then, we'd whirl the bullwhips in the air.

Walking an ocean beach near Yaquina Bay, I come to a bullwhip with a curving stipe (stem) doubling back to form an eight-foot-long teardrop. The slick blades are like twirled spinach pasta. I walk barefoot around the kelp on firm brown sands as if following my life's circle back to that skinny, freckle-faced girl kicking up seafoam and dreaming of scuba diving like Jacques Cousteau.

I will never dive down to every level of a kelp forest. In college, my fellow students at the Oregon Institute of Marine Biology were relieved when at last I was ordered to stay on shore. I made three trips on the diesel-powered, fume-laden boat to collect samples in nets from different depths and spent most of the time with my head over the railing. The joke was that I was destined to study estuaries, tide pools, and beaches. There are many ways to connect to the ocean. My name "Marina" is telling—a harbor with moorings.

Still, I can daydream of somersaulting in light-filled waters and kicking my fins down to the kelp's holdfast, ringed in sea stars, snails, and anemones. There, I'd glimpse a flash of thousands of krill and maybe a seabird arrowing down from the upper to lower canopies of the underwater forest.

The seabird divers remind me of forest birds divvying up the vertical canopy without competing. Pigeon Guillemots paddle underwater on short, agile wings to catch prey hiding in the nearshore or rocky intertidal zones. Puffins, auklets, and murres feast at the edge of the continental shelf, where large schools of forage fish gather some 30 or more miles from shores.

Cormorants fold their wings and kick their webbed feet to chase sardines streaking within the shadowy bull kelp of the cold rough waters. All are aerodynamic and strong swimmers with hooked bills. Each of the three species off Oregon's coast fishes differently. The Brandt's Cormorant snaps up fish on the ocean bottom. The Double-crested dives for fish in open waters. The Pelagic hunts only for small fish. The secret to sharing is to not angle for the same spot and food.

The key to the Pacific Ocean dishing up one of the most bountiful feasts on the planet is the fabulous coastal upwelling, driven by spring northwest winds that froth the sea into whitecaps. The gusts pull cold and nutrient-filled waters from the depths to the surface. At the surface, too, are plankton, the drifting marine plants and animals that form the broth powering the ocean food web. The ocean covers 70 percent of our planet, and the photosynthesis of plankton releases half the oxygen in our atmosphere. Every breath we take is thanks to plankton and forests.

Like ancient forests, bull kelp gather sunlight and sequester and store vast amounts of carbon in their blades and stems. They are also in trouble, facing threats from a warming ocean, munching sea urchins, and suffocation from sediments entering the ocean from muddy streams in clear-cuts. But there are positive signs for kelp. A nonprofit called the Elakha Alliance is dedicated to reintroducing sea otters to Oregon's coastal waters. This campaign, with strong tribal partners, is gathering steam. The otters favorite prey? Sea urchins.

Returning to my walk on the windy beach by Yaquina Bay, I notice the tidal wrack line is thick with the husks of *Velella velella* or by-the-wind sailors. When fresh, each one is like transparent blown glass with a cobalt sail, small enough to fill my palm. They cruise the ocean at the will of the winds, sailing until driven ashore in massive numbers in springtime. Each one is a hydroid colony of polyps gathering plankton and sharing the food through canals. The polyps all have roles, some for feeding, some for reproducing, and others as protectors.

We cannot know how it all will end—our lives, our life-filled planet. But we keep sailing along and doing our best to give sustenance to the ones we love. Isn't it time to steer away from the breakers? Just then a Turkey Vulture lifts from the body of a sea lion and flies so close to my head that the two-toned wings almost caress my shoulder. Life, death, and life keep interlocking like feathers.

THIRTEEN

Woodpecker Quartet

Refugia of Standing Dead

Woodpeckers play the music of afterlife. They tune the trees when they die and become "snags"—after sap stops flowing, when bark slips off, branches break, and heartwood decays. Pileated, White-headed, Lewis's, and Black-backed Woodpeckers form a quartet. I chose these four species because of their differing connections to the life, death, and renewal of Cascadia's feathered forests.

In classical music, a string quartet comprises two violins, a viola, and a cello. Drawing their bows across strings on instruments crafted from trees, the musicians do not play trios, solos, sonatas, or concertos. A string quartet plays string quartets.

A snag quartet of woodpeckers plays snag quartets, even if not gathered on the same stage. All but one are powered by strong neck muscles and beaks to drum distinctive rhythms on the forest's wooden instruments. A Pileated hammers slow crescendos that fade away like a passing thunderstorm. A Black-backed's staccato is the snare drum, while the White-headed taps a looser and lighter cadence. The Lewis's Woodpecker drums the least, with a bill best for nabbing insects midair.

When woodpeckers drum, they are courting, signaling mates, or sounding alarms. Northern Flickers are infamous for choosing metal for ringing rat-a-tats. Meanwhile, the calls of woodpeckers are variations of free jazz, hollers, caterwauls, yodels, churrs, picks, or squeaks. I'd be wincing if a string quartet played an ode to the Picidae family. Within a wild forest, the drumming and chants are as elemental as the music of native peoples honoring ancestors, future generations, and home.

Of all the trees in the feathered forest, snags are the most endangered. They are cut down for firewood, cut down as so-called hazards, and cut down because they are considered unhealthy, diseased, and unsightly. Meanwhile, the great housing shortage continues for wildlife in the forest. If only our homes could act more like tree snags, sheltering far more than humans.

Close to a fifth (about 2,000) of all the planet's bird species depend on tree cavities as homes. More than 330 species inhabit woodpecker holes. In North America, at least thirty require drilled and chiseled holes to nest, roost, hide, or find winter warmth.[1]

Whenever I'm in a wild forest, my senses infuse with all the creatures of tree holes, hollows, dens, and broken tops. Woodpecker. Bluebird. Chickadee. Nuthatch. House Wren. Brown Creeper. Tree Swallow. Kestrel. Wood Duck. Hooded Merganser. Goldeneye. Bat. Flying squirrel. Chipmunk. Fisher. Marten, Black Bear. Spotted Skunk. Raccoon. Salamander. Black Bear. Porcupine. Pacific Tree Frog. Thousands of arthropods.

Speak their names. Then go deeper. A Pileated Woodpecker's hole high up in a snag or a large dead branch of a living tree invites Vaux's Swifts to dart in one after another and sleep in a snug cavity. When snags flake chunks and curls of bark, they offer roofed vertical shelters for bats and nest spots for Brown Creepers.

Just as growing trees offer differing habitats at every stage, so do snags as they return to earth. Scientists describe nine stages: alive, declining, dead, loose bark, clean (no bark), broken, decomposed, down material, and stump (or stub). From stages five to nine, the snag loses height. In dying, death, and returning to soil, trees become ever more life-filled. Snags of all sizes matter to birds. For example, small dead trees rot fast and soften enough for chickadees to dig nest holes, rather than waiting for woodpeckers.

In my early thirties I lived in the humming house, ringed in cottonwoods planted a century ago. Twelve miles outside of Helena, Montana, on a 2,000-acre ranch, the rickety homestead nudged against a prairie knoll below the Continental Divide. Honeybees filled an entire inner wall that bowed inward from the weight of the hive. Their pulsing wings entered my dreams in a boxy upstairs bedroom.

Hairy Woodpeckers tapped for insects on the shingle siding. Flickers drummed metallic cacophonies on rusty license plates tacked over woodpecker holes. Red-naped Sapsuckers flew from the cottonwoods to nab exiting honeybees. Cottontail rabbits burrowed beneath the house in fall. Chipmunks scrambled through the inner walls. In winter, they curled up and hibernated there. In spring, waters from underground springs in aspen groves flowed downhill to fill the dirt basement waist deep. Salamanders? Fish? Antelope raced by. Foxes and skunks prowled at night. Warblers and wrens trilled within unruly chokecherry, willow, and lilac overtaking abandoned outbuildings.

The mice had a field day scampering in kitchen drawers. Their entrances were far too numerous to patch up. Many ended up in Havahart traps only to be shaken loose in a field where kestrels hunted from fence posts. It's possible the house was haunted. Scrapes, scurries, creaks, groans, and hums woke me at night.

The house held stories, one etched in the blackened outline of an iron on the rough floorboards. I heard some of them from Gene, the eighty-year-old neighbor who'd grown up there and wept when his children sold the Lone Pine ranch in 1990. But he never really left. Gnarled as driftwood, Gene often drove over in a sputtering 1950s tractor. He'd wipe his brow with an oil-blackened hand, climb out stiffly, and limp to the old junkyard. Searching among wheels, spokes, axles, and 1940s-vintage engines half-hidden among lupine, fescue, and wheatgrass, he'd find a rusty part and mend the complaining machine.

I'd hear his riveting account of the barn burning down from an errant Fourth of July firework as if it were yesterday instead of fifty years earlier. He revered his mother, who ran the ranch and raised eight children in a house perhaps only 800 square feet in size. His father worked on the railway and rarely came home.

In the two years I lived there with my first husband, we struggled in winter blizzards when temperatures dropped to 40 degrees below zero and snows drifted deep in the roads. Often, we were stuck at home or drove cross-country over fields to get to work. What I remember most is the humming within my tree snag of a home.

It's late May in Badger Creek Wilderness on the east side of the Mount Hood National Forest, a three-hour drive north from Bend. I'm on a quest for a Pileated Woodpecker. Glamorous, with a scarlet swoop of a crest, North America's largest living woodpecker is a poster bird for saving old-growth trees. A crow-sized bird requires a home with plenty of elbow room when nesting and roosting. In Oregon, the trees must be at least three feet in diameter. Hollows are imperative.

Here is a rare valley of old-growth forest, free of roads, logging, and with a head-spinning array of tree species, many of impressive girth and height. Thanks to unsung heroes Ruth and Ken Love and David Corkran of the Mount Hood Forest Study Group, the 29,000 acres slid right into the Oregon Wilderness Act of 1984. When I reached David, the Portland retired science teacher told me that Ken Love's pivotal flight with Congressman Les AuCoin saved the day. Timber interests ruled, and designating roadless areas as wilderness was an uphill struggle. As the small plane veered east from Mount Hood, Ken extolled the virtues of wild forests fed by Badger, Little Badger, and Tygh Creeks. But AuCoin had his eye on the treeless landscape to the east, toward the small town of Dufur. "So instead of looking at the timber below him, he saw all that country without trees and figured this place wouldn't impinge on logging," he told me, chuckling at the memory.

A biodiversity hotspot, Badger Creek Wilderness is influenced by the weather of the Columbia River Gorge to the north that funnels rain off the Pacific Ocean. White oak and beaked hazelnut mingle with chinquapin, ponderosa, Douglas-fir, grand fir, western larch, and shade-loving redcedar, western hemlock, Pacific yew, and Engelmann spruce.

Backpacking up-valley with my husband, Wes, and our eleven-year-old Labrador, wearing her own pack, we take notice of the shifting array of trees with elevation. Western white pine, noble fir, and silver fir chime in as oaks and hazelnuts recede. Riparian-loving hardwoods abound too, from black cottonwoods to alders, willows, and bigleaf maples. Each tree has character and a story of living within this self-willed valley, finding microclimates tied to soils, moisture, and orientation. Snags spear the sky singly or in bunches that are gifts of spruce budworms, fire, and other creators of dead trees. Far from threats to the feathered forest, budworms and beetles are natural and essential for supporting woodpeckers that, in turn, knock back outbreaks.

This is Pileated paradise. Hiking in nine miles the first day, we pass by many rectangular holes whacked by chisel-shaped bills. The square edges are efficient for opening tunnels in decaying wood grains to expose carpenter ant tunnels. On the second day at dawn, nine miles up the trail, I hear the distinctive ululations above the rush of a side creek entering Badger. Fueled by morning coffee and without a backpack, I hurry off trail toward the sound but cannot find the bird.

Admiring a five-foot-wide living redcedar, I brush my hand across a light-switch-plate-sized Pileated hole in an old fire scar by the base. A brick-sized excavation marks a fallen Douglas-fir, where I kneel to inhale the sugar of candlelike blossoms of vanilla leaf lined up all in a row.

Western carpenter ants, favorite prey of Pileated Woodpeckers, carry sawdust from pencil-sized round holes. Shiny and black with reddish legs, the ants chew galleries within the nurse log. Essential recyclers, they do not digest wood, but instead prey on western spruce budworms, collect nectar from rhododendron petals, and farm aphids for their honey. Sometimes they might be yanked out of a tunnel by the rough long tongue of a Pileated Woodpecker.

Throughout our Badger Creek wanderings, I am slowed by May wildflowers and birds. I'm leaning over to study delicate *Calypso* orchids, purple crowned with speckle slipper pouches. I'm tilting my chin up to look for a Hermit Warbler trilling high piano keys in the conifer crowns.

A Nashville Warbler sends chips of sun song in two-part phrases out into the forest above Badger Creek. Each series ends in a trill. Seeking the sleek small bird with gray head and yellow breast, I scan first from the eye-level vine maples, hazelnuts, and white oak and then higher into the spreading wings of Douglas-fir, western white pine, and grand fir intermixed with the bigleaf maples closest to the creek. The warbler flits from the greenery to the bare branch of a snag and warbles a soprano—*see-bit see-bit see-bit see-bit see-bit* followed by a lower *titititititi*.

Among the symphony of forest, birds, and creek, the Pileated Woodpecker is the first violinist tuning the orchestra. In biology, the term is a keystone species. Without this species, an ecosystem crumbles. More than twenty wildlife species in Cascadia rely on nest holes. One is the Vaux's Swift. Toward evening on our hike, I hear telltale twittering and looked up on the ridge to see a dozen migrating swifts streaking above several tall dead trees snapped off by winds. Roost tree? The cavities they seek are home, too, for silver-haired bats that also rely on older conifer forests of structural complexity. Females, which often bear twin pups, may roost in colonies of up to twenty-five in a roomy cavity.

Pileated Woodpeckers use both chiseled nests and natural hollows with several exits for escape. Each year, mated pairs dig new nest holes, leaving the old ones open for new occupants. I've watched males and females taking turns to chip an oblong entry through outer wood. To tell the difference, I look for the red cheek stripe on the male, who also puts in more than twice the work of the females. After several weeks of tossing and carting billfuls of chips, the two-foot-deep hollow cavity is ready for the finale of a scraped cup of chips to cushion four eggs.

Wherever I am among living and dead trees of great girth and with deep hollows, I'm on the alert. I've known Pileated Woodpeckers nesting in old cottonwood trees by Rattlesnake Creek in Missoula. I've heard their sonorous piping in the deepest, darkest fir forests of Lookout Mountain roadless area in Oregon's Ochoco Mountains. I saw one pounding a driftwood log on a beach of Washington's Olympic Peninsula.

On this trip, Badger Creek hid Pileated Woodpeckers well. Instead, the stream sent her news flowing pell-mell in the snowmelt waters. An American Dipper picked up the headlines. Across from our second night's camp, Pine Creek tumbled storied words. Western Tanagers answered all questions in whistled refrains from high in the canopy. Sunlight filtered troubles away. Pepper curled next to me in a furry black Labrador bundle. I put down my notebook and pen, laid back to look up the trees, and daydreamed of dwelling forever in the bliss that is wilderness.

A trio of Black-backed Woodpeckers hitch their way up separate charcoal trunks. Hundreds of crispy burned trees streak upward from magenta fields of fireweed, a native flower often the first to bloom after a burn. Mountain Bluebirds and Tree Swallows fly in and out of nest holes. Fire morel mushrooms crowd the edges of fallen burned trees. Fire moss blazes with burned orange spores over ashy soils. Bicknell's geranium, or cranesbill, waves delicate five-petals of pink and white.

I've marveled at similar scenes in the first five years after severe wildfires in Oregon, Idaho, and Montana. Like a phoenix rising from the ashes, the Black-backed Woodpecker co-evolved with stand-replacing wildfires yielding thousands of burned trees chock full of fire-loving beetles. The cryptic coloration of black feathers on charcoal bark is living proof that high-severity wildfires have long been part of the ecology of western forests.

Everywhere are lessons, reminding us to think long term. Patient are the seeds of the Bicknell's geranium that can wait for centuries until intense wildfire burns through top layers and leaf litter to expose the seeds to sunlight. Patient, too, are the ways of ceanothus, a shrub with leathery leaves and white clustered blossoms pollinated by native bees. Their seeds, too, can rest centuries to germinate only after high heat. Fire moss is nowhere to be seen in the unburned forest, yet their wind-carried spores find their way to mineral soils postfire.

Burn morels can bide their time for fifty years for the magical moment to send their fruits upward, to the joy of mushroom pickers. Called a phoenicoid (after the phoenix), this honeycomb-shaped mushroom is the only edible one in the fire-loving group. This morel attaches mycelium to a conifer root and dwells in a companionship of nutrient exchange until a hot fire kills the tree. Then, the morel harvests the tree's energy and is ready at last to press up through the earth. But first, the burn morel needs snow in winter after the fire for water, and good drainage in spring sunshine. Conifer forests with mixed species are a favorite. If the fire is too hot, the mycelium will die, and if not hot enough, the tree host won't die.

Perhaps Black-backed Woodpeckers are less patient as they wait for the smoke plumes to rise and for the fire-loving beetles (*Melanophila*) to sense the intense heat from 50 miles away. The beetles detect fire with heat sensors on their thoraxes. They whir to smoldering trees, mate, and females lay eggs in crevices. The eggs hatch into white grubs that tunnel into the wood. Then, the woodpeckers go to work spearing the juicy treats. One Black-backed Woodpecker can eat 13,500 larvae a year.

Learning to think ahead hundreds of years is not always easy. I wept when the Lookout Fire burned through the heart of the ancient forest of the Andrews. The change within my lifespan felt too hard to bear. And yet, that following spring the bird crews recorded their first Black-backed Woodpeckers. By the next summer, biologists had tracked a family at a nest hole.

The Lewis's Woodpeckers have returned to the Turquoise Forest, home of the Grandmother Tree. It's the first of May 2025. Six birds encircle two ponderosa snags about 70 feet tall and 40 feet apart. The sun gleams on iridescent green-black backs, rosy breasts, fog-gray necks, and raspberry faces. With every flap of crowlike wings, the robin-sized woodpeckers cast a spell. Like magicians, they swirl black cloaks. In one moment they are woodpeckers and in the next flycatchers hawking insects. When backlit and facing away, the bird is a dark silhouette fringed in rosy breast feathers.

The penstemon sky fills with squeaky chatter and *churr churr churrs*! Some calls are like Steller's Jays, fellow companions of a mostly second-growth pine forest that harbors Pygmy Nuthatches, Mountain Chickadees, Hairy Woodpeckers, Dark-eyed Juncos, California Quail, and Common Ravens year-round. The woodpeckers perch, take off, land, inspect, meet up, fly apart, and chase each other. The racket comes from males. The identical females may join in with *yick-yicks*.

Whenever I come home after a long absence, I exclaim over what's familiar, longed for, and strangely different. Lewis's Woodpeckers winter as far south as Baja, Mexico, with some staying in southern Oregon, where oak trees offer acorns as winter foods. For several years, I've watched pairs nesting in two adjacent snags in the Turquoise Forest.

A couple weeks later, the first pair has settled in. I am startled to see one with a white bubble on the beak's tip. After a few flutters balancing the bubble, the woodpecker pops the spider egg sac on a tree limb and devours the tiny inhabitants. Then the pair mates in classic bird style with the male on top for a few seconds. While both genders are equally breathtaking and impossible to distinguish one from the other, I can tell from her under-the-male position, she is the one that next flies to a cookie-sized hole, 20 feet up a snag and below a sturdy branch. Here, the tree is still partially covered in thick amber bark. Tipping forward, her crimson belly is framed in dark tail feathers. Then, she slips inside.

Within a gourd-shaped cavity, typically about a foot deep, she will line the bottom with wood chips that she can peck from the soft interior. There, she will lay five to nine white eggs and incubate them for a month. After hatching, the parents have a frantic month ahead of feeding the hatchlings insects and spiders. Unlike other woodpeckers, the adults are not extracting tunneling larvae from the trees, because of the limits of their flycatching bills.

Soon, another pair is nesting in the nearest snag. In early July, I find a third nest tree closer to my home when I hear the faint cheeping of chicks within a dead ponderosa thick with witches'-brooms. All the nest trees have bark remaining. A white skeletal ponderosa has none. The holes they choose are all flicker-sized. I give thanks to Northern Flickers for their prodigious excavations.

One day early in the nesting, five Clark's Nutcrackers flew by the snags like boisterous partygoers, but dressed in somber grays, blacks, and whites. I'm surprised to see them here, probably on their way to the subalpine whitebark pines of the high Cascade lakes.

This is what it is to be drawn to one place repeatedly and out from the cavity of my roofed house. While my attention is on the woodpeckers, I take time to be with the Grandmother Tree. She's the biggest tree in the forest and likely four hundred years old. I often put my cheek on her ponderosa puzzle bark and spread my arms in a wide hug. A long drooping branch brushes the edge of the lava flow. Far above me, starry needles tessellate the sky.

Digging is not the forte of Lewis's Woodpeckers. They seek decayed snags soft enough for their bills to chip away only pliable wood. Reusing Northern Flicker and Hairy Woodpecker holes is their first choice. Across western North America, Lewis's find premier nesting homes in burned trees after wildfires. They favor streams and rivers with large dead cottonwood trees for nesting and bountiful insects hatching from waters. But seeing them here is a reminder of the significance of the dryer ponderosa unburned forest as well.

Lewis's Woodpeckers are yoked to more than a single or clusters of snags. They flap to green treetops and seek their insect prey in the air and on the branches. When the winds fluff their breast feathers, they bloom like wild roses. Without a rich understory, they would have a near-empty pantry. In Late May, bitterbrush flowers of lemony clusters scent the breeze in spicy cinnamon and invite insect pollinators. The woodpeckers glean for insects among blossoms, leaves, twigs, and trunks. Manzanitas, currants, and ceanothus are denizens, too, of central Oregon ponderosa forests. Unseen below, the mycelial network knits away without dropping a stitch.

Observing Lewis's Woodpeckers nest year after year, I've observed changes in the snags I'd miss otherwise. The woodpeckers led me to notice the sloughing of thick plates of amber bark, the latest crack, split, cavity and a whitening, barkless spire. Two years earlier, they landed on the shelves of white conks protruding from the upper trunk of one tree and sought insects there. Those fungi are gone. Yet, both trees are decaying at a stately rate. The snags stand erect with a ladder of branches, still retaining half their bark. Every nest hole I find is in the bark.

On the first of July, my neighbor Michele Kellogg and I catch our breath at the same time. A chick peeks from the round hole—mostly black beak and a bit of grayish head. The nest tree talks in chittering of nestlings within. The parents fly back and forth conveying bees, flies, and other winged catches. They even take suet from a bird feeder at a home a quarter mile away.

As the growing chicks edge toward fledging in the second week of July, the native red currants are in full berry. Michele clicks her long-lens camera as a parent flies to the hole with three shiny scarlet berries lined up neatly in the bill. Soon, two chicks peer out. The time is close.

One shard of forest bordered by a lava flow may seem inconsequential at a mere half mile long and a quarter mile wide. Three nesting pairs of Lewis's Woodpeckers prove otherwise. Hairy Woodpeckers and Pygmy Nuthatches raised young in holes in two of the snags with Lewis's. Every snag-filled patch matters, especially with a 70 percent decline of Lewis's Woodpeckers in the past fifty years.

On that early May day, with six birds circumnavigating the two snags, I hoped at least one pair would stay. What a joy this season has proved. Lewis's Woodpeckers are also raising young in a nearby island of ancient living and dead ponderosas skewering the sky amid a lava field. This is a kipuka (from the Hawaiian word *kīpuka*), where, seven thousand years ago, hot lava parted on its journey, leaving the original habitat unscathed. Kestrels nest in snag cavities. Coyotes den. To hike to this refugium takes sturdy boots and gloves for clambering among sharp and loose volcanic rocks threaded in twisting pines and junipers. When I am ensconced in this tree-filled acre-sized bowl, lined in manzanita bushes and rimmed in high lava stones, I feel far away from the travails of fast-paced life.

Like Noah's Ark in the flood, a kipuka can be a life-saving home for animal species that can later colonize lands when conditions improve. Environmental philosopher Kathleen Dean Moore, speaking at the 2025 Public Interest Land Law Conference in Eugene, Oregon, held up the kipuka as a lesson from nature for how we defend wild places and wildlife: "We will make ourselves the rocks that divide the flow, the obstruction, the slight rise in the land that diverts the forces of destruction and creates a place of safety, where the future is free to become fully itself."[2]

Each time a White-headed Woodpecker flies into our yard, I drop everything, as I did one nesting season in collaboration with my neighbor. A pair raised a chick and showed up as a family of three, but the nest snag eluded us.

White-headed Woodpeckers were frequent companions when I hiked miles as a seasonal employee conducting stand exams for the Malheur National Forest in the early 1980s. Their flights through centuries-old and glowing amber ponderosas matched the rolling slopes of fir, pine, and larch. The birds flew to the ground to drink from pools and small creeks fed by melting snow. Always there were living and dead trees of immensity.

White-headed Woodpecker havens are defined by many ponderosa snags of great width. The biggest living pines also offer the most pine seeds. Clinging to cones, the birds pry and pop out winged seeds. Landing on the trunks of smaller pines, they drill sap wells in a row like sapsucker woodpeckers seeking liquid sweets. Often the little trees are close to a commanding nest snag. To find insects for hungry chicks, the woodpeckers flake off puzzle bark and dig into softer dead wood with beaks too weak to drill into hard wood. When probing needle clusters for larvae, they often enter denser forests with closed canopies.

Every rolling flight is classic woodpecker—a burst of flapping and a quick glide with wings pinned to the body before another burst. There's no mistaking the white head and white flashes on black wing feathers and the glimpse of a cherry feather patch on the head feathers of a male. The birds fly with ease through open ponderosas that self-prune lower limbs with age, preventing wildfire flames from ascending ladder branches. Thick bark is another fire shield. Frequent wildfires at low severity are the hallmark of ponderosas of the east side lower elevations, long ignited from lightning or cultural burning by tribes.

Within these havens, White-headed Woodpecker pairs stay together year-round—feeding, drinking, and often roosting in old nest cavities they dig together. They renew their bonds with drumming, calling, and courting. Pairs excavate a new nest cavity in soft wood. By the end of May, parents take shifts warming the four or five eggs. After about two weeks, the featherless chicks hatch one at a time. Parents are soon flying back and forth every three to ten minutes with insects. Despite vigilance, typically only one to three chicks fledge after about three weeks. The tenacious adults feed their chicks most of the summer and stay close through the fall. Their young grow robust on ants, beetles, cicadas, and others.

As cones ripen by late summer, the birds switch diets and feed heavily on seeds through midwinter. When I watched Hairy and White-headed Woodpeckers among pines near Sunriver, the birds were likely seeking bark beetles active on a warmer spring day with snow still on the ground.

At the foot of the Grandmother Tree, I like to pretend she is one among many—a time when White-headed Woodpeckers flew through the open midstory with thousands of long-lived ponderosas, some reaching seven hundred years and growing to heights of 150 feet or more. There would be green-needled trees with wide bark plates in red-gold hues only possible after growing more than a century. I'd rejoice in broken-off tops regrown with flat crowns, and snag upon snag. Flammulated Owl males would call from their favored perches in the high crowns, and pairs of the pint-sized owls would nest in old woodpecker holes. Colonies of big brown bats would roost in voluminous hollow trees. California myotis, diminutive bats only two to three inches long, would rest under loose bark.

We've lost so much. Already in trouble, this stunning woodpecker has few places to turn. East of the Cascades in Oregon and Washington, only 3 percent of trees greater than 21 inches in diameter are remaining. That small fraction stores 42 percent of the carbon in the forest.

To be a good ancestor to this woodpecker is to save every big ponderosa pine and snag left and to allow fire to work her magic in this ecosystem where periodic lightning and cultural burning renewed the open stands.

Wandering by Wallowa Lake at the Fishtrap Writer's Gathering in summer of 2024, I sat down in the shade of a mighty ponderosa and pulled out my notebook to write:

> Peel off a chip of my puzzle bark. Go ahead. Peck and chisel. Find every crevice in my amber trunk. I have known you, Downy Woodpecker, a hundred times over. I am ponderosa. My age cannot be measured by the five hundred rings alone. I am river song. Whitecap on lake. Trickling headwaters. Lightning strike on high ridge bursting into flame.
>
> I carry salmon deep in my heartwood. When full moon sweeps the far away tides, my branches tremble with all that is ocean—deeper even than my taproot. Memory floods with Chinook and steelhead spawning in Wallowa River, with black bears slapping great fish and padding under my shade to feast. The bones of salmon from the Pacific 500 miles away fed me and fed my kin. So long gone. The time when the river ran red with wriggling fish coming home. So long gone, the two-legged ones who knew my language. We could talk then. I learned their name—Nimiipuu—the people. They learned mine. They knew the way of drum, of chant, of kin, of family, of elder.
>
> So many of my brethren so long gone. Felled by a sharp-toothed monster roaring, whining, cutting. Smash! I could not save them. So frantic. They called. Tapped distress root to root. I remember the Bald Eagle nest crashing, three chicks spilling out shrieking. The crushing silence.
>
> Yet still my sap flows. My cambium lives on, protected by layer upon layer of bark. And still, on a summer's day, the scent of vanilla wafts from every fissure, where you, Downy Woodpecker, might nab a striped beetle with a neat flick of tongue.
>
> I have known fire so hot, I bear a scar where trunk meets earth. I have known wind so strong, my top spire cracked and fell—only to grow a new one. I have known blizzard, ice, frost, and the softest touch of a hummingbird weaving a nest in a twig fork. But I have not ever known this relentless heat—the panting of Red Crossbill chicks, the suffering of all I carry. Even you, Downy Woodpecker, must fluff your feathers not for warmth but for cooling.
>
> We can outlive this. We can. I am strong, like the Nimiipuu. Come home again to speak to me in the language of trees. Give me your wings, your paws, and your beetle feet. I will carry all of you.

FOURTEEN

Overstory

Gathering Light

I'm lost in time within the glacially carved Crabtree Valley, among primeval Douglas-firs, western hemlock, western redcedar, and Alaska yellow cedar. The oldest Douglas-firs in Oregon are rooted here. If immortality were possible, this might be the place. The trees drink from the sponginess of bog, springs, and two small lakes. The elders know the way of sun and shadow, snag and hollow, gnarl and crown.

Wavering reflections of conifer spires in Crabtree Lake draw me closer. The lake is the oval eye with lashes of vine maples flashing leaves turned to flame and ember. Closing my eyes and listening to the jingle of Golden-crowned Kinglets, I'm once again lifted out of my human self. If I've ever wondered what climate refugia looked like, this is it. A circling Red-tailed Hawk halos the breathing trees. Hidden in the tree crowns, surely there are red tree voles lapping droplets from Douglas-fir needles.

Northern flying squirrels will paper the dusk in downward glides, evading Northern Spotted Owls. The imperiled owls have long known the Crabtree Valley. With few ancient forests left and Barred Owls advancing into their last strongholds to outcompete them, Spotted Owls are teetering toward extinction. I can only hope this sanctuary is inviolate.

If Shangri-La existed in Cascadia, this would be the mystical valley. But without environmental activism, the timber industry would have paid loggers to cut down every big tree, as they did for mile upon mile in the western Cascades, leaving a patchwork quilt of roads and clear-cuts. I give a silent prayer as if I could speak in the language of trees. "Please, stay this way for another millennium. Be the grove that seeds the surrounding places with all the biodiversity you are guarding."

I wish the Crabtree Valley forest extended far more than two square miles, but I'm grateful for every square inch. Once owned by a timber company, its fate seemed sealed. In the 1970s, people who loved this place did not shrug and walk away from the impossible. They fought for it. Years later, the Bureau of Land Management bought the Crabtree Valley via a land swap, to become an Area of Critical Environmental Concern.

Turning to my companions John Cissel and Chandra LeGue, I feel privileged to be here with them. They are knowledge keepers, old-growth defenders, and educators who share the wisdom of ancient trees. Six feet, five inches tall, with a trim silver beard and wire-rim glasses, John is still dwarfed next to the trees escalating above us. He's the co-author with his wife, Diane, of *Best Old Growth Forest Hikes: Washington and Oregon Cascades*. They're updating the book by hiking many trails he'd not seen since the 1990s, when he covered 2,000 miles, now adjusting for wildfire and logging incursions. John's a forest ecologist, past director of the Andrews Forest, and a bit like J. R. R. Tolkien's character Treebeard, leader of the Ents, who said "Nobody cares for the trees like I do."

Chandra, of nonprofit Oregon Wild, is one of my favorite tree huggers. She's leading us to the "King Tut" tree that could well be a thousand years old, measured at 270 feet tall with a diameter close to 8 feet, and 29 feet around. Named by activists to draw attention to Crabtree Valley's significance, the tree is elusive. To get there, we depend on Chandra's savvy ability to find her way off trail.

I'd become friends with Chandra through our mutual love of forest wilds and teaming up on a series I wrote for Oregon Wild's fiftieth anniversary in 2024 called Every Wild Place Has a Story. In her forties, she's a steady and seasoned eco-warrior for more than two decades of activism with Oregon Wild. As the author of the 2020 book *Oregon's Ancient Forests: A Hiking Guide*, she's come to know most of the state's wildest groves. Like me, she'd rather not hustle along on a trail when there are plants to identify and curiosities of scat, tracks, and feather piles. We'd also backpacked in Badger Creek Wilderness in midsummer, when we were slowed by enticing ripe huckleberries and native blueberries.

This time, we find bear scat puckered with huckleberries, elk tracks in mud, porcupine-chewed chips below a small tree, and a mountain beaver burrow with a tidy pile of fresh clipped leaves and twigs at the softball-sized entry among ferns. This primitive forest rodent, related to squirrels (not beavers), lives a shy life in underground tunnels and, above ground, never strays for more than a few meters from any of the multiple entries.

Pressing through forgiving red elderberry, we avoid the chest-high, thorny Devil's club. We come to several great redcedars forming an imposing wall as if one fused family. Loose, rich soils burst with brainlike coral mushrooms and angel wings, delicate white fungi shaped as the name suggests. Encircled by a half dozen hemlocks, redcedars, and Douglas-firs, each wider than the six- to seven-foot wingspan of a bald eagle, the three of us fall into revery. A bit later, I ask John how he feels here.

"We all come from somebody and somewhere, but we all come from Mother Earth," he tells me. "We only have one, and we need to take care of her. For me, old growth is where I feel that connection come alive."

I'm nodding. We're elfin and childlike in comparison. Scrambling over barrels of mossy nurse logs, Chandra, John, and I come to King Tut. A ridge of bark like fusilli pasta wraps from the base and coils upward as far up as we can see. While spiraling wood grain helps trees withstand stress and distribute nutrients, why would the pattern appear in the craggy bark? John suggests an old fire scar might have been the source. For me, this tree is not King Tut from far away Egypt, but Spiral Tree.

Spiral is the way of birds wending around the trunk like the shaft of a feather. Spiral are pinecones, snail shells, and galaxies. At night, lying on my back to look at constellations, I'm spiraling into the fourth dimension of time with starlight emitted two billion years ago.

Gazing up the cliff of the thousand-year-old tree, I see my life as one blink of the eye of Crabtree Lake. I'm a tiny mite clinging to the barb of an owl feather. No matter. With every second remaining, I seek the winding way—flying with birds into the overstory.

FIFTEEN

Vaux's Swift

Hollow Trees and Chimneys

What is it to flutter into a brick chimney among thousands of your kin, to hook your clawed feet on the inner wall, fold your arched wings closed, and rest until dawn? You know the way of the vertical. Even your tail feathers are tipped with spines to support your upright sleeping. Do you dream of your ancestors whose hearts beat within the hollows of giant trees? Do you whisper stories of migration? Or are you too dizzy to do anything but find your center in the whorl of time?

As day slips toward dusk in early September, twittering Vaux's Swifts twirl like ashes from wildfires burning on the east slope of the Cascades. Time rewinds in their counterclockwise circling around the chimney—fifty, a hundred, and then two hundred years ago, when all roosts were trees, a time before buildings, roads, railroads, and when the people were of the forest and lived by nature's rhythms.

Vaux's Swifts take us swiftly to the trees most maligned by those who see only board feet, disease, and hazard. Long live the ancient forest in all her glory of young and old, of dying and dead, of burned and blackened, of broken tops, peeling-off bark, mistletoe clumps, conks and softening heartwood. Long stand the towering snags carved by woodpeckers. May the older forests preside with abundant snags and living trees with hollows just right for nests and roosts.

May the Vaux's Swifts of the west and the Chimney Swifts of the east lead us to the wonder of living trees thriving with cavernous centers—trees that know swifts shingling their sapwood in feathers and heartbeats. Trees that keep roosting and nesting swifts not too hot and not too cold—microclimate refugia essential in a warming world. May our threatened trees be protected from all who would cut them down.

I've joined Mary Ann Kruse and Bob Johnson in downtown Bend for their nightly count of swifts entering a capacious chimney stack. The flocks come in waves each evening as they wing from Canada to Venezuela for the winter. They may fly 50 to 150 miles in a day before a night's rest in a chimney or, where they can find one, a tree-hollow roost.

The smallest swift in North America dazzles the sky in aerial pursuits of insects. Four inches long, with a tube-shaped body and wings like bows for shooting arrows, a Vaux's Swift strobes the air with intermittent quick glides. One key to the agile turns, banks, and veers is the wing shape, with proportionately larger wingtips than most birds. Their batlike erratic flights give the illusion that wingbeats are alternate rather than synchronous.

A swift pursues "aerial plankton," tiny flying insects as essential to the planet's food web as marine plankton is to the air we breathe. Among the prey are ballooning spiders kept aloft by single silken strands. The bird's overall brown plumage with a paler breast and rump remind me of the cryptic shelf fungi growing on dead trees. Feathers can be clues to habitat belonging.

All members of the bird family Apodidae (meaning footless) cannot perch. Instead, their feet are like Velcro, with four toes in the front with spines for clinging to rough, perpendicular surfaces. Of the 109 swift species in the world, four inhabit North America. Whereas Vaux's and Chimney Swifts seek tree hollows, Black Swifts nest behind waterfalls and are often fellow denizens of ancient forests. White-throated Swifts hurtle along canyon rims and nestle in cliff crevices.

The world's population of Vaux's Swifts is estimated to be between 200,000 and 300,000—breeding in Cascadia and wintering as far south as Venezuela. The Bend chimney joins some 150 on the Pacific Flyway from Canada to Mexico, where volunteers record numbers and send in their data to the one and only Larry Schwitters. Without this dedicated man, we would know very little about swift migration. Larry is more than a coordinator of data through his project, Vaux's Happening, which he founded in 2009. The health of the migrating population is far better off because of him. He's keeping the lifeline going, supporting communities to restore and maintain chimneys, and giving quirky talks on all things swifts.

For more than a decade, Bob and Mary Ann have monitored Vaux's Swifts cindering the sunset and pluming into a chimney. They tally birds nightly without fail in spring and in fall—each stint lasting from three to six weeks. The two have become fast friends. Mary Ann, a retired nurse, rides her bike to the parking area below the Boys and Girls Club, a brick building that once served as an infirmary during the 1918 flu pandemic, right after the doors opened as the new Bend Amateur Athletic Club Gymnasium. The swifts add to the ghostly feel.

When I arrive, Mary Ann is sitting on the sidewalk with her back against a nearby building's stone wall. Her silvery hair is pulled back in a bun. Slender and strong, she wears a flamingo pink workout top and black-and-gray tights. Hands folded below the binoculars around her neck, iPhone balanced on her outstretched legs with ankles crossed, she's at once relaxed and alert. Her cloth mask patterned in strawberries is a wise addition in the acrid smoky air. I sit down next to her and tilt my head back against the wall.

Bob tends to arrive closer to dusk. Mary Ann prefers the hour or two buildup when tremolos fill the air and swifts whorl, scatter, and whorl in again. Nearby, two young women are lying on their backs on the sidewalk with arms crossed behind their heads and looking up. I hear their murmured exclamations. The sky is Michelangelo-worthy, a blush of rosy clouds in the haze.

Our ears tune to the flicker of high-pitched calls and our eyes to the zips, zings, skitters, and scatters of swifts hawking winged ants and beetles, flies and moths—all too tiny for us to see. As the light lowers, the swifts converge. Their randomness becomes a harmony of circling.

Walking over to Mary Ann, Bob stands with full attention on the chimney. Neither uses binoculars for the count or scribbles tallies until after the last bird drops in. Now the flock carousels around the stack faster and faster. One or two birds billow down into the chimney and then a few more. The birds are funneling into the chimney. Bob and Mary Ann are laser-focused, silently counting by tens and then hundreds. At the finale they turn to each other.

"How many?" Bob asks Mary Ann, his eyes merry behind wire rim glasses. He wears a dapper cap over his silvery hair.

"I counted 805."

Bob grins. "I got 820."

Mary Ann springs to her feet. The two give each other a high five. To be that close is a nod to experience. The next evening, I return to a tripling of swifts—2,400 according to Mary Ann's count, with Bob's a bit fewer. They split the difference.

I ask how to learn the craft of estimating swift numbers. Bob suggests tossing dry beans on a table to get a sense of what ten and a hundred looks like. Later, I give this a try with red kidney beans. Starting with handfuls, I'm pleased at my estimates of tens. Then I make ten piles of ten beans and push them altogether. A hundred looks daunting. After random scatters and guesses I see how easy it is to fall short.

There's also the depth-of-field problem. When swifts are raining down into a chimney like winged maple seeds, how would I account for the width of the flock? I start dropping handfuls into a bowl to mimic birds entering a chimney. Impossible. At least birds slow their downward flight with wingbeats and angled short tails. They enter headfirst but then flip around to drop feet-first and grasp a chosen part of the textured wall for a face-up sleep, overlapping with their brethren in cozy protected warmth.

While counting takes practice, the spell of the swifts is instantaneous. A gyre. A ring. An incantation. Or, as Bob calls the shape before the birds flutter into the chimney—a donut.

All day long, the swifts are flying. To bathe, they skim a lake or river's sheen, parched feathers wetted in baptismal sprinkle. In courtship, birds snap their wings upward to form V shapes and glide several seconds. To mate in the air, two birds become one in a twirling descent almost to the ground before separating and flying upward. Their nests are half-baskets glued with sticky saliva inside a hollow tree or chimney. Both parents build the nest, using their beaks to break off twigs in mid-flight. To feed their chicks efficiently, they capture a hundred or more insects at a time to form a bolus (a ball) at the back of their throats. The bonds of mated swifts are strong, lasting several years.

In late October, after the migrating swifts had all flown south, I met Bob and Mary Ann at the Strictly Organic coffee shop a few blocks away from the downtown chimney. I wanted to know more of what motivates them to come night upon night. They are likely the most dedicated of all swift watchers who count the chimneys along the Pacific Flyway.

Curiosity drew Bob and Mary Ann to the watch two decades earlier, in 2004, when the swifts roosted in a chimney of the old library. Local birders had taken notice, but counts were informal. The site was only blocks from Mary Ann's home, and she was attracted to the spectacle and the ease of bicycling over to join in the count. She worked night shifts as a nurse, so could only come on her off days until retirement.

Bob had questions that kept him coming back. He wondered why their numbers rose and fell. How could you tell if birds stayed an extra night? How did swifts handle wind, rain, smoke, heat, or cold? What about their links to insect numbers? He credits a psychology degree for his love of methods, sampling, and data. In summers, he switches from swifting to mothing, joining individuals across the world in a meticulous community-science project.

Over coffee, they shared stories of early swift watches and the puzzling chimney-shifts, from roosting in the old library to a downtown business in an older house called Christmas Presence. The enamored owner even crafted swift ornaments for sale. In 2009, the swifts moved to the spacious chimney at the Boys and Girls Club.

For swifts to roost, a chimney must be as treelike as possible, without light coming in at the bottom (a signal that a climbing predator could come from below). Within, the birds line up in layers with heads facing upward. One of the challenges is the demise of mortar chimneys. Swifts cannot get a grip in newer metal-lined chimneys.

Only during migrational treks north and south do the swifts gather in communal roosts of up to 55,000, the record for one stunning night at a San Francisco Bay chimney. For thirty years, Portland's Chapman Chimney attracted hundreds of humans to picnic on a grassy slope, mesmerized by up to 20,000 swifts wreathing their roosts. Adding to the drama, sometimes a Cooper's or Sharp-shinned Hawk would wing in to nab a bird. In September of 2024, the swifts abandoned the chimney. A high level of predation there could have been one factor, according to Schwitters, who also pointed to rising numbers of birds roosting 30 miles to the north in the Rainier Riverside Chimney, which reopened in 2019 (closed by a grate before that).

Wherever they roost by thousands in cities and towns, swifts have become unknowing ambassadors. My hope is that the wonder of watchers translates to advocacy for protecting both the old chimneys and our ancient forests.

Seeing great flocks of migrating birds tugs at our deep past. I feel an instinctive yearning when thousands of Snow Geese and Tundra Swans rise like white clouds from a prairie lake, or bugling Sandhill Cranes form flying necklaces above my house.

I'm wearing my stiff new uniform of Montana Fish, Wildlife & Parks—a long-sleeved gray shirt with a big yellow patch featuring a grizzly bear on one sleeve and dark green pants. I'm at Canyon Reservoir near Helena, where I'd recently started my new job as a "nongame information specialist." Hundreds of Bald Eagles chitter, circle, and land to devour the carcasses of a huge run of kokanee salmon. TV cameras from a national network are pointed at me. I take a deep breath, and my jangled nerves calm just enough. I speak of our endangered national symbol that, in the fall of 1989, edged closer to recovery. What I say matters far less than the eagles flying, fishing, and perching in trees. They are majestic. They are scavengers.

Another day, I'm there with a busload of second and third graders, giving my education spiel on the eagles. On the weekend, I return on my own. Several children tug at their parents' hands and urge them over to the water's edge. The eagles are everywhere, but the children are down on their knees with the bright red kokanee salmon—staring glazed eyes and hooked jaws and torn by eagles. I hear the kids repeating what I'd told them about the salmon spawning and dying. I'm thrilled. They brought their parents and were teaching them. I also had an epiphany. Of course they were attracted to the salmon over the eagles. Children love to touch, feel, and be close. I put my hand on a cold clammy fish and my nose wrinkles from the stinky scent. I look up at the eagles flapping wide wings. There is no separation between living and dying and renewing. Touch death. Be like a child, still openhearted, curious, and unaffected by all we deem unpleasant.

Once, 30 to 60 million bison rumbled over the plains. Up to 5 billion Passenger Pigeons gusted over oak and chestnut forests. In the eastern half of the country, their nests covered 870 square miles of oak forests—weighing down and breaking branches. They were keystone species critical to a thriving ecosystem. Hunters shot them from the sky. Loggers cut down the forests. Martha, the last passenger pigeon, died in the Cincinnati zoo in 1914 at age twenty-nine. Like the swifts, they relied on wild forests. There's no second chance for an extinct bird.

Aldo Leopold knew the relationship of pigeons to trees well, as he lamented in a 1947 tribute within his *Sand County Almanac*, "On a Monument to the Pigeon": "Men still live who, in their youth, remember pigeons; trees still live who, in their youth, were shaken by a living wind. But a few decades hence only the oldest oaks will remember, and at long last only the hills will know."[1]

For every starry assemblage of birds that still exists, I am grateful to be alive—staggered by blizzards of snow geese, murmurations of starlings, and a fling of sandpipers. A collective of swifts is not what I would have guessed—a scream. How can that be, when I hear the faint music of the spheres? The reference comes from the high-pitched, wheezy calls of Common Swifts, also suffering from loss of ancient forests across their range in Europe and Asia. A scream sounds straight from Alfred Hitchcock's, *The Birds*. But it gets your attention.

Named for William S. Vaux (1811–1882), a member of the Academy of Natural Sciences of Philadelphia who never saw the bird, the swift deserves better. If I were to choose a name, I'd evoke snags as counterparts to the eastern Chimney Swift. Maybe the Tree-hollow Swift? The renaming ought to come from those most intimate with the birds—like Bob and Mary Ann. Once, when it was stormy and they knew birds might roost early, the pair met at noon and stayed until 7:30 p.m., counting swifts entering not all at once but a few at a time. "We froze our butts off!" Mary Ann recalls. And still the two keep coming back, in wildfire smoke, rain, snow, wind, and heat.

"I like the muted light, sunsets, clouds, moon cycles, seeing satellites and that I can ride my bike or walk here," Mary Ann said. "I'm an outlier in the birdwatching world. I don't drive and blow exhaust into the air to reach the next spot for the next bird, to check off a bird."

"For me it's the spectacle and the miracle," she said. "It's a religious experience."

Bob nods. "Sometimes we see the moon through all the phases and the full moon twice." He's become so fond of the swifts he called them "darling little things."

When the swifts are away, the two continue giving back to the natural world. Bob cares about moths and swifts equally. In North America, there are some 12,000 kinds of moths, compared to about 800 butterfly species. With feathery antennae, furry stocky bodies, nocturnal habits, and a tendency toward the drab, moths tend to be brushed under the rug in favor of butterflies. But among them are spectacular variations like the luna moth, North America's largest, with translucent pale green wings. Some have evolved echolocation to baffle pursuing bats accompanied by barrel rolls, loops, and dives.

To catch moths, Bob sets light traps with egg cartons where the moths find cozy spots to rest. In the morning, he snaps photos, and shakes out the moths unharmed. The photos are his source for identification and reports sent to an international community-science event held the last week of July called Moth Week. His counts are showing a sharp drop in diversity in the last four years. The numbers are similar, but they tend to be the more common moths. Something is going on. He suspects the rapid pace of development in Bend is tearing up their habitats, including the soils, with vulnerable pupae only a few inches down.

Moths suffer from light pollution, toxic sprays, and likely losses we do not yet know. Diminishing moths harm the swifts that depend on them as part of their winged insect diet. Songbirds feed caterpillars to their young. Wildflowers need certain moths for pollination. Every kind of moth has a role. Extinction of one leads to an unraveling of the web.

Mary Ann has not caught the moth counting bug, but she has taken her love of swifts to educating others on the importance of dark skies and turning off lights that disorient and lead to the deaths of a billion nocturnal migrating birds annually. Even swifts are not safe. In 2019, hundreds of Chimney Swifts died when they crashed into the brightly lit NASCAR Hall of Fame in North Carolina. The swifts were out past dark, possibly because they could not find a roost chimney to rest. Buildings with reflective glass deceive swifts and many birds into flying right into them. They're caught in wind turbines, too. Given all the obstacles we throw in their way, the least we can do is save historic chimneys and the great forests, too.

I have known swifts in the wild, but only overhead. When I'd first shared my longing to see swifts roost in a tree, Mary Ann forwarded a September 9, 2024, email from Larry Schwitters. The subject line was "Into the Wilderness." There he shared his initial musing of a possible missing roost in a forest. In the past year, the swifts changed their southbound course from Vancouver, Washington, after finding a chimney opened by birders in the town of Rainier on the Columbia River, an hour's drive west of Portland. The new chimney meant the birds had found a shorter route south, but now they were short a roost in between.

Right away he thought of Olympic National Park. "No chimneys in the park but lots of big old trees," he wrote. On cue, he received an email from Melinda Wood, new to the watching of swifts. She'd found a tree roost in the park—off a popular trail by Lake Cushman, and right in line from Victoria, BC, to Rainier, Oregon—a little less than halfway. The first night [illegible]he was able to count about 500 and then, on returns, 4,100 and 3,300. "That's [illegible]ld," wrote Larry.

[illegible]he fall southward migration wasn't quite over. I entered the destination [illegible]y phone's Google map—six hours northwest of Bend. Could I get to [illegible]Cushman and join her on this west side of Olympic National Park? I [illegible]ommitment to speak about kingfishers at the Wings Over Willapa bird [illegible] on the Long Beach Peninsula of Washington. There, I'd also be hiking [illegible] Island in Willapa Bay among some of the oldest remaining western [illegible]—some a thousand years old—and protected at the last minute [illegible]g. But I couldn't add the three hours it would take, because of a [illegible]o return to Bend. I contacted Melinda, who first sent me two [illegible]eos.

[illegible]ave pegged the tree for a swift roost. In one video clip, the [illegible]r with a slight lean and a plethora of green needles in the [illegible]ue. About 15 feet down from the top, a sturdy limb grew off [illegible]m bent at the elbow. There at the juncture with the tree was [illegible]ed by needles. The swifts swarmed into the hole like bees [illegible]

[illegible]Melinda on Zoom, I noticed an Audubon print of Belted [illegible]e wall behind her—a good sign for a sympatico interview. [illegible]ith wide-set eyes of forest green, long dark hair the color [illegible] a last name of Wood, she seemed destined to be the finder. [illegible] and her acuity for birds that led her to the rare sight of swifts [illegible] like fish into the depths. On the fateful evening, she was hiking by Lake Cushman with her boyfriend.

"We had just started and I heard twittering and looked up at a cloud of swifts," she said. They searched and stayed until dark and strained to see the birds. "We could see tons of snags in the forest, but it was hard to get a good visual from the trail." They estimated at least five hundred birds gathered. She was back the next day, navigating the hour-and-fifteen-minute drive from her home in Olympia. She'd checked with the park ranger to assure she had permission to head off-trail. "Then I saw them pouring into the hole!" From September 5 through 26, she hiked to the tree at least twice a week. It felt eerie to be alone, she said, hearing strange sounds, and stumbling off-trail in the dark.

New to counting swifts but not to bird counts, Melinda brought her write-in-the-rain notebook and put a tally for every hundred, noting the birds

in groups of ten plus stragglers. She took videos to document the coun
Melinda noticed some swifts appeared to land among the high-up branc
for a few seconds and "flutter up like bats and then funnel down" befor
descent into the hollow.

However, from so far below perhaps landing was an illusion, since
cannot perch. But perhaps they did find purchase on an outer edge of th
for an instant? Some evenings, the swifts tumbled in and others in shor
Once, an osprey landed on a nearby treetop. Melinda heard Norther
Owls and Barred Owls.

Olympic National Park is a bastion of biodiversity among a
ging and development. The coastal park protects close to a mil
95 percent is designated wilderness. Within the boundary is a
tem, ranging from lowland ancient forests to the high glacier
National Park. More than 300 bird species find home here.

The swifts from Melinda's roost would journey south ov
tations, second growth, interstates, industry, and towns.
the older forest and staying for hours to watch and listen, s
loss beyond the park. But young and at the beginning of he
optimism for all that's still left in the world.

Birds came into Melinda's life naturally, growing up wit
gist father who tracked endangered Marbled Murrelets at se
Evergreen State College, earning an undergraduate degree i
studies and a master's in ornithology. Among other fieldwork, s
Pigeon Guillemot nests around Puget Sound as a volunteer for the
Guillemot Network. Her dream is a full-time job working with birds on the Pacific Flyway. Speaking with Melinda at the cusp of a career with birds in uncertain times, I asked her if she had any last thoughts about the watch.

"I wish I had found the roost sooner and wish I had been on more counts."

Scrambling through bushes, hiking out in the dark, and driving in traffic—all this was worth it. Planning to return the next spring and autumn, Melinda demonstrates the intrepid nature of a field biologist.

Far from Olympic National Park in northeastern Oregon, a woman biologist defined the meaning of intrepid starting in the 1980s. In a male-dominated field focused on deer and elk, Evelyn Bull studied the underdogs or "nongame"

the inside and conducting water upward) and the phloem (toward the outside and transporting sugars and nutrients from leaves downward).

Swifts depend on trees living with the fungus for at least 120 years. The cooler and moister the forests the better for the fungus, too, along with trees of different ages and structures. The natural hollows of living and dead trees buffer them from rising temperatures. Evelyn documented that the ambient air temperature within tree cavities is 5 degrees Fahrenheit cooler than inside nest boxes.[6]

As part of my early 1980s seasonal work examining stands of trees on the Malheur National Forest (a couple hours from Evelyn's study forests), I counted the conks on grand fir trunks to label a tree as a "cull" or worthless. Now I know that a single conk indicates about 40 feet of decayed heartwood above and below. Trees with multiple conks all the way up mean the entire tree could be a chimney. Even then, I felt disturbed by the term "cull." If timber "stand exams" were wildlife exams, the multiple conks would earn not the lowest but the very highest of values. Native fungi steer the forest like the feathered tails in flight. Our wild forests are not a collection of trees to be cut and planted anew or thinned like carrots in a garden.

Isn't it time to see through the eyes of swifts? Up high in the branches of Traverse in the Andrews Forest, I had a swift's-eye view of the living and dead spires, broken tops, spreading crowns, and canopy gaps. I could hear the song of Lookout Creek. As seekers of hollows, the birds traverse the tops of trees and swoop down into the forests. Not any woodpecker hole will do—only the Pileated creates the openings big enough for entry. Not any broken top will do—the tree must have a deep enough hollow without light from below.

While the grand firs are exceptional, other trees can yield roosts, like the Douglas-fir in the Olympic National Park. I found a video of Vaux's Swifts entering a hollow cottonwood tree in Washington north of the Columbia River. The chimney by San Francisco cocooning 50,000 swifts hints at what a gargantuan redwood tree once provided.

As the great forests have fallen, so Vaux's Swift numbers have dropped, estimated to be half as numerous since 1970. In the east, the saga of Chimney Swifts is similar, with even more plummets—70 percent fewer than in 1966, the year our family moved to Mount Rainier National Park, still a wild citadel for swifts in the ancient forests. Within a 1939 "Nature Notes" for the park is this entry about Vaux's Swifts:

> They have not yet shown much attachment to our civilization, but we have one or two chimney-nesting records. Their natural nesting site is some hollow snag in the forest into which they drop from above. The birds may be considered almost common in the park, and are recorded near the boundaries on all sides.[7]

Back then, the Vaux's Swifts were the wild ones compared to the Chimney Swifts, with few chimney-nesting records. After the felling of forests, both species need chimneys in our diminished world. National Wildlife and other conservation nonprofits have put out calls to preserve old chimneys for the birds and to build nest towers. A friend who is an expert in home efficiency installs an insulating kind of balloon at the base of chimneys to prevent drafts of air, while still providing birds with roosts.

But chimneys will never be enough for swifts. Like all living beings, three components are the essentials for survival—shelter, water, and food. Insect numbers have dropped a frightening 75 percent worldwide in what scientists are calling the insect apocalypse.

If the sweep of swifts over chimneys is to continue, we must care a whole lot more about insects. Pesticides are deadly to nature's aerial insect bird predators—swifts, swallows, flycatchers, nighthawks, poorwills, and whip-poor-wills keeping this Earth in dynamic balance. If statistics fail to move us to change, then perhaps birds in abundance can awaken all who sleepwalk.

Bob and Mary Ann's nightly vigil at the Bend chimney is more than a tally. It's prayer, an offering, and a homage to the wild birds. The counters are taking the wild pulse of the planet. When the pulse weakens, our pulse becomes fainter, too.

Diversity is refugia. What happens in the forest happens to us. Every species that goes extinct harms the web on which we cling like roosting swifts. Keep the chimneys. Keep counting. Become guardians of hollows and snags. Know that a tree's heartwood can fill with the hearts of birds.

SIXTEEN

Hermit Warbler

Beacon of Two Worlds

I'm holding a Hermit Warbler—my right hand cupped gently under the bird as my left forefinger and middle finger cradle his neck. The fine feathered warmth pulses with radiant life. When I open my left hand, he rockets upward in a dandelion-yellow and black fluff. Landing for a nanosecond on a hemlock branch, the newly banded bird wings high into the overstory. My heart skips a beat. I turn to the bird banding crew and see my grin reflected in their expressions. On a sunny early June day in the higher elevations of the Andrews Forest, I knew astonishment.

Joining a small flock of fellow Hermit Warblers, this valiant songbird felt far too fragile to have flown thousands of miles, touching down in late April or early May. The window is narrow for defending a territory, courting, mating, nesting, and raising chicks to depart by late June to mid-July.

One Hermit Warbler, banded at the Andrews and equipped with a data logger weighing less than a paperclip, completed a round trip of 6,475 miles. The fall route to Mexico took three months, to give time for molting and renewing feathers in the early part of the trek south. In spring, he was bursting with speed, reaching the Andrews in fifty days, averaging about 62 miles per day.[1]

The male flew home to the same trees where he had been caught a year earlier. To return to the same nest site is to be philopatric, a quality many kinds of birds share. "Philo" stems from the Greek *philos* (love of) and the Latin *patria* (homeland or fatherland). So often, trees are treated simply as "renewable resources." What if we thought of each one as a homeland for a returning bird?

Susceptible to the effects of heat and reliant on the cool microclimates unique to ancient forests, a Hermit Warbler is the lemony beacon of ancient tree crowns. Preferring mountainous terrain and nesting trees at least 150 feet tall, the songbird gleans for insects among the tousled, spired, living, dead, and canopy gardens. Sun finds a rival in the canary yellow face, dapper black chin, and white breast. The polished eye, back, and wing feathers match the darkest of nights. Wingbars are moon-white.

I can think of no better poster songbird for protecting our tallest, heaviest, and most carbon-capturing forests in the world. I'm not pushing out the resident Northern Spotted Owl as the endangered icon of the Pacific Northwest. Rather, I'm adding a bird with tropical panache and a love of high places. Declines are worrisome—a rate of 4 percent per year, or almost 30 percent in the past fifty years. But that drop in numbers is lower or even reversed for Hermit Warblers lucky enough to nest in the relict old-growth forests.

As every wild place has a story, so does every bird. Some hold their secrets close, like the Hermit Warbler singing far above the forest floor. When I listen to the piccolo notes, I hear *sing-song-sing-song . . . triple-time-tuee!* But what are the birds really saying?

Nina Ferrari took to the trees to expand bird field studies from the ground into three dimensions. After the Lookout Fire, Nina returned in 2024 to scale several unburned trees for a new chapter of her PhD dissertation. Pausing every 15 meters up, she played birdsongs and recorded responses to map territories. She soon noticed patterns. Hermit Warblers tended to favor the crowns but would wing down to check out a territorial recorded call. Western Flycatchers preferred the midstory, where they could foray out from a branch in an airy opening to snatch a flying insect and then zip back.

Pacific Wrens and Swainson's Thrushes stayed low, but Hermit Thrushes would fly up a little higher. Golden-crowned Kinglets bounced around every level. Chestnut-backed Chickadees surprised her with how high up they tended to stay. The birds appear to have niches, and some show more elasticity than others.

Of all the songbirds responding to playback calls at every 15 meters, the Hermit Warbler males are the feistiest and most territorial. "They like the canopy but would come down to every part of the tree and were glued to me during playback," she said. "I'd have three or four Hermit Warblers coming in."

The willingness of the warblers to check out an aggressor may be a clue that males, females, and fledglings are flexible enough to fly lower for heat relief, too. The feathered forest acts as an air conditioner. High in the canopy, millions of needles release water the trees have sucked up all the way from roots. From redcedars with their winglike branches and western hemlocks with feathery nodding tops to Douglas-firs with candelabra trunks, the trees are misting the air. Air streaming across the ocean of treetops trips up on the pointy, ruffled tree crowns. As turbulence pushes warm air up, a cooler downdraft forms. That's where the deep pool effect comes in tier by tier until reaching the lowest haunts of Pacific Wrens and Varied Thrushes.

From Nina's analysis of her prefire studies recording temperature and humidity at different tree heights, she's finding patterns. Every night, the forest cools and resets temperatures to be similar from canopy to understory. In summer, a thermal gradient forms during the day. For the second-growth trees, it's a smooth gradual line from warmest at the top to coldest at the bottom. However, in the taller, multidimensional old-growth forest, there's a cool plateau in the midstory with lower temperatures at the forest floor.

The canopy creates a microclimate. Among the shadows, light, branches, trunks, and twigs, songbirds are sorting, sifting, preening feathers, weaving nests, hiding, probing, roosting, hovering, hawking, flicking, snapping, leaping, laddering, and winging.

In winter, Hermit Warblers know tropical montane forests as home without the responsibility of raising a family. When it's time to head north in early spring, they loft into the night on flight paths that vary. Lightness, strength, and oxygen are the superpowers of migrating birds. Hollow bones gain support from internal struts. To breathe, birds have nine air sacs extending from the lungs throughout the body and into bone cavities. The sacs work like bellows that store air and deliver oxygen, assuring lungs are constantly refreshed. I can inhale the forest air fragrant in ferns, moss, and leaves, but on the exhale my lungs deflate and then refill. Not so for birds. Imagine what the world record for the mile might be if runners' lungs were constantly oxygenated.

To wing back to the Andrews from Mexico, the warbler I held had navigated by the stars, the Earth's magnetism, and cues that scientists have yet to grasp. Headwinds, downdrafts, and storms posed hazards, worsened by climate change. He'd survived a gauntlet of artificial lights, skyscrapers, glass windows, and stalking outdoor cats. To rest and refuel during the daytime, the avian ultramarathoner looked down from the sky for welcoming green canopies. Perhaps he sheltered in a native-plant-and-tree-filled yard. Like steppingstones across a river, the wild habitats must not be too far apart or the birds can't make the jump.

What I could not know from cupping the warbler in my hands is another likely miracle located within the bird's gut microbiome. A study of Blackpoll Warblers in western Canada found the bacteria shifted before fall migration, from multiple microbes to one kind that specializes in genes facilitating building muscles and metabolizing carbohydrates for energy.[2] Doubling their body mass before liftoff, the Blackpoll Warblers perform legendary migrations, the longest known of any North American warbler. Some fly 5,000 miles one way from Alaska to Brazil. Two thousand of those miles are over the Atlantic in nonstop flights of up to eighty-eight hours. Their lives are enmeshed with the boreal forest stretching across Alaska and Canada and the tropics. In winter, sightings have ranged from cloud forests to mangrove forests to coffee plantations that retain native tree diversity. They may be most plentiful on island trees of major rivers. Like every kind of neotropical migratory bird, Blackpoll Warblers point to what we must save—diversity, diversity, diversity. Globally.

Hermit Warblers, too, add body weight for migrations and likely have changes in their microbiomes. The bird I held faces a challenge that especially affects long-distance migratory songbirds. Climate mismatch. Warmer temperatures in spring are leading to flowers blooming and insects emerging earlier. Warblers time their nesting periods so chicks will hatch when insects are most abundant. The farther away they spend their winters, the less likely they are to have any warnings of an earlier spring.

However, the ancient forests have backups, because of high arthropod diversity. Plants are leafing and insects emerging throughout the nesting season. A logged and simplified forest hosts far fewer species. There, birds could easily miss a singular peak and struggle to keep their chicks fed. It's like an organic farm that provides daily harvests of the latest ripening vegetables compared with an industrial farm growing monocultures.

Our central Oregon yard stirs with birds and bumblebees as I write about distant Hermit Warblers on a July day. If I drove an hour west, I'd find their homes in the verdant Cascades. Meanwhile, thickets of goldenrod and aster that will bloom in fall are hip to head high. Native clematis vine blooms in creamy clusters that twine over the tops of manzanita and ceanothus shrubs. Bunchgrasses spray like fountains from the sunniest spots. Milkweed, penstemon, Oregon sunshine, blanketflowers, fireweed, lupine, columbine, spirea, wild strawberries, and yarrow are flowering. Each have their own strategies in shape, color, fragrance, and timing to call in just the right pollinators Caterpillars co-evolved with native plants like fireweed, which hosts the larvae of Yellow-Banded Day Sphinx, a hawk moth that mimics a bumblebee. An iridescent green fly the size of a peppercorn lands on a leaf. A spiderweb links our mason bee house to the clematis vine. We are still waiting for imperiled monarch butterflies to find our milkweed.

I'm a giantess walking in a mini-forest. Spotted Towhees, Dark-eyed Juncos, American Robins, and California Quail often burst from deep cover of ceanothus and manzanita bushes. The more native plant diversity, in kind, number, heights, clusters, and varied times of blooming, going to seed, and producing berries, the more varied the insects will be, and the more birds will find the smorgasbord they require to raise chicks. Still, our yard is a one-story home. The feathered forest skyscrapers supply vertical living arrangements to please the choosiest of residents. Everywhere there is multiculturalism sparking the creativity that is evolution.

From watching birds outside my home, I know intimacy. Red Crossbills that often cross the sky from pine to pine drink from our water baths, one with a bubbler feature. A Rufous Hummingbird hovers by my ear as I fill feeders. A second male bursts in from a bare branch. The two zip sideways and upward in a tussle of two lit matches never touching.

We often have two nesting pairs of hummingbirds finding mini-refuge. Like the Hermit Warbler, the dervish of a bird dwells in two worlds, multiplying risks. The Rufous has the record for longest hummingbird migration, some nesting as far north as British Columbia and Alaska and flying to Mexico. As coppery and light as one US penny, the slip of a bird whizzes south by way of mountain wildflower meadows filled with wild nectar. But with lower snowpacks melting faster, the flowers dependent on snow have a precarious future. Along coastal mountains, there are toxins from herbicides sprayed by the timber industry on the flowering shrubs coming up in clear-cuts. Rufous Hummingbird numbers have dropped by 65 percent since 1970, with losses accelerating twofold in the past couple decades. In their presence, I'm at once in awe with an undercurrent of worry.

In our yard, I can channel feathered forests like the Andrews. There, a Rufous Hummingbird flew right up to Nina's enticingly orange helmet as she spidered her way up a very tall tree. The day before I held the Hermit Warbler, I'd tagged along with Nina, helping pack ropes and gear to several hefty and very tall firs she climbed to retrieve temperature, humidity, and audio data as part of her larger study.

When Matt Betts invited me to join a bird-banding crew, I was thrilled. Pedaling my bike from Mona Campground at dawn, I thought of the last time I'd helped banders, in 2019 at Big Bald Mountain.

I'm at the Big Bald Banding Station on the Appalachian Trail bordering North Carolina and Tennessee. The dawn sky is the brooding gray of catbirds. My arms ache from lugging bird-banding gear. A singing Chestnut-sided Warbler kindles the flame azaleas emblazoning green grassy ridges. Soon, we're setting up the banding table and twelve mist nets. There's no hanging back. Under the guidance of biologist Mark Hopey, the small crew flurries into action. While not trained to free birds caught in the net, I learn to place them in paper bags, label each one, and hustle to the banding station.

Best of all, Mark sends me off to release two Tufted Titmice close to where they had darted into a net, one after the other. I am alone and thinking of my father who had backpacked this Appalachian Trail section more than once. In his journals, he often wrote of the vireos, warblers, and tanagers gracing his spring hikes. How I longed for him to be standing by me on this June day of 2019. When I'd pulled each bird from their paper bags carefully, as taught, it was as if my father's hands held the silky gray birds with the dashing crests. When the birds flew one after the other down into a thicket, my spirit longed to race after my father's to see him again.

Parking my bike at the Andrews Headquarters at dawn, I waved at Matt Betts. As a hands-on director of Long-Term Ecological Research, he likes nothing better than to be in the field humbly lending a hand. This was twenty-year-old Adlai Herrera's day to shine as an undergraduate from Cal Poly Humboldt.

She'd taken on a study to identify insect diets of ten songbird species, including the Hermit Warbler. The six of us were there to help her.

To know who eats what gives insights into the dynamics of predator and prey within a wild forest. What role do different birds play in the well-being of the ecosystem? The questions are big. The sampling sounds far simpler. But collecting bird poop for later DNA analysis can be hit or miss.

Adlai, who is of Mexican descent, wore her thick brown hair pulled back from her smooth oval face. She smiled often. Growing up in the Central Valley near Fresno, she never paid attention to birds until taking a freshman introductory science class. The professor assigned the students to spend a half an hour alone with the Merlin app listening to birdsong. "I started realizing the world is filled with birds and I wanted to know them," she said. "At home, I'd sit by canals in wetlands and watch and listen to herons, egrets, ducks, and blackbirds." Adlai took more classes, worked in ornithologist Matt Johnson's lab, and applied for and got a funded research position through him. Humboldt is one of several universities that come to the Andrews for studies. Matt was there on this day to give her a hand and guidance as needed.

That morning, Adlai hoped to catch a Black-throated Gray Warbler, a nimble bird of leafy hardwoods able to find shade under a branch or fly to the canopy to bask in the sun. We headed to low-elevation forest within earshot of Lookout Creek. Bigleaf maples cloaked in moss and cottonwoods intermingled with Douglas-firs. The air felt as alive as maidenhair ferns spreading their feathery hands. The riparian trees offer nesting habitat for Black-throated Grays that winter in western Mexico and follow coastal ranges north to arrive by April, one of the earlier warblers. They also fare well in dryer, brushy forests. Females line their nest cups with hundreds of feathers from a multiplicity of birds.

I helped set up one of the two sets of mist nets, remembering how to take nets out of the bag without tangling, slip them onto tall poles, and pull the fine black mesh across an opening. Divided into two groups, we were silent as Adlai played calls of a male Black-throated Gray Warbler. Right away, a male landed 40 feet above where I crouched. But he would not fly to the net. Instead, we were treated to his song of *zeedle zeedle zeedle zeet-chee!*

After more unsuccessful tries, the teams switched gears and lured in two Pacific Wrens, two Hammond's Flycatchers, a Swainson's Thrush, and a Warbling Vireo into the mist nets. The banders followed ethical protocols to untangle, take measurements, and band each bird with a numbered ring.

Adlai's study also required poop collecting by placing a bird in a paper bag fitted with a simple white card at the bottom. She set the timer for five minutes to reduce stress. After releasing the bird, she'd pull out the card, hoping for droppings to scrape off and into an alcohol-filled vial. The vial would be analyzed in a lab using DNA techniques to identify spiders, mites, caterpillars, and a kaleidoscope of other protein-packed delicacies. Often the white card was bare. When a Hammond's Flycatcher left a sample, Adlai and Matt cheered.

Gathering up nets and gear, four of us drove higher along Lookout Creek to the trailhead for the Carpenter Mountain fire lookout. A short way up, we set up a net. Right away, we caught a MacGillivray's Warbler, a Dark-eyed Junco, a Hermit Thrush, and the Hermit Warbler that flew from my hands like a wish.

When finished, we hiked to the lookout. Valley clouds puffed by like white smoke above conifers packed tight as a jostling crowd. High-elevation Pacific silver fir and noble firs slendered the sky over headwaters. I drank in the top-of-the-world feeling and views of wild forests that have never seen a road, even while lamenting distant clear-cuts.

The fateful lightning strike that started the Lookout Fire was still two months away. The first low-elevation bird banding site would be spared, but not where I held the Hermit Warbler. The nesting season is short, so likely the birds had left. But what would it be, upon return, to find a familiar home drastically changed?

When bird field crews surveyed in 2024 and 2025, their inventories showed the long-distance migrants did come back, including Hermit Warblers, and sometimes even in higher numbers.[3] The fire burned in a mosaic, leaving unburned areas as refugia. It's possible the birds displaced by the fire packed in with neighboring warblers into smaller spaces. The burn also attracted new postfire-loving birds, from Mountain Bluebirds to Black-backed Woodpeckers and Lazuli Buntings.

The death of centuries-old trees when so few remain is still hard no matter how much I value their afterlife. When the verdure of a familiar forest is gone, it takes training to regard the forest after the burn anew. Birds can take me there. Life goes on—if we honor the sanctity of natural renewal.

At Cape Meares on the Oregon coast where I wrote of the Climate Guardian Sitka spruce, the Hermit Warblers are faring poorly. Each year, they're raising Brown-headed Cowbird chicks twice the size of the warblers. While the 15-acre refuge is a critical ancient forest headland, it's popular with visitors, small, and too near Tillamook, where sprawling dairy farms attract the native cowbird that evolved the lay-eggs-in-other-birds'-nests strategy to keep up with moving herds of elk or in places where bison kick up swarms of insects. Yellow Warblers, long familiar with cowbirds sharing forest edges and streamsides, can spy an unwanted cowbird egg and will build a nest on top and start over. They also give an alarm *seeeet* call when spotting an intruder—a signal to guard a nest and sit tight. The alarm benefits other birds. But interior forest nesting birds like Hermit Warblers have no defenses.

Always I grapple with the fault of being human and wreaking such havoc. Then, I'm comforted by the fine scientists who are making a difference on behalf of our winged brethren. We can't save what we don't understand.

Hankyu Kim, an assistant professor of biology at Kyung Hee University in Seoul, South Korea, studied the migration and summer homes of Hermit Warblers, detailing their flight paths and wintering forests for the first time. His meticulous research for his 2021 PhD also offered the first empirical evidence of Hermit Warblers and several other songbirds benefiting from the microclimates and biodiversity of ancient forests.[4]

I interviewed him in late 2020 for an assigned *BirdWatching* magazine article on tracking tools for bird migration. To catch, band, and equip 150 Hermit Warblers with geolocators over two seasons was far from easy. He caught the birds at six sites, in Washington, Oregon, and northern California, including Yosemite. The Andrews Forest was formative for much of his research. To lure a warbler down from high up in the canopy, Hankyu would set up a painted male decoy on a branch and play the male's song recording. If fooled, a male would fly down from upper branches to confront the intruder and end up in a mist nest. They soon became wary. "One bird took six hours to catch," he said. We tried many different net formations."

Hankyu used nontoxic eyelash glue to attach geolocators to the backs of birds, and smooth looped cords he designed for harnesses. As the first to track Hermit Warblers long distance, he took care to prevent any possible tangling or skin abrasions from the harness. "I've worked with so many birds, I have confidence on my tagging techniques," he said. "The main principle is to be safe for the bird and safe for the tag."

At the nesting season's close, the warblers flew south with their mini-packs recording ambient light levels periodically to determine locations. The next summer, his team recaptured twenty-two males right where they had banded them. Nine were at the Andrews Forest. In their slower trek south, while molting along the way, the Oregon and Washington warblers tended to follow the Cascades and the Sierra Nevada Mountains through the Central Valley, into Arizona and New Mexico and then Mexico. One flew all the way to Los Angeles before shifting southeast. The birds had scattered to winter far apart from each other in Mexico, from Chiapas near the Guatemala border to the western Chihuahua. Migration is hard on birds and some didn't make it back, while others eluded recapture. Not all the tags stayed on.

A brief breeding season adds to the Hermit Warbler's vulnerability. So much must click in like clockwork—defending territories, courting, mating, nesting, and fledging. Hankyu and co-authors, in a separate study at the Andrews Forest, found that the complex structure of old-growth forests combined with micro-topographies of swales and nurse logs, along with higher elevations, all add up to critical microclimates for Hermit Warblers, Wilson's Warblers, Chestnut-backed Chickadees, Swainson's Thrushes, and Varied Thrushes.[5]

Hankyu also documented evidence of the "insurance effect" for Red Crossbills and Wilson's Warblers.[6] Crossbills count on bountiful conifer seeds to coincide with raising chicks hatched within cup nests high up in trees on branches close to the trunks. Warmer, dryer conditions lead to earlier cone ripening, which could spell disaster within a monoculture of planted Douglas-firs. Add multiple tree species and the birds are assured there will be closed cones to crack open with those precise crossed bills. The older the trees, the more cones they produce. The generous crowns of centuries-old Douglas-firs proliferate in cones, with twenty to thirty times more than found in second-growth trees of less than a hundred years.

Far below the crossbills, Wilson's Warblers conceal nests at the base of shrubs, logs, saplings, wildflowers, ferns, or grasses. Because the understory is swimming in leafing, flowering, berrying, fern unfurling, crisscrossed stems, saplings and shrubs, the warblers can raise chicks with a full pantry. If some caterpillars hatch earlier with climate change, others will be munching later.

All is connected—from crown to ground. Where Hermit Warblers sing dawn songs in the high canopies, the great trees stretch their branch wings, fluff their feathers, and guard all who live far below. When I'm in a wild forest I feel as safe as a bird chick in a concealed nest. Here, too, Red Crossbills crack open ripe cones. Golden-crowned Kinglets trip along nipping insects. Vaux's Swifts waft like smoke from a tree chimney. Chestnut-backed Chickadees pop up from the midstory to join the feasting on arthropods crawling, hopping, and spinning silk. All is in dynamic balance of predator and prey.

A showy close relative of the Hermit Warbler dwells in the canopies of the oldest trees of the Andrews Forest in summertime too, a bird with a stunning yellow ring around a black ear patch. Covering a much larger nesting range of Cascadia, the Townsend's Warbler has an affiliation for the mixed conifer forests I've come to know in the Blue Mountains. Like clouds are to rain, bees are to pollen, and sun is to shadow, so are these warblers to lush, unlogged, and naturally dense ancient forests. A female Townsend's Warbler laces spider cocoons, lichens, moss, and animal fur to form a cup nest on a concealed branch of a tree of great girth. Her mate shields her from harm. Ethereal melodies give voice to the wind stirring the unfolding of bud, cone, and hatching insects. In the presence of this warbler, I know the meaning of inseparable.

We are inseparable from the great forests of Cascadia, and from all who share the planet. To change course toward a far safer pathway, we might look to neotropical migrants—warblers, tanagers, vireos, flycatchers, buntings, swallows, thrushes, hummingbirds, swifts, and nighthawks. Flying without passports, they erase the artificiality of walls and international borders with every wingbeat. There's no enemy on the other side. Why not dismantle all standing military armies? Be like Costa Rica. Open our borders. Share humanitarian aid. Build schools and libraries. Protect nature with half the planet at least as wild. Dream big of a more peaceful, tolerant future. Birds fire up our imagination without a nagging little voice saying, "that's impossible!"

On a hike below a singing Hermit Warbler in another Cascades forest by the South Santiam River, I jotted down the mnemonics as *sleepyhead-sleepy-head-sleepy head . . . are you getting up?* Shake ourselves awake. Stop looking at our feet and trudging the set trail. Run our fingers through a fallen feather. Be alert for a flashing beacon in the trees. Find our flock and fly so close we give uplift to every companion.

SEVENTEEN

Marbled Murrelet

Sea to Tree to Sea

Marbled Murrelets are flying overhead on fast-beating wings that never glide. As dawn unfolds, the seabirds are whizzing to and from the Pacific Ocean a mile away. Alone in a hidden mossy bed on a wide platform branch high up in a Sitka spruce, a fuzzy chick waits for a parent to land with a fish. Perhaps the imperiled murrelets should be called sea-tree-birds. Their flights bind two ecosystems into one. They nest at dizzying tree heights and ride the stormiest of ocean waves.

I catch my breath at the first sighting of my life. Dove-sized. Very dark. Pointed wings are a blur of speed. A murrelet's cruising rate is 50 miles per hour and double that at full power. During peak feeding times before fledging, each parent may feed their chick up to four times daily, typically at dawn and dusk, but occasionally midday as well. While some birds raise their young in conifers near the ocean, others fly far to find sanctuary. The farthest occupied nest found in Oregon so far is 47 miles inland. In Alaska, murrelets may nest 60 miles from the ocean. Doing the math for one parent alone, that would be 120 miles round trip times four, or 460 miles in one day. Unfathomable.

Two more birds hurl across the ancient forest gap above me. In a half hour, I'd counted a baker's dozen of thirteen. They flew singly or in twos or threes. Sometimes their flights were like darts flung at a target and at other times a wide circling. By 6:30 a.m., the sky caught the eastward glance of sun and turned from gray to flax blue tinged in wispy clouds. Chestnut-backed Chickadees sprinkled notes and Steller's Jays rained guttural calls into the new day. Rimmed in droopy hemlock and stiff spruce tops, the gap formed a free-form window. As my craning neck stiffened, I kept staring up. One blink and I'd miss a murrelet.

I'm at the Cape Perpetua Campground of the Siuslaw National Forest in Oregon, and within a murrelet mecca. Nearby at Devil's Churn and Cook's Chasm, waves funnel, shoot, and spray like geysers from the black basalt volcanic rock. Extending from the Cape five miles south to Tenmile Creek and three miles out to sea is a Marine Reserve, teeming with life. There, wildlife catch the fish and people do not. The feathered forests include the sumptuous trees of Gwynn Creek, where earlier in spring I'd hiked among trillium blooms seeking chickadees.

For two hundred years, the seabirds kept their nests a mystery to Euro-Americans, but not to the Indigenous peoples. Of all North America's birds, the Marbled Murrelet eluded western scientists longer than any others. The "discovery" of a chick in a nest in 1974 rippled through the world. The unwitting finder was expert climber Hoyt Foster, a tree surgeon cutting snowstorm-damaged limbs 148 feet up an enormous Douglas-fir, a half mile from the visitor center of Big Basin Redwoods State Park. He'd almost cut a big mossy branch when he noticed a fuzzy chick with webbed feet. When Hoyt tried to rescue the bizarre bird, the chick fell—fluttering and bouncing down through needled limbs and landing unharmed. The park, about eight miles inland in California's Santa Cruz Mountains, proved to be a hot spot for an isolated population of murrelets until a massive 2020 wildfire. Some still nest there, and others are trying to pack into the islands of old redwoods to the north. Their choices are slim.

Marbled Murrelets range from coastal Alaska and British Columbia south to Washington, Oregon, and California. No one knows the historical population, but likely well over a million birds flourished when Cascadia coastal forests were wild and the seas swarmed with krill, sandlance, herring, and anchovy—all part of the birds' diet. The Tlingit of Alaska revered the Marbled Murrelet as the Mother of Raven. One name meant they "just ruffle up the water," according to author Maria Mudd Ruth in her 2005 book, *Rare Bird: Pursuing the Mystery of the Marbled Murrelet.*[1]

In a 2014 published study of southeast Alaska, researchers tracked thirty-three murrelets and made the surprising find that half nested not in old-growth trees but instead chose steep talus slopes with waterfalls and hanging glaciers. Biologists have found just one ground nest in the Lower 48, on a cliff within the Olympic Mountains.[2]

About 70 percent (around 300,000) of Marbled Murrelets are in Alaska, according to BirdLife International.[3] Oregon's bird numbers are second, at about 9,500, double the populations in Washington and California. The International Union for Conservation of Nature (IUCN) lists the Marbled Murrelet as globally endangered and declining. The murrelet's future is tied to the 1973 Endangered Species Act (ESA) remaining strong, to preserve older coastal forests the birds cannot live without.

In 1992, Marbled Murrelets in Washington, Oregon, and California were added to the ESA as a threatened species. With climate change causing havoc, protecting wild forests and restoring depleted fisheries is critical. The murrelets lead us to the meaning of sustenance—for all species and for this planet in peril.

To witness a bird at the edge of extinction is an uneasy kind of thrill—like tossing love, heartbreak, exuberance, sorrow, reverence, and a dash of hope into a blender. The concoction fuels a commitment to activism that's no longer existential. I desperately want murrelets to recover. Right along the Oregon coast, flocks of Brown Pelicans soar, flap, and lift on cushions of air above the waves. They, too, teetered on the edge after plume hunting, killing, overfishing, and then the pesticide DDT sent numbers plummeting. Listed under the Endangered Species Act in 1970, Brown Pelicans flew off the ESA list in 2009—a success story of banning DDT in 1972, combined with protection and careful management. Still vulnerable, the fish-eating birds have recently suffered from waves of starvation.

Behind every species' recovery story are the scientists, environmentalists, Indigenous stewards, and volunteers stepping up not for financial return but for moral, ecological, and spiritual return. Whether a profession or not, the work generates a shared calling. To join in is akin to clinking cups around a campfire in camaraderie.

I'd come a day early to participate in the annual mid-July community-science Marbled Murrelet survey, organized by the Bird Alliance of Oregon (formerly Portland Audubon). Arguably one of the most effective bird advocacy groups in the United States, the century-old alliance led the efforts in the late 1980s to add murrelets to the ESA and to up-list them in 2021 as an Oregon state endangered species.

In the prelude of my solo watch, I gave a start. A Belted Kingfisher swooshed by at eye level, giving a definitive "I know you are there!" rattle, and landed on a red alder limb flexing over the mossy stony creek. I took the visitation from my favorite bird as a sign of good luck.

Indeed, the next morning our group would detect murrelets ninety times, likely from forty to fifty birds coming and going from nests. The survey is precisely from 5:10 a.m. to 7:10 a.m. Often, the birds gave clarion *keer keer* calls, carrying the voice of the sea inland. It helped to have more than twenty of us. Like looking for shooting stars, it's easy to miss them if scanning the wrong direction.

The first community-science murrelet survey was in 2005. I'd joined for the twentieth anniversary along with almost a hundred volunteers. Joe Liebezeit, statewide conservation director for Bird Alliance of Oregon, organizes the annual mid-July event. He's a mild-mannered biologist laser-focused on advocacy for protecting bird habitat on land and at sea. Joe is a believer in the value of community science leading to personal investment in the future of bird life. He also oversees Snowy Plover and Black Oystercatcher surveys.

Oregon's premier Marbled Murrelet scientist, Kim Nelson, and Bird Alliance's Paul Engelmeyer founded the annual survey. They joined Joe and Lindsay Adrian of American Bird Conservancy at the community center for our early evening training on murrelet biology, conservation, and identification. While Kim is retired from Oregon State University, her commitment is lifelong. She would lead our group at the Cape Perpetua Campground.

Following the training, some volunteers mingled at the campground group site. A young woman with dangling albatross earrings wore a sundress covered in flying birds. "It's a booby dress," she told me with a laugh and sure enough, it was. Joe looked relaxed, a pro at juggling all the volunteer details. We sipped beer or wine around a bonfire that fended off mosquitos. I was with my nerdy bird tribe and happy. Somewhere in the night were the murrelets.

Brodie Cass Talbott (also with Bird Alliance) set up a white hanging curtain with a UV light to attract moths. We clustered close as he snapped photos for uploading to iNaturalist, a nonprofit network for sharing biodiversity information. Looper moths with exquisite patterns resembled tree bark. Brodie pointed to a moth with a fuzzy bristly head indicating an ability to fool bats by jamming their echolocation signals. Like Marbled Murrelets, certain kinds of moths and bats depend on deep interior forests over fragments. Pull one strand and the biodiversity web reverberates.

After restless sleep, I joined the flock of watchers in the parking area of the group site. Above the bubbling creek, a Western Flycatcher sang first, a high-pitched *tps-SEET ptsick tseet*. The first murrelet crossed the sky at 5:30 a.m. I kept my eye on Kim to pick up on her technique. In the chill of coastal dawn, she wore a black puffy coat over a turquoise button-up shirt. With her freckled complexion, curly shoulder-length auburn hair, and sturdy stance, she embodied the word capable. Standing in the center of the opening, she slowly turned and never took her eyes off the sky, except to record observations on her phone's voice recorder. At one point, I turned on my Merlin app. When I played it later, I realized I'd caught more than the *Keer* . . . *Ke* . . . *eer* sounds: "All of those last *keers* were three different detections, but are probably the same birds," said Kim. An observer added, "two . . . three . . . four . . . and two went that way!" Then loud and clear, "*ke—eee—er! Keeeeer—Keer!!*" You can hear the excitement in Kim's lowered voice. "Calling, calling. Right over us!" Another volunteer, "There's two more ahead of that one—so three." Then Kim, "Coming around again and circling."

For the last half hour of the survey, ten of us joined Ethan Woodis on a third of a mile hike up the creek on a trail built by the Civilian Conservation Corps in the early 1930s and leading to the Giant Spruce of Cape Perpetua. Ethan had just completed his OSU master's degree. His thesis demonstrates the strong negative effects of edges (like campgrounds and clear-cuts) on Marbled Murrelet nest selection.[4] Kim was on his committee. Wearing brown rubber boots, a yellow rain jacket, and black ball cap, he was ready for the coast's often fickle weather.

Tall and rangy with dark hair, a mustache, and the beginnings of a beard, Ethan is at home on the sea as well as land. The day before, he'd been out on a bird research boat off Gold Beach, a small town on the southern Oregon coast, and had seen a blue whale and ten thousand Cassin's Auklets, rocky island nesters and relatives of Marbled Murrelets. To know the leviathan whale is still surfacing, spouting, and diving and that auklets form a great living raft is more than gratifying. Yes, we live in a time of loss, and yes there are splendors for now—including the giant spruce.

This giant spruce, an Oregon Heritage Tree, measures 40 feet in circumference, 185 feet tall, and is about six hundred years old. The base forms a tunnel you can duck in—the space left from the nurse log that nurtured the sapling long ago. The trunk on the inland side is fuzzy with lichens and moss. Ferns burst from the bark in places, and far above we could see a classic platform branch with a new leader shooting straight up. Likely the tree is too exposed as a popular recreation destination for a nest.

At the foot of the spruce, and hugged by the great forest, we noticed Vaux's Swifts darting after insects. Looking up Cape Creek, I could see multiple snags that might host nests within the hollows. Whenever a murrelet sped by, we noted a similar blur of wingbeats, but the light-bodied swifts threw in glides and batlike turns that would be impossible for the chunky seabirds. A Varied Thrush sang chords on three different pitches and a Pacific Wren fountained his spray notes from the creekside. Adding the murrelet to the familiar ancient forest bird repertoire felt akin to finding a missing piece of my personal life.

Wes joined in the murrelet survey along with our easygoing Labrador, Pepper. The rest of the time, they hiked Cape Perpetua's trails, leaving me to immerse myself in the feathered forest. For three mornings, we rose to snippets of sea shanties of murrelets passaging up and down the creek and often high above. Their calls melded with a forest chorus of Swainson's Thrush, Western Flycatcher, American Robin, Chestnut-backed Chickadee, Pacific Wren, Varied Thrush, Steller's Jay, Banded Pigeon, and Wilson's Warbler.

Cape Perpetua's exceptional coastal forest is as feathery as feathery gets. Hemlocks flex winglike branches and Sitka spruce steady the sky with sturdy, ladderlike limbs. The understory surges in temperate tropical exuberance. Like strutting peacocks, sword ferns wave five-foot-high fronds as if to impress the lacy lady ferns gracing the shadows. Both are caespitose (pronounced sess-pi-tose), the botanical term for growing in a clump. Wilson's Warblers hop and give chip calls among a tangle of salal and red elderberry with bamboolike leaves and scarlet clusters of fruit that robins plucked.

With the sea on my mind, the great forest shape-shifts into a fleet of schooner ships hoisting masts of varying heights and sizes, the better for the wind to billow the sails. While I slept cocooned in the comfort of the pop-up camper, a chick dreamed on a mossy mattress, lulled by the crooning of all that dwells in the overstory.

Marbled Murrelets in the Lower 48 nest only in mature and old-growth coastal forests, and often in the crowns of Mother Trees—the largest of all in a stand. The birds have high site fidelity, returning to the same groves throughout their lives. A female lays a single speckled lichen-green, chicken-sized egg (huge for a small bird) on a bed of luxuriant moss, in turn reliant on coastal fog or heavy winter rains. To assure the egg does not roll off, the platform must be at least four inches wide and is typically close to the trunk, the better for staying hidden. The parents also select sites with umbrellas of thick-needled branches overhead to shelter the chick from rain and the notice of predators.

The specialized branches unique to the tall and old trees form by epicormic sprouting from a dormant bud in the trunk's cambium as a hormonal response to more light. Some become sprays and others are muscled biceps, with the forearm held straight up as the tree forms a new leader. Where dwarf mistletoe graces a tree, the branch grows large enough to be an ideal nest platform, too.

The parents take turns incubating the egg with twenty-four-hour exchanges for about thirty days. If Hermit Warblers are heat sensitive, Marbled Murrelets are extremely so. Their dense plumages are meant to keep the birds toasty in the icy Pacific waters. If nests are too exposed, the incubating birds can overheat, with beaks open and panting. The closed canopy, multiple tree heights, and branch shapes offer pleasant microclimates even in the overstory, where moisture is essential for mosses, ferns, and aerial gardens.

After the chick hatches, it's go time. Murrelets fish mostly in the nearshore, diving with wings flapping underwater pursuing fish close to the surface, but can dive 200 feet if need be. Like whales, they also eat the shrimplike krill—too tiny to carry to chicks. An adult flies with an anchovy, herring, or sandlance gripped crosswise in the beak. Approaching the nest, the seabird awkwardly stalls out to zoom down or up. The sound is like whipping a rope overhead in a circle. The chick has waited in stillness, looking like a brindled hedgehog with a beak instead of a nose. To swallow a whole fish—the bigger the better to save trips to the nest—might take several gulping tries.

A fecal ring of white guano from the chick gradually becomes a circle around the moss compressed into a shallow cup. Murrelets are feeding the forest with fish from up high, while salmon fertilize from low down. As fledging nears, the parents increase their fishing trips, sometimes at midday as well as dawning dusk. The number of flights may depend on the size and quality of prey. With luck, the growing chick will fledge a month later and make it to the sea in one perilous flight. In a video from a nest camera, a Steller's Jay lands to inspect a chick as if to give the docile-looking bird a peck, but this young one is old enough to stab at the jay. Danger averted. But in another clip, a Red-tailed Hawk lands, grabs the chick in a scimitar beak and flaps off.

Predation is now the number one direct cause of murrelet chick mortality, because of logging forests into fragments that expose murrelets to predators that are not deep forest birds, like the Red-tailed Hawk. Campgrounds and picnic areas are magnets for ravens, crows, and jays munching on left-out food. Since no one wants to camp or have lunch in a clear-cut or a tree plantation, the popular forest sites tend to be in murrelet habitat. The birds often fly inland above creeks that serve as aerial runways to the nest trees—and wherever there is water, people are not far behind.

To address the problem of campers and picnickers leaving food, California State Parks started a "Crumb Clean" campaign, now extending to Oregon. During my stay, I decided to be a murrelet ambassador—chatting up women waiting at the restroom door, passing dog walkers, hikers, and fellow campers. All were amazed. I don't believe in keeping birds a secret—we need every advocate we can get.

After the dawn survey and a breakfast break, the returning groups packed onto an observation deck overlooking the Pacific at the confluence with the Yachats River, close to town. A documentary film crew joined us, too. Everyone was in high spirits after a bountiful morning at each of the five sites. Now it was our chance to see the birds floating on the sea. Squinting through spotting scopes at a choppy olive sea under light cloud cover, we saw several murrelets bobbing along. I could discern the marbling of the breeding plumage of adults—like Mexican chocolate with white flecks on undersides, cryptic colors for nesting. There were also birds in nonbreeding plumage sporting white collars and wing patches that break up their shapes to elude hunting Bald Eagles and Peregrine Falcons from above and sea lions from below. The murrelets are two or three years old when males and females court, mate, nest, raise young, and remain paired.

The more you look and the longer you stay, the more you see. Ten Brown Pelicans slid into single-line formation to glide so close to the sea their wingtips flicked the low waves Among the tide pools, a Wandering Tattler had stopped in during a southbound migration from the Arctic to pluck prey from between barnacles, a perfect match for the shorebird's feathers. At first glance, the waves looked empty until dark shapes emerged. Pigeon Guillemots, Brandt's Cormorants, Western Grebes, and Surf Scoters bobbed in the swells. The murrelets tended to be floating a bit farther out. Admiring the elegance of grebes, I thought of the rescued female from Cape Lookout 90 miles to the north. Perhaps she was swimming in safe waters with a chick tucked on her back and an attentive mate nearby.

At the deck, I had a chance to talk to Kim. Her decades of seabird research include the Alaska study finding the ground-nesting Marbled Murrelets. There, too, she heard stories of the Tlingit tribe's reverent relationship with the bird. While I'd read of Kim's finding the first Oregon murrelet nest in the *Rare Bird* book, I wanted to hear the story. Out surveying for woodpeckers for an old-growth project in 1985, Kim heard strange calls with a seabird quality but not a gull. She knew about the 1974 Big Basin find, but 30 miles inland seemed too far for a murrelet. She was inventorying ancient forests of Marys Peak, highest in the Coast Range at 4,100 feet, and 25 miles west of Corvallis, where she was working on her master's degree in wildlife ecology at Oregon State University. Kim called a northern California birder friend who knew murrelet calls, and he suspected murrelets.

The next spring she returned to Marys Peak and saw murrelets, a finding she shared in 1986 with the Pacific Seabird Group, composed of seabird researchers and managers. The enigmatic seabird set Kim's career trajectory. Soon, she had a funded study to identify ancient forest habitats and nests along the entire Oregon Coast Range. Woodpecker treks in coastal old growth gave her a head start on where to look. Kim's crew included Paul Engelmeyer, an expert tree climber from years of cone-picking for the Forest Service to grow and plant new trees after logging.

In 1990, persistence prevailed. Dawn stakeouts led to Kim and her survey crew seeing a murrelet whir into high tree branches and a second bird fly off. It was time to call a tree climber to take photos and pinpoint the nest site. Paul arrived with his arborist gear to ascend an adjacent tree. Dangling on a rope with binoculars and camera, he spotted the egg in the nest. He returned three to four more times to document the hatching and growing chick. Sadly, this one did not make it to fledging—likely snatched by a predator. Soon after, Kim would find Marbled Murrelets in five of the original old-growth project's survey sites, including Gwynn Creek.

Looking for the murrelets from the deck, I asked how our view compared to the 1990s. There was lament in her good-natured tone. She used to see two hundred murrelets from this same spot and now is lucky to see twenty-five. In early days, climate change rarely came up. Today, rapid warming of the North Pacific is harming fisheries, along with plastics and overfishing. Studying Marbled Murrelets across their entire range, she's convinced their future lies in both intact marine and old-growth ecosystems. The nesting trees inland must align with excellent fishing. Murrelets can't afford to expend energy flying north or south along coastlines. Marine reserves and wilderness are one continuum.

From the Oregon Marbled Murrelet Project (2015 to 2021), Kim and co-investigators made an astonishing finding the first year of research designed to follow birds to better understand nesting. After capturing, banding, and fitting locators on fifty birds at sea on the Oregon coast, they were unprepared for what happened next.

The murrelets flew not to the forests but south to Point Reyes, California, a state marine conservation area. An El Niño year of warmer seas with little upwelling meant poor fishing. The birds did not nest and instead knew where to go, with an uncanny ability that fishermen have heeded for thousands of years, according to elders from Alaska tribes and Canada's First Nations.[5] The Tsimshian called the Marbled Murrelet *spipiyus*, also the name for a provincial park on the Sechelt Peninsula in British Columbia that preserved Marbled Murrelet pockets of old-growth forest.

The implications of murrelets skipping a nest year are meaningful for saving their trees from logging. Carl Sagan's adage applies, "Absence of evidence is not evidence of absence." While the protocols for surveying for nests requires two years, that may not be enough if there are two years in a row with warm ocean temperatures and weak upwelling, critical to lifting cold, nutrient-rich water to the surface. Murrelets will return to their same nesting site in any year when fish are abundant. It would be far better to protect all forests with murrelet habitat and include a buffer around them that excludes roads and logging. Since adults can live for ten to fifteen years, they can afford to miss a year, but not many. That's true, too, for the larger Common Murres that squeeze tight together as colonial nesters on top of flat rocky islands.

Later, I'd receive the official tally of murrelet detections on our survey morning in the forests—Cape Perpetua Campground with 94; Big Creek:

37; Gwynn Creek: 85 in one spot and 70 (estimate) in the other, plus the winner—Ten Mile Creek Sanctuary with 101. That's where I headed the next day after the survey, joining Paul Engelmeyer for an inland tour of the forests he has fought to save from logging on Tenmile and Big Creeks. As the founder and manager of the Ten Mile Creek Sanctuary of Bird Alliance of Oregon, he is devoted to acquiring and rewilding old homesteads for future murrelet habitat. Many have older forests or individual big trees worthy of murrelet nests.

Paul still has the wiry build of a tree climber. Meeting at the top of the 800-foot-high Cape Perpetua for the landscape overview, we instead gaze into the life-giving fog. He wears a sweatshirt hoodie the color of marmalade, a khaki vest, a pair of wire-rim glasses, and carries a poster-sized roll of maps. His prominent mustache matches his mist-silver wavy hair. "We'll come back up after the fog lifts," he says.

We head to Tenmile Creek, five miles to the south and a key linkage between two protected watersheds—Cummins Creek and Rock Creek Wilderness. Paul's vision is to stitch together the ancient and recovering forests across five watersheds—adding in Gwynn Creek and Yachats River. He and his wife Mary, a woodworker, initially lived several miles up Tenmile, off the grid, and now live closer to the creek's confluence with the ocean. They are part of a tight-knit community that staved off a proposed nuclear power plant in 1969 and then a proposed mega-resort.

Every wild place has a story, as I'd soon find out with Paul who drove us in his new hybrid Rivian truck, remarkably quiet with 55 miles per gallon efficiency—part of his personal commitment to live sustainably. He pulls over a couple of miles up Tenmile Creek and we get out. Paul often speaks with his hands, palms up or pointing to individual trees he knows as neighbors. He shows me a roadside great redcedar with burn scars—a survivor of a wildfire 150 years earlier. "This is one of the units that were slated to be cut as the citizen advisory and the public engaged with the Siuslaw National Forest," he tells me. On my own, I'd have gone right by, taking for granted the staggering beauty of 200-foot-tall Douglas-firs, bodacious redcedars, and maidenhair ferns overhanging springs. While ready to protest and climb trees to defend them in the tense timber war years of the late 1980s and early '90s, Paul preferred to build relationships in the Forest Service. He showed up, commented on plans, and, thanks to a visionary forest supervisor named Jim Furnish, the agency withdrew this and other timber sales to protect Spotted Owls and Marbled Murrelets. Today, the older forests have new significance for their superior carbon-capturing abilities.

However, without wilderness protection, they are not safe from political shifts that impact public lands. Paul worries about an aggressive approach to managing forests across the West driven by fears of wildfire, even on the coast. Thinning old-growth forests is detrimental and even destructive to the survival of murrelets and other rare species like flying squirrels gliding tree to tree. Drying winds deplete formerly lush microclimates.

"Can trees grow close? Do you have to thin them to get bigger? I think not," said Paul as we gazed up into a wall of diversity—redcedar, Douglas-fir, and Sitka spruce at every level and some trees close to 200 feet tall. "There is example after example! You don't have to do that." A few miles later, we park and take a discreet footpath past an old redcedar through alders into the Ten Mile Sanctuary right on the creek. In the late 1980s, a 120-acre old homestead included a native forest slated to be cut down. Paul had little money himself, but decided buying it was the only option. With his charismatic personality and drive, I'm not surprised he raised the money. By 1990, Oregon's first Audubon sanctuary was official, with Paul as the steward.

Paul shows me the rewilding under way. In what was once an old meadow, red alder trees give nitrogen to the spruce, first, and redcedars that fifth graders interplanted twenty years ago and now are 40 feet tall. To give the saplings more light, he brought in the Angel Job Corps to prune lower limbs on the alders. He points to the evergreen huckleberry and elderberry jostling among ferns. "My agenda is diversity," he tells me. It's a light touch he calls "soft restoration"—impossible to discern without Paul's pointing out the wilding that's supercharging the return of a wild forest capable of hosting murrelets. The forest opens into a meadow with the most enormous bigleaf maple I'd ever seen—left by the homesteaders to shade their livestock. Swainson's Thrushes are calling and singing nonstop. Clambering into the center of the multiple enormous mossy trunks, I am humbled by one living tree defying gravity with outstretched branches, each the size of a hefty tree.

We sit for a while by Tenmile Creek, running low from the summer's drought. Paul tells me of the anadromous Chinook, steelhead, coho, lamprey, and eulachon smelt that rely on the placid waters lined in forests. The sanctuary extends beyond the core to 500 acres in separate parcels. Acquisitions and land trades of private to federal lands add up to thousands of acres on Tenmile Creek. His vision is no pipe dream. It's happening.

Continuing our loop tour up and over a ridge and down to Big Creek, we see not one but two Barred Owls in broad daylight. The first is perched and the second is on the gravel road in what's called a pancake pose, crouched low with wings spread wide and unmoving. I'd never seen a sunbathing owl—a practice that adds vitamin D and helps the birds rid their feathers of parasites. The sun's heat brings the parasites to the surface so the owls can remove them through preening. The owls were stupendous with their big dark eyes, round heads, and barring on soft feathers. We knew their presence spelled bad news for Northern Spotted Owls, but we fell under their primordial spell. After all, owls evolved at least 60 million years ago, compared to our 300,000-year origins.

Back to the top of Cape Perpetua, Paul spreads out his maps on a picnic table. While it's hard not to be distracted by the see-forever views of the rugged coastline and infinite ocean, I pay attention. He's unrolling a watershed map showing all the rivers and creeks. Most are labeled as impaired by logging. He shakes his head at the salmon losses and the death by a thousand cuts. Before the trip, he'd sent me a link to a Google Earth time lapse of forests along the central Oregon coast. It's horrifying to watch the solid green of 1985 chopped up into clear-cut squares over the years until little of the wild forests remain. But still Paul is undeterred. Despair is not in his vocabulary.

"There's no sideline," he said. "You have to be in the game." Paul has seen nature healing. And he's beheld something else few people ever have—Marbled Murrelets in their nests. In those heady days with Kim Nelson, he even built platforms in neighboring tall trees so he could perch for hours watching. With his arborist skills, he'd cross from tree to tree hundreds of feet in the air. I ask him how we convince people the fate of Marbled Murrelets matters. "If the murrelets do well, the forage fish do well and the salmon fishery does well. The forests that support murrelets protect our drinking water, our climate, and the salmon."

After our day comes to an end, I'm left with an image Paul has in his head for a poster of a murrelet flying and in the wake are the wildlife tagging along under the bird's protection—flying squirrels, tree voles, salamanders, owls, warblers, thrushes, woodpeckers, swifts, moths, and salmon.

EIGHTEEN

Drift Creek Wilderness Interlude

Coastal Victory

I'm drifting back in time in Drift Creek Wilderness, the largest protected ancient forest in the Oregon Coast Range, at 5,800 acres, saved as part of the Oregon Wilderness Act of 1984. As a college student at the University of Oregon in 1980, I taught a class as an undergraduate called Oregon Wildlands, a course of the Survival Center, a dynamo student group taking on the world to save big trees, wild rivers, wildlands, and wildlife. The class was strong on field trips to endangered places. Drift Creek? Extremely threatened. The loggers coveted the last great stands. The Forest Service sided with the loggers, as did most politicians. Timber ruled. We drove in vans from Corvallis to follow the winding Alsea Highway and then on rutted logging roads through moonscapes of giant stumps, slash piles, and slumping hillsides. I'll never forget what it was to step into the arms of the wild forest and breathe in the immensity of giant trees.

Forty-three years later I am back, free from worry about impending chainsaws. It's late October. I'm with my friend Sandra to camp at the Horse Creek Trailhead and hike the next day, a round trip of eight miles to the creek and back. A Pileated Woodpecker raps a reverberant tree. Evening sun splashes waves on the masts of trunks with canopies, like sails ready to billow and head seaward. Often, we're crouching low to exclaim over mushrooms with names like Slippery Jack and Pinewood Gingertail.

The next morning, Sandra and I wake to wafting mists and lowered clouds. The trail is spongy underfoot. We hike up a gentle uphill and down a long ridge toward Drift Creek. Sandra works with Vermont Family Forests, a nonprofit dedicated to creating mutually beneficial relationships between people and forests. She calls our route "the line of grace," for a trail that hugs contours and flows with the land rather than in opposition. We find warmth in sunny glades where trees have fallen and admire survivors of past fires—some Douglas-firs more than seven hundred years old and seven feet in diameter. Redcedars are among the tall carbon-storing giants holding up the sky. Five Douglas-firs are so packed close, I suspect an origin of a Douglas squirrel midden.

Overstory. Midstory. Understory. Like the best of literature, the plots are interwoven in place and time. A Pacific Wren darts from behind a root wad. The petite singer has gone quiet in late October. A Varied Thrush, festive in Halloween orange and black, flurries through the mist at eye level. Chestnut-backed chickadees converse in undertones above us. Two hundred feet up, a string of Red Crossbill notes are flickers of light in the fog. Ahead and below are the beckoning currents of Drift Creek, harboring a surprise.

There, we come into the presence of spawning Chinook salmon as a Bald Eagle lifts from a spruce limb and flies downstream. In one pool and riffle, we count five, some four feet long. All show lacerations. I can see females with broader flat heads and males with hooked jaws. Their colors are bruised purples and loden green. Motions vary from finning the currents facing upstream to sudden bolts forward or sideways. Then, there's the vigorous splashing as a female wriggles sideways to hollow out a redd, a nest in the underwater stones of clear, cold water. The salmon have come to the wilderness, where bigleaf maple and conifers shade and crochet the banks in place.

To celebrate what it took to save what has now become a critical carbon and biodiversity reserve, I pieced the story together from my friends, environmentalist Andy Kerr and ecologist Paul Alaback. They were among the leaders of a decade-long fight for preservation ending in partial victory. The Oregon Wilderness Act of 1984 included three coastal wilderness areas—Drift Creek, Cummins Creek, and Rock Creek. By then, I was living in northeast Oregon and advocating for wildlands there. Some made it in the 1984 final bill, including the North Fork John Day Wilderness, Monument Rock, and the expansion of the Strawberry Mountains Wilderness.

The north side trail following the line of grace was pivotal in the 1970s–'80s campaign to save Drift Creek. Volunteers put many hours into maintenance after the Forest Service let it go. Without a trail, coastal forests are almost impassable. A key strategy for protection was to bring people to threatened wildlands. The adage "we protect what we love" is true.

Originally, the Forest Service inventoried 6,400 acres of roadless land, leaving out much of the old growth. Later, the agency increased the acreage to 11,252 acres, but Congress stuck to the lower figure for the final Drift Creek Wilderness. The remainder is roadless, with late-successional reserve status under the Northwest Forest Plan—a designation that could be undone.

Paul recalled being part of a small conservation group in Corvallis speaking up for Drift Creek in the 1970s and '80s—and joined by the Sierra Club chapter and Oregon Wilderness Coalition (today's Oregon Wild, and where Andy worked out of Eugene). Paul gave slideshows, appealed timber sales, attended acrimonious hearings, and led field trips on the trail. Paul often teamed up with Bob Frenkel (geography professor and local Sierra Club leader) and Glenn Juday, whose PhD dissertation focused on the remaining old-growth forests of the Oregon Coast Range. Glenn and Paul spent countless weekends in Drift Creek documenting the old growth with the help of students—another key to raising awareness. The politics were rough. Timber really did rule, and convincing Oregon's congressional representatives and senators to include the ancient or old-growth forests in any version of a wilderness bill was uphill all the way. There were losses, but there were wins, too. It's never been easy to save wild places.

As we hiked back up the line of grace, Sandra and I felt blessed. Leaning close to a Mother Tree, we listened. This heartbeat. This mycelial network underfoot. This one flicker of our lives and a friendship spanning miles and decades. Always reciprocal. This wilderness.

NINETEEN

Spotted Owl

Last Stand for an Ecosystem

The full moon balances on a ridge in the western Cascades as if ready to roll into the valley of ancient ones. A hundred feet up in the lower crown of a Douglas-fir, a red tree vole scampers from his softball-sized nest snugged within a whorl of limbs. He bites off a twig tipped in new green needles, grasps it in his mouth, and races toward safety. Unique to western Oregon and northern California, the pocket-sized rodent rarely ventures to the ground. When thirsty, he licks fog, dew, or raindrops from fir needles.

A Northern Spotted Owl glides wraithlike from a perch. She snatches the cinnamon-furred vole in her talons. White dots constellate her coffee-brown head, back, and breast feathers. The barring on her flight and tail feathers is like the blurred paths of meteors. Her brown facial disk is an orb with a milky X shape over luminous dark eyes and a curved yellow beak. On velvety wings, she breezes to a monolith among the interlacing canopy of Douglas-fir, redcedar, and hemlock. Snapped off by high winds, the broken treetop offers a natural hollow. Inside, two fuzzy owlets open their beaks and give hissing whistles. She feeds the vole whole to one chick just as her mate whisks in with a flying squirrel. Another tree vole is luckier. Concealed inside her roofed nest laced to a dwarf mistletoe broom, she's stripping freshly harvested Douglas-fir needles with sharp-teethed precision. The needles are lined with resin ducts, filled with terpenoids designed to repel herbivores. By removing the ducts, she can munch an edible meal and then weave the strips into her lopsided dome house, basketball-sized and scented in spicy sweet resin. Her pelage is lustrous, ears tiny, body plump, and tail long. She dines in a room near the ceiling, tends her two babies in another, and deposits her fecal pellets in a latrine. Three escape tunnels at the bottom lead to the Douglas-fir's wide trunk. Occasionally, a male will visit from his separate nest to see if she's ready to mate again.

Otherwise, the vole's life is solitary—except for the clouded salamander. Lounging on top of the nest, the arboreal amphibian snaps up a couple of mites. Four inches long from head to prehensile tail, and with long toes equipped with broad tips that add surface area for climbing, the salamander earned the name "clouded" for the grayish hues mingled with coppery tones on the back. The name seems apt for life in the clouds.

Vole and salamander live in reciprocity. The compacted resin ducts, twigs, needles, lichen, and pellets of the nest form a damp, warm microclimate for the lungless salamander that breathes through moist skin. The vole benefits from the salamander eating flies, mites, and beetles living in the nest.

Slinking along a sturdy branch is an ermine, or short-tailed weasel. Lithe and deadly, the ermine can invade a vole nest and tug out the babies one by one. In winter, the ermine is white with a black-tipped tail, and in summer brown and yellowish. Spying twigs pressed into the fork of a heavy branch, he slips closer, just as a Pacific tree frog hops from the abandoned vole nest. All kinds of animals join the birds of the overstory that's replete in epiphytes, nests, hollows, holes, and wrinkles in the bark of wise elders.

A cirrus cloud tendrils the moon. The owl is hunting. A northern flying squirrel peeks from a lichen-lined woodpecker hole in a tall snag. Climbing onto a branch, he leaps and sails. A flap of skin called a patagium stretches from forelimbs to hind limbs and slows his descent. To land, he brakes with his fluffy flat tail. He follows his nose to an aromatic truffle, the food of the forest. He also eats fruit, seeds, flowers, insects, snails, and even small bird eggs, but truffles are a favorite.

Ensconced in moss, a red-legged frog jumps out of the way and plops into a still pool beneath a tipped-up redcedar tree's wheel of roots. The soggy nurse log, rotund as a basking sea lion, shelters garter snakes, slender salamanders, banana slugs, and millipedes. Piles of cone scales and cores scattered among the moss where hemlock saplings grow in a line are clues to a Douglas squirrel's meal. I wonder if the tree after death still senses the drumming of Ruffed Grouse, pattering of Townsend's chipmunks, sprinting of American martens, and serenading of Pacific Wrens?

When I'm in a night forest listening for owls, I feel longing to know the sky community like the scientists who have scaled the great trees to investigate unseen lives. There's sorrow too. From all my recent wanderings in old forests of Cascades and Coast Range, I've never seen or heard a Spotted Owl. My chances are diminishing. I feel the pang of impending loss. What does the forest feel?

The future of vole, salamander, frog, ermine, flying squirrel, truffle, snake, slug, millipede, chipmunk, marten, and wren are tied to the fate of the Northern Spotted Owl. The vanishing icon inhabits ancient forests of the Cascades and Coast Range from British Columbia south as far as California's Muir Woods, north of San Francisco Bay. Divided into three subspecies—Northern, California, and Mexican Spotted Owls—the other two are imperiled from logging old-growth forests, climate-induced megafires, and development. As Barred Owls multiply, extinction looms for the California subspecies, too.

Biologist Janice Reid holds out hope for refugia where Spotted Owls are free of the deadly competitors. For more than thirty years, she researched Northern Spotted Owls in the field, including two decades working under Eric Forsman. Without the owl's listing in 1990 under the Endangered Species Act, there would be little if any magnificent forests left within the bird's range, outside of designated wilderness and national parks.

Today, Janice is the board president for Umpqua Watersheds, a conservation nonprofit based in Roseburg, an old timber town of the Umpqua Valley that's become a center for more than thirty wineries. I asked her what she's learned of the owls' habits from observing, banding, fitting them with transmitters, and releasing the lightweight birds from her hands. "I'm addicted to telemetry. I love finding things about animals without having them know," she said, stressing the importance of not changing animal behaviors.

"Spotted Owls need moisture, shade, coolness, and a closed canopy to allow them to thermoregulate their temperature," she said in our phone conversation. "We tracked the owls year-round. In summer, they are down low staying cool. When it's cold, they are often in the tops of canopy trees and sometimes sunning themselves on the upper or outer branches."

By the end of June, a little over a month after hatching, the one to two chicks face their first big challenge—how to get to the ground far below them. One at a time, they cautiously venture out of a nest that can also be in a mistletoe broom or natural cavity in a snag. "When the young owls first come out they are called branchers," Janice said. "They walk along a branch and might look for days at a lower branch until finally they jump to the next one."

Slowly, the birds gain confidence to flutter and flap all the way down. Their landings are cushioned by Pacific yew, chinquapin, or bigleaf maple drenched in mossy branches. In the southern part of the owls' range, they might shelter in madrone trees. Their first flights can be humorous, even hanging upside down when landing on thin branches. The parents attend them into August and early September, when they stop responding to begging calls for food. The young fly off to establish their own territories and find mates, typically by their third year, if they survive. Each pair requires several hundred to more than a thousand acres for hunting, roosting, and nesting, depending on the richness of prey. They avoid clear-cuts.

The owls lead to what makes a forest resilient from overstory to midstory to understory. Throughout are relationships as exquisite as salamander and vole. From Janice's days, seasons, and years in owl habitat, she's come to know the value of different trees for roosting. Golden chinquapin, a shrubby relative of the chestnut found only in western Oregon and northern California, forms an umbrella top about 30 feet high. "The owls get in there when it's raining and stay."

A Pacific yew tree, famous as the original source of the cancer drug Taxol, is a shrubby hideaway from a Cooper's Hawk or Great Horned Owl. Daytime roosts must have plenty of branches close to a sturdy trunk. Before settling in for a nap, a Spotted Owl turns around and makes sure there's no chink in the cover. The owl and the tree merge into one.

That image of owl as tree and tree as owl is fitting. No other bird has played such a pivotal political role in saving the planet's last best temperate forests. During the 1990s "timber wars" era of the Pacific Northwest, loggers and environmentalists clashed. Spotted Owls became the scapegoat as bulldozers kept churning and building roads into the dwindling last wild forests on public lands. Destruction followed with clear-cuts, choked salmon streams, and landslides. The owl was further vilified by the timber industry after the ESA listing. Loggers protested with signs reading, "To hell with owl lovers," "Owls won't feed my family," and "Loggers are an endangered species."

A reprieve from the mayhem came with the adoption of the 1994 Northwest Forest Plan, a compromise hammered out under President Bill Clinton. Of the 24 million acres covered by the plan in Spotted Owl habitat, a quarter are called "late-successional reserves" to preserve mature (eighty-plus-year-old) and old-growth forests. Despite not going far enough to protect forests that will become future old growth or including the Traditional Ecological Knowledge of local tribes, the plan is an international model for protecting an ecosystem. But the future is in jeopardy as top-down politics shift toward extraction over all other values on public lands.

Meanwhile, Barred Owls may seal the fate of Northern Spotted Owls. Native to eastern North America, the birds hopscotched across the northern plains, taking advantage of trees planted by settlers. Barred Owls were first noted in the Pacific Northwest in the 1970s. We live in a time of fauna and even flora on the move, especially to escape the heat of climate change. Corridors are essential. What happens when a new arrival wreaks havoc? Do we give things time to sort out even if there are extinctions? Does our meddling make things worse?

The debate over killing one owl to save another has become a wedge among those who have fought together to save the remnant wild forests. Like Sophie's choice, it's an agonizing moral dilemma. Janice saw her first Barred Owl on a Spotted Owl survey in 1988. Their behaviors alone suggested problems to come. "Spotted Owls are an acoustic territorial animal—talk it out, you stay in your yard, and I'll stay in mine," said Janice. "But Barred Owls are physical and aggressive when encountering other species."

Early on, a Barred Owl had trouble finding a mate and started breeding with the related Spotted Owl, producing hybrids. Once the birds had a foothold, there were plenty of their own kind. Both species mate for life. By 2000, Barred Owl numbers were multiplying fast. Now, survey crews playing recordings of hoots to listen for responding calls of Spotted Owls are more likely to hear Barred Owls. While the technique continues, it's not as reliable since the smaller owl may not hoot back if a Barred Owl is nearby. Bioacoustics technology, however, is revolutionizing monitoring. Crews set up audio recorders within two-mile-square territories of Spotted and Barred Owls. Artificial intelligence is key to analyzing the sounds to pick out the two species.

Four-legged helpers also are sniffing for owl pellets at roost sites. Back in the lab, DNA testing confirms whether the pellets are from a Spotted or Barred Owl. The pellets are dissected to look for red tree voles as part of a prey study. The dogs are part of the Rogue Detection Team, a woman-owned Oregon business that trains rescue dogs to find animal scats for wildlife inventories.

"In all my annual reports I was trying to raise awareness that Barred Owls were quickly swamping Spotted Owls," Janice said. "Human nature is to delay, and now it's really hard." As humans, we've shuffled the deck with our global trade. Highly evolved ecosystems like ancient forests suffer when newcomers enter and the residents have no defenses. What's the answer for the Spotted Owls? If they go extinct, the most muscular tool for saving wild forests is gone. One woman activist knows that well.

Francis Eatherington leans into an enormous, thick-barked Douglas-fir by the West Fork of the Millicoma River and gives the tree a kiss. She is owl-like, with cropped silver hair, earthy brown clothes, and a barred flannel shirt.

We are in the heart of the Elliott State Research Forest, inland from the coastal towns of Reedsport and Coos Bay. It's early June, when 20-foot-tall rhododendrons spill perfume from pink blossoms. A dipper dips on a flat stone at the edge of the lazy river, a stronghold for endangered coho salmon. The older forests are home to threatened Spotted Owls and Marbled Murrelets. The word "research" entered the forest's name in 2024, a promising change from logging as the priority. Founded in 1930 as Oregon's first state forest, the Elliott's steep canyons, streams, and forests are part of the homeland of the Hanis (Coos) and Quuiich (Lower Umpqua) peoples.

At seventy-five, Francis remains an unabashed tree hugger, and a force when it comes to saving ancient forests in southwestern Oregon. Back in 1979, she started Three Sisters Forestry after a stint with the Hoedads, a legendary tree-planting collective that championed women. Like Paul Engelmeyer, she climbed trees to pick cones and honed her map and compass skills trekking through trailless forests never logged before.

In 1996, she shifted to saving wild forests as a volunteer for Umpqua Watersheds, not far from her rural home on a land collective. Throwing herself into a fight to save big trees far from roads and slated for logging under Congress's 1995 "salvage rider," she applied her mapping, forestry, and field skills to find and expose the travesties. The rider reinstated former timber sales in centuries-old forests of staggering beauty in Washington and Oregon. Originally halted to protect Spotted Owls and other rare species, the sales were exempted from public challenge. The only recourse was public outrage.

My favorite description of Francis during the 1990s comes from Josh Laughlin, the director of Cascadia Wildlands, a Eugene-based environmental group willing to blockade log trucks if need be. He recalled:

> I remember first meeting Francis Eatherington the day she rolled into an Earth First! road blockade high up on the Umpqua National Forest on her motorcycle. She was wearing a leather biking jacket, had a stack of timber sale maps under her arm, a compass dangling from her neck and a ruffled brow, shaking her finger in the air, furious that the Forest Service was intent on punching roads and logging units into the adjacent Mount Bailey roadless area.[1]

Francis shifted from volunteer to conservation director and, in 2010, took on a wider role for Cascadia Wildlands. Since 2015, she's served as a part-time adviser for the Elliott State Research Forest. Retirement is not in her playbook. She couldn't be happier than when out ground-truthing timber sales to see whether what's on paper matches what's in the field. Her strongest allies are the endangered Northern Spotted Owl and the Marbled Murrelet. It was Francis who urged me to call Janice at Umpqua Watersheds.

For years, the Elliott was ground zero for protests, with tree sitters, barricades, banners, and public outcry over clear-cut logging to turn trees into cash for public schools. Finally, in 2022, after public opposition to logging old-growth trees for profit, the Oregon legislature de-coupled the Elliott from school funding. For a research forest, an approved conservation plan is meant to protect habitats for endangered species.

Francis is not backing off her vigilance. I thought our day would be a driving tour of the Elliott's 145 square miles, the size of the city of Portland. Without her, I wouldn't find the wild forest havens for murrelets and owls within a maze of logging roads snaking up ridges and down to the river bottoms. There are no designated hiking trails. About 41,000 of the 93,000 acres have never been logged. Five-hundred-year-old giants that survived an 1868 wildfire mingle with 150-year-old trees that have reached impressive heights and girths in the coastal wet climate. It's fantastic owl and murrelet habitat.

To my delight, she put me to work. Soon after picking me up at the Dean Creek Elk Viewing Area outside of Reedsport, Francis pulled over to the side of a gravel road leading into the Elliott. Propping a creased and well-worn map on the steering wheel and holding printed-out copies of planned timber sales in her left hand, she pinpointed our first destination. These are the first sales in thirteen years. None are in old growth, and most—but not all—have a goal of restoring dense, even-age plantations by cutting some of the young trees.

It is profoundly desolating to walk in 135 acres of trees doomed to be clear-cut. Every Pacific Wren song from a fern-laced creek, every Hermit Warbler gracing a redcedar, and every wild rhododendron spilling over with fuchsia bloom felt funereal. The trees were not exceptionally big, and old stumps told of past logging, but in the verdant climate, the forest was regrowing her feathers.

Not far from where she kissed the big tree is Cougar Creek, a feathered grove she helped save from clear-cutting because of owl sightings. We took the side road up the creek. She wanted to lead me a mile uphill to eight-foot diameter trees, but struggled with a bad knee. Pulling out her cane from the car, she grabbed an alder stick and broke that for her other hand, and walked partway. She told me a story: In 2009, twenty-seven of fifty activists were arrested in another part of the Elliott for their blockades and tree-sitting on platforms to stop a clear-cut. The Elliott falls in two counties—Coos and Douglas. They happened to be over the line to the north in Douglas County. All ended up in a jailhouse in Roseburg right across from Francis's office of Umpqua Watershed. The judge sentenced them to sixteen hours of community service in the nonprofit of their choice. "Well, they all just walked into my office," Francis shook her head with a laugh. Rather than assigning them, she asked what they wanted to do. They decided to build a hiking trail (the Elliott has none) into the Millicoma Cougar timber sale project to draw attention to the beauty.

They didn't ask permission. We could see traces of the old trail, but the coastal forests grow fast, lush, and thick. In the old days, Francis was known for clambering up and over huge, downed trees and parting her way through walls of salal, evergreen huckleberries, rhododendrons, and salmonberry with stickery thorns. Nothing would stop her from finding the big trees and habitat for owls and murrelets.

The trail alone did not save the stand from logging, but Cougar Creek was in the public eye. The state agency could not bury any findings, such as the Northern Spotted Owl flying right into the center of the targeted forest.

I asked Francis how it felt to be among ancient trees standing tall because of her activism. She gave a humble half smile and shook her head, pointing to the Elliott's conservation champion Bob Sallinger, who died tragically in 2024. I had to turn to others for praise of Francis, like Oregon Wild's Doug Heiken, who has watchdogged timber sales since 1995. "Francis has an amazing ability to get things done, with impeccable attention to details," he said. "She reads timber sales well, knows the ground, and then unravels their plans."

She's well connected and "equally comfortable with a bunch of lawyers in a room or a bunch of tree sitters." When Doug joined Francis in the woods, he often saw her scramble down steep ravines to the middle of timber sales where the Forest Service or BLM often hid the big trees they wanted to cut down. Together, they'd challenge proposed new roads that were deliberately placed to justify logging huge trees they were supposed to leave alone. On our day trip, I saw a playful side of Francis—kissing trees and crinkling myrtlewood leaves to sniff the bay leaf incense, catching floating rhododendron petals. There, in the old forests, we were bathed in the beauty of the moment.

Like Francis and Janice, I would grieve the extinction of the Northern Spotted Owl. But I'm uneasy about shooting Barred Owls to save Spotted Owls and the many creatures in danger from the newcomer's voracious appetite. While the latter eats voles, flying squirrels, mice, and woodrats, the Barred Owl is often lower in the canopy, hunting all kinds of prey—even coastal giant salamanders yanked out of pools. Birds Connect Seattle (formerly Seattle Audubon) wrote of the ethical dilemma this way:

> Which do we value more? The persistence of a unique branch on the tree of life, or the individual suffering of a slaughtered Barred Owl? Which is worse? The slow starvation and irreversible elimination of an entire species, or the quick but perpetual killing of thousands of Barred Owls?[2]

The group, along with several other environmental organizations, sees no other way to avert extinction. They've reluctantly favored a US Fish and Wildlife plan to shoot up to a half million Barred Owls, conceding there will have to be regular removals in the future. We wouldn't be in this place if we'd saved far more and larger ancient forests.

What we should not do is abandon science, monitoring, and studying entwined relationships the owls know from treetops 300 feet high all the way down to a hiding place in a Pacific yew. Within these forests are more cancer-fighting drugs and medicines, many that Indigenous people have known for a long time. To cut down the forests because of Spotted Owl absence would be a travesty.

We live in an era when a third of species and ecosystems in the United States alone are at risk of extinction, even as we keep finding new species—a reminder of all we've likely lost that are unknown. Only in 2017 was another denizen of Spotted Owl habitat officially recorded—the Humboldt's flying squirrel. While

I'd prefer a descriptive common name, I am a fan of nineteenth-century naturalist Alexander von Humboldt, who wrote, "Our imagination is struck only by what is great; but the lover of natural philosophy should reflect equally on little things."[3]

The Humboldt's flying squirrel is smaller, a bit darker, and genetically different from the northern flying squirrel, and lives in the coastal regions from southern British Columbia to southern California mountains. The two kinds split off from a common ancestor of the northern and southern species 1.3 million years ago.

Another ancient forest species is also named for the naturalist—the Humboldt or coastal marten. Decimated by fur trapping and logging of their closed-canopy old forests and assumed extinct, they were found again in 1997. Fewer than five hundred survive in fragile refugia—one in northern California, one in forests within the Oregon Dunes National Recreation Area, and another in a remote Oregon grove. Poking up a triangular head with perky ears, a glossy and slim marten with chocolate and caramel fur turns from a perch on a nurse log to race up a leaning tree—leading us to what makes a forest whole. The marten has not yet received protection under the ESA.

I believe our best hope for Spotted Owls, flying squirrels, and martens is to trust in the intelligence of complex forests and honor their existence. I trust in all that birds can teach us, to enlighten us and free us to create a society of restraint over greed, kindness over violence, and sharing over taking. And I trust in people who are falling for birds and reconnecting with the natural world.

In journalism graduate school at University of Montana, I wrote a regular newspaper column for the student paper, the *Kaiman*. One piece in April of 1987 showcased a commanding Barred Owl that appeared on campus and napped in a spruce by the student union building. I noticed a strange phenomenon. Students, professors, the college president, and even a US congressmen gathered to watch. Once hooked by the owl, they were looking up in the campus trees as a practice.

In the column, I quoted Professor Dick Hutto after he took his ornithology class to see the owl: "Once you start becoming aware of birds, it will change your perceptions of the world."[4]

In wild forests where the Spotted Owls should be, I'm on the alert in evenings for the pure low tones of the Spotted Owl: *hoo—hoo-hoo—hooo*. Instead, I often hear the Barred Owl's bracing *Who cooks for you?* I consider the mnemonic. Who cooks for all of us? Mother Earth does. We could at least step up to wash the dishes—cleaning up our mess to leave a better world seven generations from now.

TWENTY

Townsend's Solitaire

Ancient Juniper Wisdom

The single held note of a Townsend's Solitaire is the rung bell of junipers on this first day of February. I pause in my hike up Horse Ridge, a pilgrimage with five other tree lovers to see the oldest documented western juniper at more than 1,600 years of living. Solitaires winter here, subsisting on an exclusive diet of juniper berries jam-packed with energy.

Rumpling across about 9 million acres of arid parts of Washington, Oregon, northern California, Idaho, and Nevada, western juniper forests are wise in surviving climate extremes. About 10 percent of the long-lived trees took root before 1870. Unlike the tall, multistoried Douglas-firs, redcedars, spruce, pine, and hemlock of wetter forests, these trees tend to hunch low, growing no more than 30 feet tall, with some exceptions. The record western juniper for size grows in the Lost Forest of south-central Oregon and is triumphant at 79 feet tall, with a circumference of 19 feet. South of juniper forests, in similar dry habitats, pinyon pines grow in the Great Basin.

Here in central Oregon, rain and snow tallies to less than 15 inches of precipitation a year, a striking contrast to the state's record wettest place, Laurel Mountain in the Coast Range, with the record of 204 inches, set in 1996.

Golden Eagles soar over open country, spotting rabbits hopping among sagebrush, rabbitbrush, and bunchgrass from a mile away. Not far from Horse Ridge is Dry River Canyon, closed to entry from February through August to protect Golden Eagles and Prairie Falcons that nest on cliff ledges. The Bureau of Land Management oversees the public lands, including the nearby Badlands

Wilderness, protected in 2009, thanks to the leadership of the Oregon Natural Desert Association.

On our trek uphill, our faces sting in biting winds sending stratus clouds nipping past the sun. On trails, we are chatting. Off trail, we zigzag our separate ways among snow patches, ice, mud, rock outcroppings, and crisp bunchgrasses, along with threadleaf sedge, a plant that thrives only with little to no livestock grazing. Part of Horse Ridge is a Research Natural Area, designated in 1967 because of the outstanding plant communities. The hillsides are dotted with junipers anchored in sandy, ashy, and pumice pebble soils. Some trees overflow with clusters of powdery blue juniper berries.

Dulcet ruffles of solitaire song romp across canopies of widely spaced junipers. Like an American Dipper on an icy stream, a Townsend's Solitaire breaks the rules of melodies reserved only for the nesting season. And like dippers, both males and females sing. Slender and gray, with a telltale white eye ring, fawn-gold wing patches, and a longish tail edged in white, a Townsend's Solitaire shares the high desert's unassuming beauty.

I reach the oldest juniper first with my friend Mathieu Federspiel, who has located the hidden tree before. When he heads downhill to direct our wandering friends, I'm alone with the elder. Placing one hand on the exposed trunk of multihued grains of wood, from ashy gray to burnished cedar, I hear a whoosh overhead. Three ravens cruise by. Wind lovers.

Walking a short distance from the juniper, I take in the wizened tree with a corpulent trunk and gesturing arms. From one angle, I can discern an abstract face in the middle of the trunk and two wide arms. There are also two dead limbs forking up from the tree like antennae of a beetle.

Close up, I study the twists and turns of branches. Fluorescent green lichens whisker from bare limbs. So little of this tree appears to be alive. A healthy branch pokes upward from a strong side limb. Another fists the sky like a miniature tree. Gray wood grains curve like columnar basalt flows, and others are molded reddish clay. A dead stem forms the shape of a long-necked bird with lichen feathers.

I easily find the square hole where Rick Miller, renowned range ecologist of junipers and pinyon pine communities, aged the tree with a graduate student and field crew in the 1990s. Since most of the ancient junipers are hollow, it's rare to find one with an intact pith (the tissue in the center of the trunk). On the dead side of this tree is the plunge cut, made by a small chainsaw. They used a thin increment borer 20 inches long to remove a pencil-like sample on the living side, but it wasn't long enough to reach the center. A technique called cross dating of the two samples added up to 1,600 years. Turning to the superlative juniper, I wonder what it is like to remain rooted in place for more than twenty human lifetimes.

> You learn that one living root can quench your thirst. Many of your great twisted limbs may die and break, yet all you need is a single snaking line of sustenance to the one greening branch. Even your way of leafing is held tight to the twig, like the fine scales of sagebrush lizards also savvy in the art of dry living. You offer your berries to birds, spread your umbrella limbs to shelter elk and deer, and welcome bushy-tailed woodrats to shred strips of bark and create layered nests in the hollows and clefts of lower branches and trunks. Over time you have listened in the way a tree listens to languages—of raven, coyote, cottontail, and solitaire. You bear witness to predator and prey and the cycling of seasons.
>
> Your great taproots sense water even 25 feet below in the aquifer and those crisscrossing lateral roots are in a constant communion thanks to the fungi partners. You've known generations of bunchgrasses, wildflowers, ants, beetles, and lizards scampering along exposed roots in the volcanic soil. Those roots! So strong they can split rock and hold you up century upon century and long after death.

A companion juniper that must be well over a thousand years grows about 20 feet downslope. The upper branches are also dead. Evergreen needles form a swirled skirt lower down. This tree has a split trunk at the bottom, giving the juniper a two-legged look, as if the tree might walk off at any moment. The two trees remind me of an old couple celebrating anniversaries not by the decade but by centennials. Their way of clasping hands is underground, through roots extending their mycelium to exchange messages and nutrients—help in hard times. The old ones have eluded past wildfires on a site so rocky you couldn't put a shovel in to dig. Domes of sagebrush and fine, golden stems of cured bunchgrass protrude from shallow snow tracked by deer mice.

Our group gathers to touch the tree, to photograph, and contemplate in silence. Mathieu has brought his diameter tape—39 inches of hard-earned growth. On our return loop journey, we are admiring every older tree, including the sculpted standing dead. A flock of American Robins streams overhead. Six noisy Clark's Nutcrackers burst from a cluster of trees. We keep our eye out for Pinyon Jays, gregarious sky-blue corvids that have dwindled by 80 percent in the last fifty years, as biologists scramble to find out why.

Coyotes have left purple scat piles of juniper berries. The trickster of Indigenous myths is a connoisseur of fine dining. Why not mix in berries with meals of rabbits, quail, mice, and other carnivorous delights? Junipers have many allies in their quest to propagate. Other mammal berry eaters include foxes, striped skunks, and many rodents.

Hearing again a solitaire's pure note, I'm steered to a twisting old tree where the bird perches on a top spire. Two kinds of wolf lichens (one is called brown-eyed) fluoresce chartreuse colors from trunks and barkless branches. Shaped like scruffy arugula greens, they crave space and light, hence their attraction to bare limbs. Harmless to trees, the photosynthesizing algae share sugars with fungi that in turn catch moisture and minerals. The colors come from a toxic vulpinic acid, a repellent to insects and others who might take a bite, like mule deer. Lichens proliferating on old junipers send another signal: Breathe deep. The air is good.

Star mosses after winter's rain or snow turn stones and soil an Irish kelly green. They tend to grow close to older trees. Bending low to touch the soft felt rumpling, I'm astonished by lushness. In spring, white bouquets of sand lilies scatter across ashy soils. Wildflowers quicken the life pulse as native bees and butterflies pollinate purple penstemon, scarlet gilia, and cushion penstemon. Bitterbrush spices the air in cinnamon-scented yellow flowers. By late summer, rabbitbrush blooms in saffron panicles. Juniper berries begin to ripen.

After a winter of berry-picking, Townsend's Solitaires depart in spring to fly to higher elevations of the Cascades to nest within conifers and along rivers. Throughout their western range, they are short-distance migrants from juniper country to mountains and back. Their nests are wedged in crannies, alcoves ledges, tree roots, or by large stones.

Severely burned forests are magnets. There, solitaires find the microrefugia of natural caves formed when displaced rocks fell from unstable banks or in the hollows of tipped-over trees where roots once clenched boulders. If level ground, a female scrapes a shallow hollow, then weaves a needle basket typically with pine needles and lined with soft strips of barklike incense-cedar, or grass, rootlets, moss, and lichens gathered nearby. On a slope, she will first create a sturdy foundation of twigs. She lays three to five eggs and broods them, as the attentive male brings her protein-rich insects. Within two weeks the featherless chicks hatch and fledge a couple weeks later. Both parents feed them caterpillars and spiders. As summer advances, the birds shift more to berries and ready for their flight to juniper country.

Solitaires draw attention to the ways of young and old junipers. Pinnacles and inverted cone shapes indicate the youthful trees. Those with berries tend to be at least fifty years old. As the trees mature, their canopies change to be rounder, wider, sparser, and often with dead or spike tops. By 150 years, the once-scaly bark becomes deeply furrowed, fibrous, and often reddish, especially after the third century. To be truly ancient is to cross the threshold of eight hundred years. In groves more than five hundred years old, there are far more fallen trees that very slowly decompose and fortify the land.

Here, as in all ancient forests, the oldest trees are capturing and storing the most carbon. They are hosts for delicate relationships that become ever more sophisticated as the junipers age and offer far more nooks and crannies—twists, cavities, cracks, splits, hollow centers, dead or broken branches, and host-specific mistletoe brooms. Midge larvae feeding on twigs cause trees to form conelike galls, where the insects pupate and in spring emerge as white moths etched in dark wavy lines and speckles. More than twenty-four kinds of bark- and wood-boring beetles feed on western junipers.

Far from uniform in appearance, each juniper shines with personality ever more scintillating with age. Beneath the old ones, a fine root mat near the surface tends to keep out other plants. Where bunchgrass softens the shade can be a fine place for a nap in summer's scorching heat, according to Rick Miller when I called him to learn more.

Rick's intrigue with old-growth junipers began in the 1980s, examining specimens at the Laboratory of Tree-Ring Research in Tucson. On a trek with some of the researchers to what have long been called the badlands of central Oregon, he was shocked to find stumps dating to 1500 BCE. Now retired from Oregon State University, he continues to be on the forefront of fire and ecology studies of old junipers as well as pinyon pines of the Great Basin.

Knowing that more junipers over eight hundred years old dwell in the badlands than anywhere else in the world helped draw attention to protecting 29,300 acres as wilderness. I hike there often, especially in winter when snow deepens in the Cascades. Trails are plentiful, yet I'm drawn to cross-country ventures, careful where I step to avoid delicate mosses and soils. Once Rick was caught in a blizzard in the wilderness. Jogging back to the trailhead, he stopped to check his compass only to find he was 90 degrees off. He's never without a vest with pockets for compass, pencil, notebook, and measuring tools.

To find the old ones, Rick seeks the asymmetrical treetops and geology that favors survival. In central Oregon, tumuli are long domed ridges that formed when molten lava swelled to push crusts upward. These shield volcanoes are ideal refugia for old junipers. When lightning ignites wildfires, the rocks protect them from the flames. Sagebrush savannas also host the elder trees, spaced well apart from one another.

Hearing a solitaire singing in an old juniper, I pause to consider all who may have lived there over the centuries. Least chipmunks and golden-mantled ground squirrels curl up in cavities. Western small-footed myotis bats shelter under loose bark. Bushy-tailed woodrats (pack rats) pile their tumbling nests of juniper needles close to lower trunks. Coyotes den among exposed roots. Mountain cottontail rabbits burrow close by. Cougars leap into a juniper with a rabbit. Sagebrush and fence lizards hide below fallen old branches and trees. On a branch, a Northern Pygmy Owl deceives songbirds that might mob him with his eye-shaped feathers on the back of his head. Rocky Mountain elk and mule deer take shelter from storms. Their hooves press down fallen juniper berries. Those seeds that sprout do best in the shelter of other plants.

Juniper berries house two to three seeds encased in irresistible pulp. They offer their spicy delights to an array of other birds—American Robins, Western Bluebirds, Cedar Waxwings, Steller's Jays, and California Scrub Jays. The birds digest the juicy outer parts and then excrete the hard-coated seeds to the ground, multiplying by ten the chance of those seeds germinating. One Townsend's Solitaire can eat two hundred berries a day. I've often sampled a pungent berry with a crunch. Without juniper berries, gin would not be gin. The Northern Paiutes of the Great Basin and eastern Oregon have long harvested berries to be crushed, pounded, and mixed with deer liver to become pemmican. They boiled berries, skimmed the pitch, and breathed vapors to soothe colds, coughs, and flu.

The bountiful berries remind me of Robin Wall Kimmerer's book, *The Serviceberry: Abundance and Reciprocity in the Natural World*. As she picked the sweet and seedy serviceberries, Cedar Waxwings, American Robins, Gray Catbirds, and Eastern Bluebirds joined the banquet. The birds led to the premise of the book—a gift economy in which all flourish and none take more than their share. Every ripe berry is the result of gift exchanges. Trees drop leaves that insects and microbes break down into soil, ready for a seed dropped by a Cedar Waxwing. Her Potawatomi ancestors practiced a culture of gratitude that she continues. Birds show the way.

A gift economy would fundamentally change our relationship with junipers. No other native tree in the West is as maligned as the very one that can teach us the most. Surviving eons of dramatic shifts in climate, they are often derided as invasive. Wise in the way of conserving water in hard times, they are blamed as water stealers. Phenomenal at storing carbon, junipers and pinyon pines, too, are cut down by the thousands, often indiscriminately.

For five years when I still lived in Missoula, Montana, I served as the communications director for the Sage Grouse Initiative, a partnership with the Natural Resources Conservation Service and a model for improving habitat for the imperiled bird and for livestock grazing, too. I often headed out to far-flung ranches in multiple western states and wrote about successes for those enrolled in the voluntary programs. One aspect was tricky for me as a tree-lover. In some cases, the best way to help sage grouse is to cut down juniper trees that have expanded into the treeless sagebrush the birds require.

Before Euro-Americans, the ecosystems of pinyon and junipers naturally swelled in climatic periods with plentiful rain and shrank in times of drought. Indigenous peoples lived in synchrony with forests providing medicine, food, and materials. They respected the natural role of lightning and applied fire as a selective tool to rejuvenate plants. By the late 1800s and early 1900s, miners had cut swathes of forests for fuel and ranchers had cleared the lands to make way for huge herds of livestock. Overgrazing pummeled the native bunchgrasses and forbs that once carried flames to naturally thin out young junipers and pinyon pines. Without the plant cover, juniper and pinyon seedlings had less competition.

Fires were put out and tribal burning was banned. Given the complexity of the past practices, a changing climate, and the introduction of highly flammable cheatgrass, the role of fire is still hotly debated, and one that Rick is still sleuthing. As he told me, "A good ecologist needs to be a good detective." What most scientists do agree on is that fires were infrequent among the ancient juniper woodlands.

I believe it's time to honor junipers—every single tree. Practice gratitude, before cutting a single young tree advancing into Sage Grouse habitat. Balance what's taken by restoring life-giving bunchgrass, wildflowers, and springs damaged by cattle hooves. Honor the roles of predators and prey. Reintroduce fire with care. In some places, ending livestock grazing will allow delicate, dry lands to revive.

Close to home, I've joined fellow birders striving to prevent the cutting of mature junipers in Bend city parks—pointing out nest holes of Pygmy Nuthatches, the pouchlike hanging nests of Bushtits, small kinglet-sized songbirds, and the plethora of berries that birds need for the winter. Jim Anderson, a naturalist and champion of the natural world of central Oregon who died in 2022 at ninety-five, wrote a weekly column in the local newspaper for decades. I loved what he wrote about junipers: "What would the Juniper hairstreak butterfly do without the tree that bears its name? How about the ferruginous hawk, other raptors and even golden eagles who build nests in the very top in which they raise their young, and the mule deer who use it as a thermal shelter in winter?"[1]

Seeking the way of forest birds in three dimensions, I've become ever humbler among trees that grow very old. In a society obsessed with immortality and ways to keep us alive longer, we might learn a different lesson. While practicing a healthy lifestyle makes sense, I know anything could happen to cut my life short. With books on secrets to staying young and slowing aging, there's often a disconnect. We'd be better off focusing on living fully each day, in the ways the old junipers teach us.

What will the world be like in 500 years? What about 1,600 years? What about 2,000? Some junipers can live that long and most escape notice, with their twisted spreading trunks and hollowing cores. Old age for trees takes on a far different meaning. I think more about aging as my crow's feet deepen around my golden-brown eyes and my freckled arms bruise easily. My hair is thinner with strands that are multihued like old juniper bark—browns, blondes, auburns, and more silvery gray by the year. My body shows scars of two incisions to remove melanoma moles and the chipped tooth when I was eight that I've had repaired multiple times. Within my heartwood are the inevitable scars from loving and loss.

Like a juniper, I'm a composition in progress. While I can be flighty, I strive to root, feed curiosity, read, accept each new injury, ache, and pain, and listen with an open mind. I'm willing to let go of what no longer serves me, like an old juniper's dead wood. The structure holds the tree together, but energy flows through certain parts of the outer tree and branches. No other tree can instruct us on how to live frugally with less water, while showering others with generosity. Townsend's Solitaires of winter plucking berries turn our attention to the bounty that comes from growing slow and with patience.

TWENTY-ONE

Tall Tree Climb Return

Mourning Traverse

In the aftermath of the Lookout Fire, a part of me will always remain high up in Traverse. I'll tuck that memory in my body's inner sanctum, right there with those of my mother, father, and others I've lost. What I hadn't anticipated was the death of the Douglas-fir that survived the fire, but not a chainsaw. A crew under contract with the US Forest Service clearing "hazard trees" along the road made the decision to fell the 200-foot Douglas-fir, prioritized as a research tree and reachable by clambering down a steep slope. All Nina Ferrari's recording devices came crashing down along with thousands of tiny lives clinging to branches, needles, and bark. I assume it was a tough decision for the loggers, assessing the risk of the tree toppling and the upper branches striking the road as a vehicle or pedestrian passed by.

When I heard the news from Nina at the end of October 2025, the word "devastated" did not do justice to our shared emotions. Shock, anger, denial, and grief flooded my body as reality sank in. I could have accepted the death of Traverse in the wildfire as a rite of passage from living to dying to nourishing new life. But this? I thought of Le Guin's 1983 *Oregonian* letter. She did not fault those who cut down the horse chestnut tree in front of her home, writing, "Nice fellows, hard working men doing their job; the city sent them and they came." She did fault those who gave the orders: "The city of Portland has taken a quarter of a century of golden autumns away from me. It has killed a beloved part of my life, without a reason and without a word. This is not how it should be done. This is not how it should be."

I climbed Traverse once. Nina ascended many times. I return to her words describing her ascents. "You are small and insignificant yet connected to this huge tree you trust to keep you alive." Traverse kept that covenant of trust.

Soon after the fire ignited on August 5, 2023, the flames crept within steep terrain above Lookout and Mack Creeks, havens to ancient redcedars, hemlocks, and Douglas-firs. Some trees had stood for at least seven hundred years. A week later, temperatures would reach triple digits. Winds gusted. Once-lazy curls of smoke conflagrated into a 10,000-foot-tall column. Helicopters bearing water buckets looked like tiny toys. Researchers evacuated. Firefighters remained. The winds blew thick smoke westward across the Cascades right into my home community of Bend. Coughing, eyes burning, and breathing through my nose, I thought of the tree Nina named Wolfy and especially Traverse. I tried to take comfort in knowing that the older trees were shielded by mighty bark and filled with water. A 250-foot-tall Douglas-fir can hold about 1,000 gallons.

For months the forest was closed to all but the firefighters until autumn rains quelled the flames, except those deep within roots and tree hollows. After a winter of more than 100 inches of rain, a few plumes of smoke emerged the following spring, a reminder of fire's tenacity. About 11,000 of the 16,000 acres composing the H.J. Andrews Experimental Forest burned.

When I toured the Andrews Forest in July of 2024 with Nina and Mark Schulze, I braced myself. Safety rules were tight. We wore hard hats in case of falling limbs. We could not have gone far without Mark as Andrews Forest director and carrying his red card, qualifying him for wildland fire operations. From the pickup truck, I looked out the window, relieved to see the lower reaches of Lookout Creek as I remembered, with lush cottonwoods, bigleaf maples, and conifers tapping roots into cascading waters. That changed in a few miles. Wildfires tend to race uphill and slow on downhills, but gusting winds on a hot day can change everything—tossing embers sometimes a mile in front of flames. The fire had skipped, raced, and created a collage of scorched, sizzled land, and islands of green, especially along the creek that served as moist refugia.

As Mark drove us farther up the watershed, we saw stands of black and gray trees like feathers without their silky vanes. This is what a stand-replacing fire looks like—just what Black-backed Woodpeckers love to find. Nina had not yet seen Traverse. Hiking down from the road, taking care not to lose our footing, we passed redcedars, western hemlocks, and Douglas-firs that had all succumbed. I knew the understory would return with vigor. Saplings would sprout. Still, I felt sadness among the skeletal remains. And there was Traverse—charred and blackened. But Mark pointed to the plentiful green needles way up high, a good sign the tree would likely survive. Tough. Resilient. Nina and I linked arms as Mark snapped photos.

On another off-trail foray to inspect one of the fourteen Douglas-firs Nina had climbed many times, a Dark-eyed Junco flew up from close to Mark's foot. Peeling back the leaf of a native blackberry sprouting from the blackened soil, Nina revealed a delicate cup nest with four speckly white eggs. Renewal.

Three of Nina's second-growth trees and four ancient Douglas-firs had burned. Some would live. Others would serve the forest in new ways as homes to beetles that in turn would feed woodpeckers. Her studies continued in 2024 with adjustments for safety, but only after her sorrow had ebbed with the spring's first blooms of fireweed blazing purple among the ashes.

The toughest blow was losing Wolfy—the tree that had lived at least five centuries, grown to a six-foot-wide girth, known earlier fires, and was the hardest of all to ascend. "Wolfy was a friend and a teacher. I learned about climbing, myself, and the system around me," Nina told me on the day of the tour with Mark. "I've never felt that kind of relationship with a nonhuman. I'm sad, but I know life is just beginning for this tree." The decaying Wolfy would attract chiseling woodpeckers and some day fall to settle into a future as a mossy nurse log and home for Pacific Wrens, salamanders, millipedes, spiders, beetles, ants, and so much more. The carbon stored within Wolfy would nurture the soil and stay safely out of the atmosphere.

Her favorite moments were always in the canopy, finding tranquility in an uncertain world. There, Nina had the profound experience of feeling she was not the observer but the observed. The forest knew her. "A piece of me will be here forever," she said. "The Andrews has touched so many people and so many have loved this place."

What is tragic is losing ancient trees to chainsaws. I'd thought Nina's Douglas-firs would be safe. In other forests, I've wept as I stood on stumps the size of round dining room tables, oozing sap. I've stood in churned earth next to two-story piles of unwanted trees and branches, the "debris" to be burned. I've felt anger seeing clear-cuts from postfire "salvage logging" that tears apart nature's fabric.

Nothing compared to my feelings about Traverse. To be in the tree's high crown was akin to being in the arms of a lover. I cringe to think of the piercing whine as the chainsaw cut through the outer bark, cambium, and into the heartwood. Traverse smashed down in the way British Columbia artist Emily Carr had described as the "cry of the tree's heart, wrenching and tearing apart." The one comfort is Traverse was not hauled away, but left for a passage to the afterlife as a nurse log.

I've relived every moment of my tall tree climb, studying notes and the photos I took when high up among curtaining Douglas-fir needles and bearded lichens like pale-green scarves draping from branches. I replayed a video where I had spoken in a low voice. "I'm way up at the top of the rope. I can almost see the top. The ground is far below me. I'm not afraid at all. I love being so close to this tree but not harming her. Everywhere are beautiful lichens. The boughs are so wide I could stretch out on one and lie there. I'm feeling what it is to be embraced by the forest."

Listening closely to my recording, I could hear a single chord of a Varied Thrush far below. Never has that song sounded as haunting. In the drawn-out braided note, I heard my yearning for a world that honored the ancient groves and heeded Le Guin's words: "If the Grove were cut, all wizardry would fail. The roots of those trees are the roots of knowledge."[1]

I'm gathering my courage. I'm a writer. I will make use of my words. I will speak for Traverse and for all the bird-filled ancient trees.

TWENTY-TWO

Saving Refugia

I'm on the porch of the one cabin that did not burn almost five years earlier. Two Lazuli Buntings sing in stereo. Their staccato and fluid phrases overlap like the cadences of the Little North Santiam River below me. In the birds' harmonies, I hear renewal. Thanks to the Opal Creek Ancient Forest Center, I've come to Jawbone Flats with the first public group since the fateful day of September 7, 2020. Then, flames galloped at speeds of close to 3 acres per second. By sheer luck, the wildfire skipped over Cabin 4 and spared a sprinkling of Douglas-firs and western redcedars as well.

Upriver is a ghost forest of silvery trunks and needleless branches above seedling conifers in the shelter of wind-fallen trees. Across from me, the greening understory is in full July swing of fecundity. Willows leaning over the currents bind the soils. Bracken ferns, vine maples, bigleaf maples, red alders, and black cottonwoods grace the once-charred forest floor. Some of the maples are two stories tall, leaping to the light and fortified by the mycelial network of underground roots.

Before the Beachie Creek wildfire, Lazuli Buntings would be rare. Now, the turquoise, topaz, and moon-feathered birds spangle ebony dead trees above emerald thickets. Males are the flashy carolers. Females in gingery-tan plumage are the basketry makers, threading bark strips and leaves with tent caterpillar and spider silk to form cup nests fused to low branches of elderberry and salal. If bunting melodies had a fragrance, I'd choose the native blackberries and thimbleberries scenting the new forest like fresh jam poured into jars.

Rufous Hummingbird blurs past a vine maple, leaves shaking in the updraft of the river that exposes her rock bones postfire. Hammond's Flycatcher gives a quick uptick. Song Sparrow tips a waterfall from his beak. The sound of river falling over stone is uneven constancy. The voice of the bunting is dynamic change. Common Raven lands on a black snag ten feet away and eyes me with an eye of black. Everywhere are reminders of the burn, like the twisted piles of metal on this Jawbone Flats, an old mining claim turned environmental center that once rang with laughing children and will again.

The fire started small and simmering after a lightning strike by Beachie Creek within the Opal Creek Wilderness. When fierce winds gusting to 75 miles per hour raked through tinder-dry forests, it was like a hurricane had struck. Downed power lines along Cascades Highway 22 by the North Santiam River sparked new fires. The Santiam and Lionhead fires collided with Beachie Creek. An inferno threw embers miles ahead to set fire to buildings and treetops alike.

The megafire burned 310,000 acres. Families lost their homes and five people died, including George Atiyeh, the environmentalist whose indefatigable campaign led to the saving of one of the finest big forests left on the planet—this one. The Opal Creek Wilderness and Scenic Area, designated in 1996, is 33,000 acres. An hour and a half east of Oregon's capital city of Salem, the wild forests quickly became a destination for experiencing cathedral trees.

In that same Labor Day weekend of 2020, the Holiday Farm fire burned 175,000 acres along the McKenzie River, also in the lush west-side Cascades and east of Eugene. Quenching rains put out the last wisps of smoke in early December for all fires.

Ultimately, nature is in charge. Our charge is to listen to birds that show us a better way of living in relationship with Mother Earth. Wild forests teach the way of resilience and natural renewal. Just as the Lookout Fire in the Andrews Forest created a mosaic of unburned, lightly, and severely burned lands, so did the Opal Creek burn. Within are the suites of birds finding home.

Because of the preservation mandate at Opal Creek, no damaging new roads or salvage logging will rob the land of shade, roots, nurse trees, and nutrients. On the drive up a winding road to the locked gate where our group of ten began our three-mile walk in, we'd passed private lands clear-cut after the fire. The hillsides were a bereft sea of stumps and weeds exposed to relentless sun and heat.

Still, I'd braced myself for loss when I made my plans to join the field trip. Forty years earlier I was here with conservation and scientist heroes, including Jerry Franklin, father of old-growth ecology. George Atiyeh was the leader. We hiked at a naturalist's pace. On whitewater wings, Opal Creek swooped down to the Opal Pool, a translucent deep sapphire fringed in tall conifers. When we reached Cedar Flats among thousand-year-old trees, all conversation stopped. Reverence spoke. I remember a forest dripping in every shade of green and the animated conversations on how to keep the wilds safe from the Willamette National Forest's intentions to log it all.

I am looking through a new lens. Etched in the ancient forest's memory are the instructions for returning from cone, seed, root, stem, and charred trees that hold soil, shade saplings, and new life. The birds are the troubadours of rebirth. A MacGillivray's Warbler scolds from her nest within tangled branches of a burned fallen tree. Hairy Woodpeckers tap for beetles in charcoal snags. A knee-high sapling with an inch of the summer's growth of green needles shades up by the trunk of a Douglas-fir as black as the raven and as wide as the wingspan of an eagle. I wonder if this new postfire Douglas-fir is kin to the elder? Vaux's Swifts curve above the icy river as if inscribing calligraphy.

A new lens takes time to break in. When our group walks to Opal Pool at sunrise of our second day to help with a bird survey, the fairyland of memory had shattered into a riot of strewn pickup sticks, remnants of a firestorm. And yet, the song of a Swainson's Thrush twines upward like a blooming clematis vine. First light over the ridge spotlights ashy gray and black trunks standing straight as porcupine quills. The bird chorus swells. We'd divided into small groups to listen for ten minutes of silence and record birds on the Merlin app. From above the hush-rush of Opal Creek, we hear the buntings joined by White-crowned Sparrows, Western Tanagers, Western Wood Pewees, and Cedar Waxwings. The birds conjure a resurgence of life.

I run my fingers over the tight, white clustered blossoms of pearly everlasting, named for the flower's way of becoming a natural dried arrangement on the stem. What is everlasting? Is there anything that will last forever? The romantic in me believes in that possibility. Birds lifting me up to every level of a feathered forest remind me to suspend left-brain thinking.

On the three-mile uphill walk on the two-track pathway into Jawbone Flats, a little boy in our group had picked up a lone feather. Soft as a suede buckskin jacket with brushed bands of dark brown, the feather bore a message from the unseen owl. Looking closer, we noticed a pearly brooch of fourteen tiny eggs attached to the vane. To be everlasting, there must be new beginnings at every scale.

In my journeys with birds and the verticality of great trees in Cascadia, I'm coming to know the meaning of the word ephemeral, too. Like yin and yang, everlasting and ephemeral seek a spirited balance. Lately, ephemeral seems far too prominent.

Take the Vaux's Swift tree in Olympic National Park. I'd aimed to meet Melinda Wood at dusk in September of 2025 in hopes of watching a mini-tornado of birds vanishing into the woodpecker hole of a tall Douglas-fir. Instead, the human-caused Bear Gulch wildfire in July barreled right toward the ancient trees. Because the youthful biologist had alerted the park rangers to the tree's significance, firefighters wrapped the Douglas-fir in a fireproof wrap and set sprinklers to water the tree. That giving act alone alleviated some of the sorrow. Always, I lament we have not protected far more older forests.

Ephemeral, too, is the Doerner Fir, the tallest Douglas-fir on the planet at 327 feet, with a diameter of 11.5 feet, and more than 450 years old. The tree is a half hour from Francis Eatherington's home near Roseburg, Oregon. She had urged me to go see the tree, and I was sure I'd have plenty of chances for an outing. Two months after our trek into the Elliott State Forest, the Douglas-fir caught fire without a lightning strike. A vandal? Who would do this? I can't fathom why. I'm reminded of the famed Sycamore Gap tree by Hadrian's Wall in Britain, senselessly cut down by two men.

For every troubled person, there's a heavier counterweight of goodness. Two brave climbers hauling a fire hose ascended the Doerner Fir and shot water down the hollow top to douse the last of the flames. The tree is no longer the tallest, but lives on.

I've come to know people who care deeply about birds, roadless wilderness, and the last big trees. Young world changers give me hope, like Nina Ferrari aloft in the highest trees to study birds in three dimensions. She's the emerging scientist, willing to show her emotions and love for the great tree Wolfy who was her teacher. Thanks to her, I learned the meaning of serene while 175 feet off the ground in Traverse.

Singular trees have become meaningful—and Traverse most of all. I care for the Climate Guardian Sitka Spruce of Cape Meares, the Grandmother ponderosa pine of the Turquoise Forest near my home, the oldest western juniper on Horse Ridge, and the Douglas-fir that fell across the Imnaha River while we were sleeping and revealed a cougar's cache of an elk calf in upper branches.

And yes, I fell hard for the Western Grebe tapping the box in my camper as hard rain pummeled the roof. A month after that night, volunteers with the Wildlife Center of the North Coast set her free in the bay, protected by the peninsula where I camped at Cape Lookout State Park. While not able to join them, I did see an earlier photo of the recovering grebe swimming in a tank. From a bedraggled, brown, and sandy mess, she'd become a fashion queen with a snowy elegant neck, velour black cap, and fluffy gray back. Even her red eye and yellow beak seemed brighter. Behind her makeover were hours of volunteer time cleaning and washing her plumage until the grebe could take over to preen. Care for one grebe. Care for the oceans linked to the wild trees by the passaging of Marbled Murrelets nesting in the highest platform branches.

At my home, I'm tracing a familiarity of birds courting, nesting, and raising their young. Mountain Chickadee fledglings beg to be fed with wings quivering and beaks open. A Dark-eyed Junco feeds two Brown-headed Cowbirds twice her size, painful to watch even as I respect the ingenuity of a bird laying eggs in another's nest. I resist the temptation to interfere when a Cooper's or Sharp-shinned Hawk snatches a junco. Predators must eat, too. Drawn to the flame-red eyes, steering long tails, and sharp talons, I've become more adept at identifying the smaller Sharp-Shinned by the pencil-like yellow legs and the Cooper's by the black cap.

To notice, to pay attention, to name, and to go deeper into the way of birds and trees are steps toward our own rewilding in the web of life, never in the center. Since my meditations with the spruce and grebe, I've returned often to the philosophical question of why it is compelling to act on behalf of an individual but not on behalf of the whole. The answer may lie in human evolution or in tapping into our empathy. Why not turn kindness into our superpower? Once our emotions are tapped, we're primed for specific actions. We crave positive solutions that fend off despair.

Save every wild feathered forest left, every roadless area, every big tree, old tree, dead tree, and all the secret relationships that birds can divulge if we attend. Renew and heal what we have harmed. As humans have heated up the world, the very Earth is responding and striving to keep our planet stable. The forests are taking up 30 percent of the additional carbon dioxide we've added. The largest trees are capturing and storing the most. To cut them down is to be cavalier with the future. When they burn, they still can hold carbon for centuries if left alone. If standing, they are homes for multitudes of birds, from woodpeckers to nuthatches.

Oceans, estuaries, marshes, prairies, and every natural system left on Earth are all part of the great natural carbon capture and biodiversity lifeline. As alarmingly fewer birds trace our skies, I believe they are signaling us to act. Isn't it time we looked up from our feet, our phones, and took notice?

There are positive signs. The delegates to the International Union for Conservation of Nature in 2024 voted overwhelmingly to pursue the goal of protecting half of the Earth's lands and seas, starting with 30 percent by 2030. The strategy is laid out as a clear solution by E. O. Wilson in his book, *Half-Earth: Our Planet's Fight for Life.*

Even if we've passed tipping points for climate, our actions matter at every scale. What we do at this moment of life on Earth will be felt for thousands of years. Dr. David Mildrexler, a systems ecologist with Eastern Oregon Legacy Lands, puts forward a tangible vision for saving climate refugia that resonates every time I hear him speak. I'm fortunate to have learned from him in the field.

David, who is tall, lanky, and good-natured, has a gentle lilt to his voice, especially when in the field sharing natural wonders. He's equally at home mapping, charting, analyzing data, and collaborating with other scientists. Like me, he's intrigued by the promise of climate refugia. While refuge means safe, sheltered from pursuit, danger, or trouble, refugia are places biodiversity retreats to, persists in, and expands from when environmental conditions improve.

Taking E. O. Wilson's half-Earth call seriously, David and fellow scientists mapped out a proposal for strategic forest reserves in eleven western states, with the majority on federal public lands.[1] Wilderness is key, but there are far too few. Roadless areas compose more than a third of the mapped reserves. For wildlife they are havens, linkages, and corridors ever more critical for finding elusive refugia in a warming world. Mountainous refugia may distribute water that spreads subsurface, unimpeded by roads.

Across national forests, roads add up to 380,000 miles. All the zigzags and horizontal road cuts are shuffling water away to be channeled elsewhere. Roads make the forests drier and more prone to burn. They also make it easy for people to enter. Most fires are human-caused and most start near roads. For interior forest birds, roads are entries for edge predators like jays and ravens that seek nest eggs and chicks.

Our momentous task is to save all the roadless areas we can here in Cascadia and elsewhere. I turn again to the 2025 clarion call from environmental philosopher Kathleen Dean Moore, when she exhorts the crowd at the annual Public Interest Environmental Law Conference to "get in the way of the forces of destruction," like the kipuka in a catastrophic lava flow that then becomes a refugia.[2] Whenever I need inspiration, I can clamber to the close-by kipuka. Every trek there is different. Bonsai ponderosa pines and junipers twist their roots into crevices seeking water far below. In the moist lava tubes with roofs long gone are rock penstemon, ferns, moss, and saxifrage flowers. They teach me a tenacity for living and give me hope, too, that those microrefugia will persist. Earth will survive and rewild.

In 2023, I wrote a series of interpretive displays overlooking a restoration project along several miles of the Middle Fork of the John Day River, winding through the Blue Mountains not far from where I lived in my twenties in Prairie City. The Confederated Tribes of the Warm Springs owns and stewards this stretch, part of their ceded lands from the Treaty of 1855.

The John Day River is the longest free-flowing tributary of the Columbia—from headwaters in northeast Oregon streaming 281 miles to enter the great river above the John Day dam. Chinook salmon still must navigate three Columbia River dams to reach the confluence and turn upriver. Within three years, the tribes and their partners had transformed a damaged stretch of river artificially confined to a narrow channel and separated from the floodplain by an old railroad grade that once hauled lumber. On my first field visit in August of 2023, I witnessed six adult Chinook salmon resting side by side in a constructed pool that had not been there a year earlier. Beavers soon moved in to build stick dams, backing up water into ponds and irrigating meadows. The cold-water refugia of beavers creates a fire-resistant landscape, where species can persist and recolonize severe burns.

Thousands of new native plants are growing there; many are important to the culture of the tribe, from dogbane for baskets to chokecherry and serviceberry. Heavy machinery, gentle nudges, and knowledge of hydrology combined with Traditional Ecological Knowledge have led to a stunning recovery. Birds polish the renewed river with their bright presence, from Western Tanagers to Belted Kingfishers and Sandhill Cranes.

In Kathleen's powerful speech, she also offered this wisdom: "Don't ever think that a sanctuary, no matter how singed or damaged, no matter how small or struggling, doesn't matter."

I believe that's true for our individual actions, whether adding a native plant for birds and pollinators or speaking up for a local park. Share every success, no matter how small. Joining community actions often leads to camaraderie, laughter, and creativity—like the "green ribbon protest"—an impromptu campaign to save sixty-five trees. Our local parks department had deemed them in the way of a planned wide-paved bike path through Drake Park in the heart of downtown Bend by Mirror Pond. A group of intrepid women, frustrated that our concerns were being disregarded, took action. Snipping big strips of green ribbon, we wrote on them, "Don't cut me down. Go around." Using a map of the plan that showed each potentially doomed tree, we tied the ribbons to the trees and then called the local TV and radio station. They promptly came and the news was out. In the hour before the parks department rushed to take down every ribbon, we noticed dog walkers, hand-in-hand lovers, families, and others, stopping, reading, and registering shock, especially when they saw the ribbon on one of the park's few magnificent ponderosas. To the park's credit, they altered their plans and did go around more trees than they would have otherwise. They avoided the centuries-old ponderosa, but the tree died two years later—the roots too damaged by the construction. Yet, despite losses, we made a difference with our rebellious camaraderie.

The course is charted. We know what we must protect and renew. Portals and touchstones connect us to what's at stake. Touch one grand tree in a city park and multiply that tree by thousands far away in roadless wilds of Cascadia threatened by logging. When the amorphous becomes intimate, we open ourselves to kinship and action.

At every turn, we have a chance to bridge the familiar to the unfamiliar, even the domestic to the wild. Take the most common domestic bird—the chicken. While writing this book I tended a free-ranging flock for my friends Dawn and Ram. One sassy golden hen flew over the fence every day to join White-crowned Sparrows pecking sunflower seeds below the feeders. I called her Dorothy for her ability to leave Kansas for the other side of the rainbow.

A white chicken with a limp from a damaged foot fooled me, even as I cajoled her with special treats. Unbeknownst to me, she began laying eggs in an unused chicken coop, and a few other co-conspirators joined her. When my friends returned, they found two dozen still-good eggs hidden there. I'd wondered why there were fewer eggs in the main coop. Coming to know chicken personalities, I'm determined to shun factory farms.

In that same sanctuary, I spent time with wild Band-tailed Pigeons, the closest I will ever come to picturing Passenger Pigeons clouding the sky. Sitting by the edge of the bend of a dreamy slough where Wood Ducks glide, I heard a *coo coo* and looked up to see a courting pigeon pair on the bare limb at the top of an alder tree. One puffed up his head and neck feathers, then leaned toward the other with a seductive croon. She turned away.

Seeking to know more about their courtship, I looked up the "Birds of the World" account and, sure enough, the male performs those classic moves. Add a strut and neck swinging and an intrigued female might bob her head. I smiled when I read this scientific sentence: "Sequence of actions leading to copulation may vary, but all seem unhurried." Perhaps that's the pigeon way, as if to say, let's not get too excited here. Chill out. Be mellow. Patience is the way.

Bigger than city pigeons, Band-tailed Pigeons are lavender and gray with white crescents on the backs of their necks, and the namesake tail. When they coo loudly, I can be deceived into thinking I've heard hoots of owls. Their favored homes are the older, unlogged forests. Knowing they travel in flocks of a hundred or more to find nuts, fruits, and flowers, I couldn't help but compare them to their extinct Passenger Pigeon kin.

To see a living relative is both a blessing and a warning of this time of the Sixth Mass Extinction. Band-tailed Pigeons are considered common but in steep decline, likely from a combination of legal hunting and the decimation of forest habitats. I've only observed small flocks of this coastal population. A separate group lives in the Four Corners area of the Southwest. The coastal pigeons nest from southeast Alaska through Oregon and winter south in California, where they mingle with year-round birds.

Before Euro-Americans arrived with guns and indiscriminate shooting, there were millions of Band-tailed Pigeons, as dependent on Cascadia's enormous coastal conifers as Passenger Pigeons were to the massive oaks of the eastern United States. The living birds nest in multilevel forests with saplings and pole-sized trees. In their "not hurried" way, a pair will take almost a week to create a sloppy saucer-shaped nest lined with needles, moss, and breast feathers, secured to a branch in a tree from 10 to 180 feet off the ground. Both parents care for the one or two squabs (chicks), born helpless, without feathers. They feed them curdlike "milk" formed in their crops, often derived from sodium minerals the birds must find in springs. The birds also feast on the fruits of elderberry and huckleberry. Wherever I dig deeper to learn about one forest bird I find tangled relationships.

We will never know a living Passenger Pigeon. It's up to us to save the native cousin. The natural touchstone for the Band-tailed Pigeon? A Rock Pigeon. Rather than malign the urban bird introduced to North America in the early 1600s, we might note the way a male courts a female with bows, coos, struts, and inflating throat feathers. Praise the iridescent purples and greens on their necks. Imagine their wild kin flapping through monumental forests instead of skyscrapers.

As I close the circle of writing about birds and forest refugia at every level, I turn again to the wisdom of Ursula K. Le Guin, who wrote in her novel *The Word for World Is Forest*, "In diversity is life and where there's life there's hope."[3]

Recently, I returned to her fantasy novel *Always Coming Home*, an "anthropology of the future" featuring the matrilineal culture of the Kesh, who lived in the Valley on the northern Pacific Coast. On the first page, I read, "In Sinshan babies' names often come from birds, since they are the messengers."[4]

Birds as messengers of wild forests turn our attention to thousands of beings as hooked together as the barbs and barbules on a feather vane. In the understory, American Dipper teaches the way of flowing waters quenching thirst of roots transporting drinks hundreds of feet above to the highest crowns. Pacific Wren sings odes to tip-up trees, mossy springs, and origins of freshwater. Varied Thrush song chords the slanted light of the redwoods and life-giving fog. Sempervirens. Ever living.

In midstory, Great Gray Owl ghosts into trees on velour wings, every flap defining beauty as dense lodgepoles, rumpled meadows, and leaning trees as ramps for owlets. Chestnut-backed Chickadee flicks our attention to inchworms, spiders, and mites. A quartet of woodpeckers chants the mystery of afterlife.

Highest of all, Vaux's Swifts circle what we must save—every big, old, hollow tree. Hermit Warbler teaches fidelity to homes across international boundaries. Marbled Murrelet traces ocean to forest to ocean, flying with fast wingbeats conveying messages of inseparability and sustenance. Spotted Owl is the dimming star, the bird that saved so much, the bird we must save, and yet the choices are heart-rending as Barred Owls proliferate in remnant hideaways. Among the old juniper forests of winter, Townsend's Solitaires lead to the wisest of all elders that in turn teach the lessons of thinking in very long timespans.

Every bird carries a message. "Attend! Our future is your future." Some may think we can live without the wild forests in fortresses of concrete, glass, and plastic. They may put their faith in big brains to come up with technology to capture carbon dioxide while continuing to decimate the atmosphere.

Will we listen? Will we look up to the trees? Find our inner child and climb one—even if small—to feel birdlike? We are in servitude to gravity tethering us to the ground. Our bones dense. Our steps crushing. Our two-legged way awkward. We have no feathers or fur. No wings. We are bald as some chicks hatched naked and vulnerable. Some would protest. Our big brains invented airplanes, spaceships, and even satellites to course above the atmosphere. Who needs wings? But we are, like Icarus, flying too close to the sun.

We are more like each other than we think. The rise of birding is widespread and far from partisan. In 2024, the US Fish and Wildlife Service reported 96 million people are watching birds—or three out of ten Americans. That same year, 331 million people visited national parks—many with wild forests.[5] During COVID, birding took off for young and old alike who stayed home and spent far more time outdoors than before. We've become a murmuration of bird lovers for advocacy and funding. Still, we can and will flex our muscles far more, supporting grassroots and national conservation groups and taking personal actions locally and globally.

I envision all who love birds and the wilds converging like tributaries entering a swelling river on her way to the sea. As a river washes over and around stones, funnels through clefts, pools, eddies, and twists through feathered forests, so we can ride the flow, finding beauty and exulting in our commonality.

When environmental crises seem overwhelming, I remind myself that I am one person trying to live the best life I can and can't control all outcomes. I turn to my tiny refugia at home, where hummingbirds sip nectar from columbines in August, readying for their impossibly long flights to the tropics. I walk to the Grandmother ponderosa and listen to her wisdom by the lava rocks where a Canyon Wren sings a rainbow of falling notes. I find solace every time I cross a boundary sign into wilderness, even as I vow to do more for the unprotected wilds. Among birds of the feathered forests, I have come to know a refugia of silence, solitude, dark skies, shelter, and desire.

Connecting the phases of my life to birds among vertical layers of trees, I could not trace a straight-line chronology. Memories mingled, overlapped, and surprised me like forest patterns revealed. Growing up in a peripatetic family helped me learn skills of navigation, adaptation, and a smidge of the courage of migratory birds. Circular paths emerged, like climbing trees as a child and an adult. Sparks lit the flames for becoming an environmentalist. Attending the University of Oregon honed my activism on behalf of wild places. In Montana, I raised my son, followed kingfishers, and helped conserve natural open space lands. To return to Oregon in my fifties felt like the closing of a circle and an opening of unforeseen wonder, as if entering a shaft of sunlight beaming down from the canopies of tall trees.

On May 5, 2025, I joined Mary Ann and Bob for the spring migration north of Vaux's Swifts through Bend. Already, they'd counted for a month with many nights of zero swifts or only a handful. But the night before was an uptick in numbers to 212 birds. Spring is more unpredictable, with fewer high numbers than in fall. Only the three of us looked skyward at sunset. The first swift flew directly to the brick chimney and dropped in as if exhausted. Slowly, the birds flittered and twittered closer, ten or twenty at a time.

Swiftly comes the night. Swiftly come the arrow birds scattering scraps of daylight to quilt the sky in tangerine gold. Their whirling around the chimney is an incantation as if shape-shifting their roost into a magnificent hollow tree. Looking upward, I'm closing and opening my hands, as if all the birds of Cascadia feathered forests might spill between my fingers and find refugia forever.

Epilogue

The trees are flying.

I hold a photo of an airborne ancient ponderosa pine in a circular sky of robin egg blue that's fractured at the edges. Guggenheim award-winning photographer Nancy Floyd created the illusion. We had become friends through her long-term photography project, "For the Love of Trees," that regularly takes her to the Andrews Forest. "If Trees Could Fly" is her name for this creative series she began in 2023. After so much time in their company, she easily shifts to thinking like trees.

Meeting at her home studio in Bend, Nancy had printed out several photos to show me, explaining her concept. "What if trees could fly? What would they want to do?" She envisions an exercise for viewers of an exhibit where the images would be blown up very large. "Why would they want to go? Where would you imagine they go?"

Flying trees seem fitting in 2025. Escape is on my mind. Magical surrealism appeals. Why wouldn't trees want to lift off the ground and spread their bird-like branches and wing to safety? After all, they are the feathered forests.

I had one foot in the immersive beauty of ancient forests raining birdsong and the other in a pile of anxiety. I wondered if I was writing of a world that will be lost to future generations. Then, I'd redouble my efforts to name, to celebrate, to evoke wonder, and invite others to slip in and join me. I would be remiss not to account for the source.

The 2024 US elections marked a sharp turn away from a green energy future, and toward the removal of environmental laws and accelerated logging on national forests—including rescinding the Roadless Area Rule of 2001. Despite the turmoil, I'm finding strands of hope. People who love wild nature come from both sides of the political divide. They stood up together to oppose the selling of public lands and that unifying groundswell worked.

The concept of climate refugia becomes ever more important as a cultural refugia for creativity and solutions for a future beyond our time. As a board member of the nonprofit Greater Hells Canyon Council, I've seen our youthful staff pivot to creating alliances and good will among neighbors through beaver and stream restoration. They're inviting people to bumblebee surveys near the rim of Hells Canyon and fostering relationships with members of the Nez Perce tribe, the Nimipuu, who are leading the return of the California Condor to once again soar over Joseph Canyon and a vast ecosystem defined by the wild Snake River cutting through Hells Canyon. In the Nimipuu language, Joseph Canyon is called Ananasocum, the place where condors nested.

Our group also created the Blue Mountains Trail, 550 miles and connecting northeast Oregon's seven wilderness areas and many roadless areas from John Day to Joseph. With no need to build new trails, the route across public lands via trails and old secondary roads offers long-distance and day hikers far more than recreation. When hikers fall in love with backcountry wilds, they can become advocates for saving one of the few places left in the United States that's large enough to support the home ranges of wide-ranging animals like wolverines and bighorn sheep, and migration corridors for wildlife and even plants to move and adapt to a changing climate.

Small towns along the way are welcoming hikers and seeing new ways of a blossoming economy, one based on keeping the wilds wild. Our group hasn't backed down one iota on defending ancient forests and roadless areas, while bridging differences to find commonality with all who live and share that gorgeous nook of the planet.

When we come to know one another—to shovel driveways of snow in winter, borrow butter, and exchange garden plants—we are erasing artificial borders and finding we are more in synchrony with nature's daily miracles than we might think. I often recite what I care deeply about in the natural world and feel energy flooding through me. We will be the upwelling of the Pacific Ocean bearing nourishment of deep icy waters to the surface. We who care deeply will continue to stand up for the birds, the forests, and for each other. I believe in wild birds to gift us with spiritual uplift as we return gifts to their lives.

Writing in late summer, a wildfire to the north sent choking smoke across central Oregon. Several times a day, I changed the water in the bird baths. So many flew in to drink and wash their smoky feathers—Red Crossbills, Black-headed Grosbeaks, Pygmy Nuthatches, Mountain Chickadees, and more. A mule deer spotted fawn nudged the gate open and sipped water too. Always I turn to the immediate. This is my solace as I contemplate what's next.

When democracy fractures, there's opportunity to create a better society where nature is not an afterthought, where everyone is an environmentalist, and where the values of living simply so others may simply live are paramount. Like birds in guilds gleaning in mixed flocks, we will find safety and synergy. In August I watched thirty Common Mergansers fishing in unison on the high-elevation Paulina Lake. They sped across the water on webbed feet, circled, splashed, reared up like stallions, dove, and herded a school of jumping fish close to the shore lined in lodgepole pines. Cooperation led to plenty for all. At every turn, birds seem to be telling me, "Observe! We will show you a hundred ways to live far better than you do now."

Heeding the lessons of birds, we will hold one another aloft and care for our feathers so we can keep flying. We will say the names of birds, of plants, of trees, and bring them into everyone's consciousness until the word "kinship" is on all our lips.

Finally, we will not fall into fear, or apathy, or turn our backs. We will return to the stories of good ancestors who overcame impossible odds for civil rights, and those who stood up for the rights of rivers to run free, of wild places to be wilderness with the big W, and of birds to be free of pesticides like DDT. To keep our spirits renewed in hard times, we can turn to beavers rewilding streams and Black-backed Woodpeckers enlivening severely burned forests.

In the summer of 2019, I tagged along with a small crew from the nonprofit conservation groups Appalachian Trail Conservancy and MountainTrue as they selected and then treated white ash trees with chemicals to protect them from the deadly invasive emerald ash borer, introduced accidentally from Asia. Their ongoing work marks the first backcountry effort to save legacy trees. Since 2016, they've mapped and injected more than 1,400 trees by the Appalachian Trail, returning every three years to treat them again.

The premise is for the trees to outlast the borers and for the mountain winds to carry their seeds to plant new trees when it's safe. Seed-eating birds, too, can fly even farther with the gift of ash trees to be. Like the birds winging from Greenland to northeastern North America and back again generations later with the seeds of another ash, they are emissaries. Climate refugia works.

That day in 2019, we entered a refugia of a cove forest in the southeast. I love the word "cove," like an ocean bay protected from winds and storms.

The fluting of a Wood Thrush coiled pure notes among buckeye, sugar maple, basswood, yellow birch, and white ash patterning the sky. I soft-stepped among shade-loving and delicate blue cohosh, mayapples, and Goldie's fern, some understory plants growing hip-high. When we came to a stalwart white ash, Matt Drury of the Appalachian Trail Conservancy suggested we name this one after my father, Dave Richie. Sometimes, naming a tree for a person is just fine, especially when there would be no plaque or mark on a map. I put one hand on the gray corduroy bark and the other on furry moss and gave thanks.

When Hurricane Helene slammed into the southern Appalachian Mountains with high winds and a deluge of rain in late September of 2024, I feared for the cove. The next spring, Josh Kelly of MountainTrue sent me an email with news. He'd made it back to treat the trees, only to find high winds had knocked down twenty of the ash trees they'd worked so hard to save, including some of the largest. But not all was lost. The Dave Richie tree is in an "exceptionally sheltered location, and it not only survived, but it is over 40 inches in diameter now and has grown over an inch in diameter since we started treating it." Many other large and lovely trees lived. It's true, I thought—there is hope for safe harbors, for nature's marinas.

Matt and Josh never met my Dad, but they knew of his leadership in conserving more than half a million acres of wildlands along the Appalachian Trail (AT) from Georgia to Maine when he served as the National Park Service AT project manager in the 1970s and '80s. I can think of no better tree to be named after a forest lover, birder, naturalist, backpacker, environmentalist, anti-bureaucrat, and quiet visionary. Aching for my dad still, some twenty-three years after his passing, I remember his rapt expression when out hiking and listening to warblers. He knew dozens of species by ear and taught me a lasting love of birds and wild places.

Love is the word with the greatest power of all, one that no amount of money can overcome. I will keep showing up for the love of trees, for the love of birds, for the love of this still wondrous Earth. I will act out of love for all who are kin, from mites stirring in aerial moss gardens where Marbled Murrelets nest to Great Gray Owls hooting among the shadowy grand firs of the Blue Mountains.

ACKNOWLEDGMENTS

A bird flies best with a full assemblage of feathers. A book takes flight with the uplift of people. Scientists, naturalists, environmental advocates, birders, friends, family, and editors all feathered my writing. As signature birds guided me to vertical realms, scientists led me through a labyrinth of ancient forest ecology. At the H.J. Andrews Experimental Forest, Matt Betts first introduced me to the vertical world of birds in ancient forests. His vision inspired my direction and his suggestions improved the manuscript. Nina Ferrari assured I would succeed in climbing a tall tree, invited me to tag along in the field as she ascended immense trees, and brightened my days with her courageous spirit. Mark Schulze led a postfire tour and interpreted tree ecology. Thank you to the bird banders for my field day featuring the undergraduate research of Adlai Herrera, with help from her adviser Matt Johnson. I'm grateful to Hankyu Kim (Hermit Warblers) and saddened by his passing in April 2026.

Tim Schowalter awakened me to insects, spiders, and mites dwelling high in the canopy. Rick Miller interpreted ancient juniper forest ecology. Charles Lefevre with his dogs Dante and Lucca unearthed truffles, the food of the forest. David Mildrexler provided invaluable insights on climate refugia and the interconnected wildlands of the Blue Mountains. Ian Wilson shared beaver and river restoration expertise and Brian Kelly his knowledge of forest ecology. Dick Hutto contributed to my understanding of Black-backed Woodpeckers and severe fire renewal. Janice Reid brought Spotted Owls to life through her stories from decades of field research. Kim Nelson generously shared her Marbled Murrelet expertise in the field and afterward. Megan Selvig and Jennifer Johns led our Opal Creek group in bird surveys revealing wondrous diversity after wildfire.

Environmentalists are often unheralded heroes. Here's to Francis Eatherington, who put me to work ground-truthing planned timber sales in the Elliott State Research Forest. Cheers to Paul Engelmeyer, stitching together sanctuaries for coastal forests to grow old and support biodiversity. Thanks to

Joe Liebezeit for his conservation leadership and organizing the community-science Marbled Murrelet Survey for the Bird Alliance of Oregon. Brodie Cass Talbott revealed moth diversity at that event. Chandra LeGue of Oregon Wild is a favorite hiking companion in the ancient forests she works to protect. Her book, *Oregon's Ancient Forests: A Hiking Guide*, has become a well-worn field guide and ecology source. I'll never forget my day with Chandra and forest ecologist John Cissel in Crabtree Valley as we stood so very small below the "King Tut" tree. Josh Kelly of MountainTrue and Matt Drury of Appalachian Trail Conservancy led me to the cove forest where the Dave Richie ash tree lives on.

A tiny Pacific Wren has more than 1,200 feathers. Similarly, the people who have influenced this journey are too many to list—thanks to all, including the staff and volunteers of nonprofits: North Coast Wildlife Center, Greater Hells Canyon Council, Oregon Wild, Umpqua Watersheds, Cascadia Wildlands, Eugene Natural History Society, Bird Alliance of Oregon, and Opal Creek Ancient Forest Center. I'm indebted to the H.J. Andrews Experimental Forest in partnership with Oregon State University.

Kathleen Dean Moore gave me permission to quote from her powerful speech. Wendy Probst, my former editor for essays I penned for *A. T. Journeys*, helped shape my book proposal with encouragement to venture into magical surrealism. Thanks to Suzanne Johnson and Ellen Santasiero for helping lift "Feathered Forest" from concept to the beginnings of a book, and to Suzanne for thoughtful reviews of several chapters. I appreciate Mike Beaty, my fellow Ursula K. Le Guin fan, for steering me to certain passages and books. Thanks to the Ekphrastic Poetry Group led by Laurel Benjamin for critiques of poems I turned into prose for the book, and to poet Annis Cassells for leading me to the group and for the warmth of her friendship.

Mary Ann Kruse and Bob Johnson are two of the most dedicated community scientists I know. I treasured sunset evenings as they counted Vaux's Swifts funneling into a downtown chimney in Bend. Melinda Wood shared the marvel of watching swifts descend into a hollow ancient Douglas-fir in Olympic National Park. Michele Kellogg's photography of Lewis's Woodpeckers nesting in our neighborhood forest illuminated behaviors I would have missed. Seeking Great Gray Owls with Sevilla Rhoads and her children Ander and Chloe, we found nature's intricacy at every turn. I met Nancy Floyd through her "For the Love of Trees" long-term photography project, and through her artistic lens I've gained new perspectives—even flying trees. Robin Coen and I teamed up as artists-in-residence for the Greater Hells Canyon Council. Joining Robin at her Good Bear Ranch and writing prose and poetry to accompany her watercolors for a *Refugia of the Blue Mountains* traveling exhibit sparked ideas.

David Liberty helped me attribute certain tribal homelands and names. Sandra Murphy, dear friend since 1987, joined me in several ancient forest excursions. I'm indebted to her for the book's subtitle, too. Mathieu Federspiel led our group to the oldest western juniper. I cherish my local friend Gail Sabbadini for her support, keen eye for birds, and environmental activism.

As a bird seeks refuge, so I crave time alone to write. Several friends gave me that gift through house-sitting stays. Thanks to Dawn Harris and Ram Papish, Margie Ryan and Jamie Fereday, Jan Hodder and Mike Graybill, Colleen Matt and Larry Aumiller, and Susan Sterrenberg.

The talented team at Chelsea Green Publishing shepherded my book through every stage. Editors Matthew Derr and Amalia Herren-Lage honored my writing style, while streamlining and improving the flow. I'm grateful to Matthew for his encouragement throughout—from proposal to feedback on draft chapters to developmental editing. Thanks also to Chelsea Green for contracting with my favorite copyeditor and insightful naturalist, the brilliant Susan Campbell.

Always I find refuge in family, beginning with my kind and loving husband Wes Pyne. I'd be remiss not to include our sweet Labrador Pepper, who accompanied us on ancient forest hikes with her nose sensing the passages of wildlife. My son Ian Oberbillig pursued American Dippers with me, and thanks to his partner Felicity Jerman partakes in birding expeditions. My brother Rob Richie and sister-in-law Cynthia Terrell joined trips to childhood homes for memoir sections; and brother David Richie offered childhood memories and support from afar. My parents Dave and Cate Richie have passed, yet they light a candle within as I write. So much of who I am today stems from my upbringing, raised to be independent, at home in feathered forests with birds, and to speak up on behalf of wild nature.

NOTES

Introduction

1. Karen Price et al., *BC's Old Growth Forest: A Last Stand for Biodiversity* (Veridian Ecological Consulting, 2020), https://veridianecological.ca/wp-content/uploads/2020/05/bcs-old-growth-forest-report-web.pdf.
2. Ursula K. Le Guin, *The Farthest Shore* in *The Books of Earthsea: The Complete Illustrated Edition* (Saga Press, 2018), 256.
3. Ursula K. Le Guin, *The Finder* in *The Books of Earthsea: The Complete Illustrated Edition* (Saga Press, 2018), 599.
4. Ursula K. Le Guin, *The Word for World Is Forest* (Berkley Books, 1976), 35.

Chapter 1. Tall Tree Climb

1. Roberth H. MacArthur, "Population Ecology of Some Warblers of Northeastern Coniferous Forests," *Ecology* 39, no. 4 (October 1958), 599–619, https://doi.org/10.2307/1931600.

Chapter 2. Feathers

1. Kristin C. Ruegg et al., "Mapping Migration in a Songbird Using High-Resolution Genetic Markers," *Molecular Ecology* 23, no. 23 (December 2014): 5726–39, https://doi.org/10.1111/mec.12977.
2. Linda Hogan, *Dwellings: A Spiritual History of the Living World* (Simon & Schuster, 1995), 20.

Chapter 3. Refugia

1. Barry Lopez and Debra Gwartney, eds., *Home Ground: Language for an American Landscape* (Trinity University Press, 2013), 293.
2. Sarah J. K. Frey, Adam S. Hadley, and Matthew G. Betts, "Microclimate Predicts Within-Season Distribution Dynamics of Montane Forest Birds," *Diversity and Distributions* 22, no. 9 (September 2016): 944–59, https://doi.org/10.1111/ddi.12456.
3. City of Melbourne, Urban Forest Visual, http://melbourneurbanforestvisual.com.au.
4. R. Glenn Ford, Gina K. Himes Boor, and Jennifer Caylor Ward, *Final Report: Seabird Mortality Resulting from the M/V New Carissa Oil Spill Incident February and March 1999*, (U.S. Fish and Wildlife Service Oregon Fish and Wildlife Office, 2001), https://www.doi.gov/sites/doi.gov/files/migrated/restoration/library/casedocs/upload/OR_New_Carissa_Seabird_Mortality_01.pdf.

Chapter 5. American Dipper

1. Ferris Jabr, *Becoming Earth: How Our Planet Came to Life* (Random House, 2024), 169.

Chapter 6. Pacific Wren

1. "End-the-War Demonstration," House of Representatives Congressional Record, January 22, 1973, 1756, https://www.congress.gov/93/crecb/1973/01/22/GPO-CRECB-1973-pt2-3.pdf.
2. Donald Kroodsma, "Winter Wren" in *The Singing Life of Birds: The Art and Science of Listening to Birdsong* (Houghton Mifflin Harcourt, 2007), 214–25.

3. "Species Distribution Models," Betts Forest Landscape Ecology Lab, https://flel.forestry.oregonstate.edu/research.

4. Thor Hanson, *Feathers: The Evolution of a Natural Miracle* (Basic Books, 2011), 36.

5. Emily Carr, *Hundreds and Thousands: The Journals of Emily Carr* (Clarke, Irwin and Company, 1966), 132–33.

6. Pablo Neruda, "Ode to Bird Watching," in *All the Odes: A Bilingual Edition*, trans. Margaret Sayers Peden (Farrar, Straus and Giroux, 2013), 102.

7. Molly Lewis: Whistler, https://www.molly-lewis.com/information-zo9fp.

Chapter 7. Varied Thrush

1. Frank J. Keim, "Varied Thrush," Yupik Bird Book, Alaska Native Knowledge Network, http://ankn.uaf.edu/Resources/mod/glossary/view.php?id=23&mode=letter&hook=V&sortkey=&sortorder=.

2. David George Haskell, *Sounds Wild and Broken: Sonic Marvels, Evolution's Creativity, and the Crisis of Sensory Extinction* (Viking, 2022), 111.

3. Alana R. O. Chin et al., "Shoot Dimorphism Enables *Sequoia sempervirens* to Separate Requirements for Foliar Water Uptake and Photosynthesis," *American Journal of Botany* 109, no. 4 (March 2022): 564–79, https://doi.org/10.1002/ajb2.1841.

4. Robert G. Lake, *Chilula: People from the Ancient Redwoods* (University Press of America, 1982), xvi, https://www.waterboards.ca.gov/water_issues/programs/tmdl/records/region_1/2003/ref993.pdf.

5. Lake, *Chilula*, 8.

6. *The Redwoods: A National Opportunity for Conservation and Alternatives for Action* (United States National Park Service, 1964), 35–39, https://npshistory.com/publications/redw/prof-rpt-1964.pdf

7. Drew M. P. Peltier et al., "Old Reserves and Ancient Buds Fuel Regrowth of Coast Redwood after Catastrophic Fire," *Nature Plants* 9 (2023), 1978–85, https://doi.org/10.1038/s41477-023-01581-z.

Chapter 8. Truffle

1. Shimona Starling, "The Wood Microbiome Inside Living Trees," *Nature Reviews Microbiology* 23, no. 618 (2025), https://doi.org/10.1038/s41579-025-01236-0.

2. Chris Maser et al., *Trees, Truffles, and Beasts: How Forests Function* (Rutgers University Press, 2008), 89.

3. Marcos V. Caiafa et al., "Discovering the Role of Patagonian Birds in the Dispersal of Truffles and Other Mycorrhizal Fungi," *Current Biology* 31, no. 24 (December 2021): 5558–70, https://doi.org/10.1038/s41579-025-01236-0.

4. Suzanne Simard, *Finding the Mother Tree: Discovering the Wisdom of the Forest* (Knopf, 2021), 5.

Chapter 10. Great Gray Owl

1. Christopher J. Clark et al., "Great Gray Owls Hunting Voles Under Snow Hover to Defeat an Acoustic Mirage," *Proceedings of the Royal Society B* 289, no. 1987 (2022): 20221164, https://doi.org/10.1098/rspb.2022.1164.

2. Mark E. Swanson et al., "Distribution of Western Hemlock Dwarf Mistletoe in Mature and Old-Growth Douglas-fir Forests, *Northwest Science* 80, no. 3 (2006): 207–17, https://research.fs.usda.gov/treesearch/34606.

3. Evelyn L. Bull et al., *Resource Partitioning Among Woodpeckers in Northeastern Oregon*, Research Note PNW-RN-444 (United States Department of Agriculture, 1986), 20, https://doi.org/10.2737/PNW-RN-444.

NOTES

Chapter 11. Chestnut-backed Chickadee

1. Timothy D. Schowalter, "Canopy Arthropod Communities in Relation to Forest Age and Alternative Harvest Practices in Western Oregon," *Forest Ecology and Management* 78, no. 1–3 (1995): 115–25, https://doi.org/10.1016/0378-1127(95)03592-4.
2. Kathryn E. Arnold et al., "Parental Prey Selection Affects Risk-Taking Behaviour and Spatial Learning in Avian Offspring," *Proceedings of the Royal Society B* 274, no. 1625 (2007): 2563–9, https://doi.org/10.1098/rspb.2007.0687.

Chapter 13. Woodpecker Quartet

1. Yntze van der Hoek et al., "The Diversity, Distribution and Conservation Status of The Tree-Cavity-Nesting Birds of the World," *Diversity and Distributions* 23, no. 10 (2017): 1120–31, https://doi.org/10.1111/ddi.12601.
2. Kathleen Dean Moore, "The Arachne Project: Conservation for an Interwoven World, Unraveling," introductory speech for panel at the annual Public Interest Environmental Law Conference, Eugene, OR, March 2, 2025.

Chapter 15. Vaux's Swift

1. Aldo Leopold, *A Sand County Almanac: With Essays on Conservation from Round River*, (Oxford University Press, 1949; repr., Ballantine Books, 1986), 116. Citations refer to the Ballantine Books edition.
2. Evelyn L. Bull and Howard D. Cooper. "Vaux's Swift Nests in Hollow Trees," *Western Birds* 22, no. 2 (1991): 2, https://digitalcommons.usf.edu/western_birds/vol22/iss2/2.
3. Douglas W. Tallamy, "The Chickadee's Guide to Gardening," Opinion, *New York Times*, March 11, 2015, https://www.nytimes.com/2015/03/11/opinion/in-your-garden-choose-plants-that-help-the-environment.html.
4. Evelyn L. Bull and Roy C. Beckwith, "Diet and Foraging Behavior of Vaux's Swifts in Northeastern Oregon," *Condor* 95, no. 4 (1993): 1016–23, https://doi.org/10.2307/1369437.
5. Bull and Cooper, *Western Birds* 22 (2): 2.
6. Evelyn L. Bull, "Use of Nest Boxes by Vaux's Swifts," *Journal of Field Ornithology* 74, no. 4 (2003): 394–400, https://doi.org/10.1648/0273-8570-74.4.394.
7. E. A. Kitchin, "Descriptions of Individual Species," *Mount Rainier National Park Nature Notes* 17, no. 3–4 (United States National Park Service, 1939): 94–200, https://npshistory.com/nature_notes/mora/vol17/vol17-3-4c10.htm.

Chapter 16. Hermit Warbler

1. Hankyu Kim et al., "Annual Migratory Movement, Apparent Molt-Migration, Migration Schedule, and Diffuse Migratory Connectivity of Hermit Warblers" *Avian Conservation and Ecology* 19, no. 2 (2024): 6, https://doi.org/10.5751/ACE-02622-190206.
2. Brian K. Trevelline et. al., "Convergent Remodelling of the Gut Microbiome is Associated with Host Energetic Condition over Long-Distance Migration," *Functional Ecology* 37, no. 11 (2023): 2840–54, https://doi.org/10.1111/1365-2435.14430.
3. Matthew G. Betts, email message to author, May 16, 2026.
4. Hankyu Kim, "An Examination of Climate and Land-Use Change as Drivers of Population Dynamics in Breeding Bird Populations" (PhD diss., Oregon State University, 2021), https://ir.library.oregonstate.edu/concern/graduate_thesis_or_dissertations/mp48sm758.
5. Christopher Wolf et al., "Temporal Consistency of Undercanopy Thermal Refugia in Old-Growth Forest," *Agricultural and Forest Meteorology* 307 (2021): 108520, https://doi.org/10.1016/j.agrformet.2021.108520.

6. Hankyu Kim et al., "Forest Microclimate and Composition Mediate Long-Term Trends of Breeding Bird Populations," *Global Change Biology* 28, no. 21 (2022): 6180–93, https://doi.org/10.1111/gcb.16353.

Chapter 17. Marbled Murrelet

1. Maria Mudd Ruth, *Rare Bird: Pursuing the Mystery of the Marbled Murrelet* (Rodale Books, 2005), 55.
2. Blake A. Barbaree et al., "Nesting Ecology of Marbled Murrelets at a Remote Mainland Ford in Southeast Alaska," *Condor: Ornithological Applications* 116, no. 2 (2014): 173–84, https://doi.org/10.1650/CONDOR-13-116.1.
3. "Species Factsheet: Marbled Murrelet Brachyramphus marmoratus," BirdLife DataZone, accessed May 20, 2026, https://datazone.birdlife.org/species/factsheet/marbled-murrelet-brachyramphus-marmoratus#Population.
4. Ethan Woodis, "Nest Site Selection and Nest Survival of the Endangered Marbled Murrelet: A Multi-Scale Analysis" (master's thesis, Oregon State University, 2026).
5. Mudd Ruth, *Rare Bird*, 55–56.

Chapter 19. Spotted Owl

1. Josh Laughlin, "Marching in Francis' Army," Cascadia Wildlands, September 24, 2015, https://cascwild.org/2015/marching-in-francis-army.
2. "Barred Owl Management Strategy," Birds Connect Seattle, January 23, 2024, https://birdsconnectsea.org/2024/01/23/barred-owl-management.
3. Wikiquote, "Alexander von Humboldt," last modified June 2025, 13:02 (UTC), https://en.wikiquote.org/wiki/Alexander_von_Humboldt.
4. Deborah Richie, "Unseen Lives Around Us," *Montana Kaimin* (Missoula, MT), April 21, 1987, https://scholarworks.umt.edu/studentnewspaper/7923.

Chapter 20. Townsend's Solitaire

1. Jim Anderson, "Western Juniper: A Weed or What?" *Source* (Bend, OR), November 28, 2013, https://www.bendsource.com/outside/western-juniper-2301716.

Chapter 21. Tall Tree Climb Return

1. Ursula K. Le Guin, *The Finder*, in *The Books of Earthsea: The Complete Illustrated Edition*, (Saga Press, 2018), 599.

Chapter 22. Saving Refugia

1. Beverly E. Law et al., "Strategic Reserves in Oregon's Forests for Biodiversity, Water, and Carbon to Mitigate and Adapt to Climate Change," *Frontiers in Forests and Global Change* 5 (2022): 1028401, https://doi.org/10.3389/ffgc.2022.1028401.
2. Kathleen Dean Moore, "The Arachne Project: Conservation for an Interwoven World, Unraveling," introductory speech for panel at the annual Public Interest Environmental Law Conference, Eugene, OR, March 2, 2025.
3. Ursula K. Le Guin, *The Word for World is Forest* (Tor Books, 1972), 125.
4. Ursula K. Le Guin, *Always Coming Home* (Harper and Row, 1985; repr., Harper Perennial, 2023), 8. Citations refer to the Harper Perennial edition.
5. *Birding in the United States: A Demographic and Economic Analysis, Addendum to the 2022 National Survey of Fishing, Hunting, and Wildlife-Associated Recreation*, Report 2022-4 (United States Fish & Wildlife Service, 2022), 6, https://www.fws.gov/sites/default/files/documents/2024-11/2022-birding-in-the-us-demographic-and-economic-analysis.pdf.

FURTHER READING

Ackerman, Jennifer. *The Bird Way: A New Look at How Birds Talk, Work, Play, Parent, and Think.* Penguin Press, 2021.

Ackerman, Jennifer. *The Genius of Birds.* Penguin Press, 2017.

Ackerman, Jennifer. *What an Owl Knows: The New Science of the World's Most Enigmatic Bird.* Penguin Press, 2023.

Birkhead, T. R. *Bird Sense: What It's Like to Be a Bird.* Knopf, 2012.

Bjornerud, Marcia. *Turning to Stone: Discovering the Subtle Wisdom of Rocks.* Flatiron Books, 2025.

Bradfield, Elizabeth, CMarie Fuhrman, and Derek Sheffield, eds. *Cascadia Field Guide: Art, Ecology, Poetry.* Mountaineers Books, 2024.

Brodie, Nathaniel, Charles Goodrich, and Frederick J. Swanson, eds. *Forest Under Story: Creative Inquiry in an Old-Growth Forest.* University of Washington Press, 2018.

Cox, Christopher, ed. *Old Growth: The Best Writing about Trees from Orion Magazine.* Orion Magazine, 2021.

Dunne, Pete. *The Courage of Birds: And the Often Surprising Ways They Survive Winter.* Chelsea Green Publishing, 2024.

Goldfarb, Ben. *Crossings: How Road Ecology Is Shaping the Future of Our Planet.* W.W. Norton & Company, 2024.

Goldfarb, Ben. *Eager: The Surprising, Secret Life of Beavers and Why They Matter.* Chelsea Green Publishing, 2019.

Hanson, Thor. *Feathers: The Evolution of a Natural Miracle.* Basic Books, 2011.

Haskell, David George. *The Forest Unseen: A Year's Watch in Nature.* Viking, 2012.

Haskell, David George. *The Songs of Trees: Stories from Nature's Great Connectors.* Viking, 2017.

Haskell, David George. *Sounds Wild and Broken: Sonic Marvels, Evolution's Creativity, and the Crisis of Sensory Extinction.* Viking, 2022.

Heinrich, Bernd. *The Homing Instinct: Meaning and Mystery in Animal Migration.* Houghton, Mifflin, Harcourt, 2014.

Heinrich, Bernd. *Winter World: The Ingenuity of Animal Survival.* Ecco, 2009.

Herring, M. L. *Born of Fire and Rain: Journey into a Pacific Coastal Forest.* Yale University Press, 2024.

Hogan, Linda. *Dwellings: A Spiritual History of the Living World.* Simon & Schuster, 1995.

Hutto, Richard. *A Beautifully Burned Forest: Learning to Celebrate Severe Forest Fire.* Springer, 2025.

Jabr, Ferris. *Becoming Earth: How Our Planet Came to Life.* Random House, 2024.

Kimmerer, Robin Wall. *Braiding Sweetgrass: Indigenous Wisdom, Scientific Knowledge and the Teachings of Plants.* Milkweed Editions, 2015.

Kimmerer, Robin Wall. *Gathering Moss: A Natural and Cultural History of Mosses.* Oregon State University Press, 2003.

Kimmerer, Robin Wall. *The Serviceberry: Abundance and Reciprocity in the Natural World.* Scribner, 2025.

King, Greg. *The Ghost Forest: Racists, Radicals, and Real Estate in the California Redwoods.* PublicAffairs, 2023.

Koberstein, Paul, and Jessica Applegate. *Canopy of Titans: The Life and Times of the Great North American Temperate Rainforest*. OR Books, 2023.

Kroodsma, Donald. *The Singing Life of Birds: The Art and Science of Listening to Birdsong*. Houghton Mifflin Harcourt, 2007.

LeGue, Chandra. *Oregon's Ancient Forests: A Hiking Guide*. Mountaineers Books, 2019.

Le Guin, Ursula K. *The Books of Earthsea: The Complete Illustrated Edition*. S&S/Saga Press, 2018.

Le Guin, Ursula K. *The Word for World Is Forest*. Berkeley Books, 1976.

Lopez, Barry. *Embrace Fearlessly the Burning World: Essays*. Random House, 2023.

Leopold, Aldo. *A Sand County Almanac: With Essays on Conservation from Round River*. Ballantine Books, 1986. Originally published in 1949.

Lopez, Barry, and Debra Gwartney, eds. *Home Ground: Language for an American Landscape*. Trinity University Press, 2013.

Luoma, Jon R. *The Hidden Forest: The Biography of an Ecosystem*. Oregon State University Press, 2006.

Macfarlane, Robert. *Is a River Alive?* W.W. Norton & Company, 2025.

Maloof, Joan. *Nature's Temples: The Complex World of Old-Growth Forests*. Timber Press, 2016.

Mapes, Lynda. *The Trees Are Speaking: Dispatches from the Salmon Forest*. University of Washington Press, 2025.

Maser, Chris. *Forest Primeval: The Natural History of an Ancient Forest*. Sierra Club Books, 1989.

Maser, Chris, Andrew W. Claridge, and James M. Trappe. *Trees, Truffles, and Beasts: How Forests Function*. Rutgers University Press, 2008.

Moore, Kathleen Dean. *Earth's Wild Music: Celebrating and Defending the Songs of the Natural World*. Counterpoint, 2022.

Nardi, James B. *The Hidden Company That Trees Keep: Life from Treetops to Root Tips*. Princeton University Press, 2023.

O'Kane, Trish. *Birding to Change the World: A Memoir*. Ecco, 2024.

Powers, Richard. *The Overstory*. W.W. Norton & Company, 2019.

Rawlence, Ben. *The Treeline: The Last Forest and the Future of Life on Earth*. St. Martin's Press, 2022.

Reid, John W., and Thomas E. Lovejoy. *Ever Green: Saving Big Forests to Save the Planet*. W.W. Norton & Company, 2022.

Rix, Harriet. *The Genius of Trees: How They Mastered the Elements and Shaped the World*. Penguin Random House, 2025.

Ruth, Maria Mudd. *Rare Bird: Pursuing the Mystery of the Marbled Murrelet. Rodale Books*, 2005.

Schlanger, Zoe. *The Light Eaters: How the Unseen World of Plant Intelligence Offers a New Understanding of Life on Earth*. Harper Perennial, 2024.

Sheldrake, Merlin. *Entangled Life: How Fungi Make Our Worlds, Change Our Minds and Shape Our Futures*. Random House, 2020.

Simard, Suzanne. *Finding the Mother Tree: Discovering the Wisdom of the Forest*. Mountaineers Books, 2021.

Simard, Suzanne. *When the Forest Breathes: Renewal and Resilience in the Natural World*. Alfred A. Knopf, 2026.

Tallamy, Douglas. *Bringing Nature Home: How You Can Sustain Wildlife with Native Plants*. Timber Press, 2009.

Walker, Charlotte Zoe, ed. *The Art of Seeing Things: Essays by John Burroughs*. Syracuse University Press, 2001.

Wilson, E. O. *Half-Earth: Our Planet's Fight for Life*. Liveright, 2016.

Wohl, Ellen. *Deadwood: The Afterlife of Trees*. Oregon State University Press, 2022.

Yong, Ed. *An Immense World: How Animal Senses Reveal the Hidden Realms around Us*. Random House, 2022.

INDEX

C

INDEX

G

INDEX

Y

ABOUT THE AUTHOR

James Hutchens

Marina Richie is an award-winning nature writer with a passion for birds and wild places. Her book *Halcyon Journey: In Search of the Belted Kingfisher* received the 2024 John Burroughs Medal for distinguished natural history writing, a 2022 National Outdoor Book Award (gold), and a Foreword INDIES Book of the Year Award (silver). Through prose and poetry, Marina seeks to bridge the divide separating people from nature. Her essays, blogs, and poems appear in popular and literary magazines. Marina has a master's degree in journalism from the University of Montana and an undergraduate degree in biology from the University of Oregon. She lives in Bend, Oregon, with her husband, Wes, and tends a bird-friendly yard.